Formal Approaches to Poetry

Phonology and Phonetics
11

Editor
Aditi Lahiri

Mouton de Gruyter
Berlin · New York

Formal Approaches to Poetry

Recent Developments in Metrics

edited by

B. Elan Dresher
Nila Friedberg

Mouton de Gruyter
Berlin · New York

Mouton de Gruyter (formerly Mouton, The Hague)
is a Division of Walter de Gruyter GmbH & Co. KG, Berlin.

♾ Printed on acid-free paper which falls within the guidelines
of the ANSI to ensure permanence and durability.

Library of Congress Cataloging-in-Publication Data

> Formal approaches to poetry : recent developments in metrics / edited
> by B. Elan Dresher, Nila Friedberg.
>   p. cm. − (Phonology and phonetics ; 11)
>   Includes bibliographical references and index.
>   ISBN-13: 978-3-11-018522-5 (cloth : alk. paper)
>   ISBN-10: 3-11-018522-9 (cloth : alk. paper)
>   1. Versification.   I. Dresher, Bezalel E. (Bezalel Elan), 1950−
> II. Friedberg, Nila, 1972−   III. Series.
>   PN1042.F59   2006
>   808.1−dc22
>   2005036815

Bibliographic information published by Die Deutsche Bibliothek

Die Deutsche Bibliothek lists this publication in the Deutsche Nationalbibliografie;
detailed bibliographic data is available in the Internet at <http://dnb.ddb.de>.

ISBN-13: 978-3-11-018522-5
ISBN-10: 3-11-018522-9
ISSN 1861-4191

© Copyright 2006 by Walter de Gruyter GmbH & Co. KG, D-10785 Berlin.
All rights reserved, including those of translation into foreign languages. No part of this
book may be reproduced in any form or by any means, electronic or mechanical, including
photocopy, recording, or any information storage and retrieval system, without permission
in writing from the publisher.
Cover design: Christopher Schneider, Berlin.
Printed in Germany.

Acknowledgements

This volume is a collection of selected papers presented at the conference on Formal Approaches to Poetry in Toronto in 1999 and other papers submitted to the volume at a later occasion. Our first thanks go to the conference participants and the contributors to the volume, without whom this book would have been impossible. Second, we gratefully acknowledge the support of the Social Sciences and Humanities Research Council of Canada for an Aid to Occasional Scholarly Conferences grant, the University of Toronto Connaught International Symposia/Colloquia fund, the Offices of the Dean of Arts and Science and of the Vice-President and Provost at the University of Toronto, and the Department of Slavic Languages and Literatures at the University of Toronto. Their sponsorship enabled us to organize the conference, with the aim of creating a greater awareness of the study of meter in North America. Special thanks go to Aditi Lahiri, Ursula Kleinhenz, and anonymous reviewers at Mouton for their helpful comments and for making this publication possible, as well as to Keir Moulton and Rebecca Smollett for proofreading and Peter Gebert for typesetting the volume.

We are especially grateful to Michael Getty, who served as one of the co-organizers of the conference and was helpful in formulating its rationale, which we have incorporated into the introduction. We would also like to thank other members of the organizing committee of the conference, Daniel Currie Hall, and William Idsardi, who gave of their time to review and comment on the papers. Thanks are due also to Christopher Barnes, Edward Burstynsky, Gordon Easson, Diane Massam, Nicole Rosen, and the volunteers and session chairs Mohammad Haji Abdolhosseini, Naomi Cull, Jean Balcaen, Susana Bejar, Patrick Fothergill, Wenckje Jongstra, Do-Hee Jung, Arsalan Kahnemuyipour, Catherine Kitto, Steve Zeidel, and Joy Zhou.

Finally, we thank our families for their support, their words of encouragement, and for teaching us to appreciate poetry. This volume is dedicated to them.

Table of contents

Acknowledgements — v

Introduction — 1
B. Elan Dresher and Nila Friedberg

1. Music and meter

A modular metrics for folk verse — 7
Paul Kiparsky

2. Metricality

What is "metricality"? English iambic pentameter — 53
Marina Tarlinskaja

3. English meter

Generated metrical form and implied metrical form — 77
Nigel Fabb

Anapests and anti-resolution — 93
Michael Hammond

Shakespeare's lyric and dramatic metrical styles — 111
Kristin Hanson

Longfellow's long line — 135
Gilbert Youmans

4. Old Norse

The rise of the quatrain in Germanic:
musicality and word based rhythm in eddic meters — 151
Kristján Árnason

5. Mora counting meters

The function of pauses in metrical studies: acoustic evidence from
Japanese verse   173
Deborah Cole and Mizuki Miyashita

Iambic meter in Somali   193
Colleen M. Fitzgerald

6. Modelling statistical preferences

Constraints, complexity, and the grammar of poetry   211
Nila Friedberg

Modelling the linguistics–poetics interface   233
Daniel Currie Hall

7. Russian meter

Generative metrics and the comparative approach:
Russian iambic tetrameter in a comparative perspective   253
Mihhail Lotman

Structural dynamics in the Onegin Stanza   267
Barry Scherr

8. Classical and Romance metrics

The ancient iambic trimeter: a disbalanced harmony   287
Maria-Kristiina Lotman

Author index   309
Subject and language index   311
List of contributors   313

Introduction

B. Elan Dresher and Nila Friedberg

This book focuses on formal approaches to poetic meter. It is well known that poetic language involves the repetition of items in artistically significant ways. Poets can repeat syllables at the ends of lines (the phenomenon called rhyme), or consonants at the beginnings of stressed words (alliteration), or they can alternate perceptually strong and weak syllables (meter). By 'formal approaches' we mean analyses that aim to shed light on the nature of these aspects of poetic language. Some of the questions that the book is concerned with include: 'What are the rules that govern formal elements of poetic language in particular traditions or poets?', 'Which line types do poets never produce, and why?', and 'Why do certain metrical patterns sound better than others?'. It is very common in literary studies to make intuitive statements about a poet's style; it is said, for example, that Milton sounds 'complex', or that Pope sounds 'light', or that some Russian poems of Joseph Brodsky sound 'English'. Formal linguistic study offers an objective way to measure such intuitions with the help of rules or constraints.

The major purpose of this book is to bridge the gulf that exists in much Western literary scholarship between the purely literary and the purely formal study of poetic composition. Within scholarly traditions in Eastern Europe such a gulf never came about. In fact Roman Jakobson, a leading Russian linguistic theorist associated with the Prague School and one of the precursors of generative linguistics, was a prolific literary scholar. In Western Europe and North America, however, the study of literary technique is split into different schools that rarely interact: scholars in linguistics departments tend to focus mainly on formal studies of meter, and scholars in English and literature departments study other aspects of literary technique. The result is that interesting formal studies of verse are often confined to linguistics conferences and publications, and so are relatively inaccessible to literary scholars.

The aim of this book is to create greater public awareness of some recent exciting findings in the formal study of meter. The last influential volume on the subject, Rhythm and Meter, edited by Paul Kiparsky and Gilbert Youmans (Academic Press, San Diego, 1989), appeared over fifteen years ago. This volume brought together leading exponents of the theory of generative metrics with representatives of other approaches to the study of meter. Kiparsky and Youmans' (1989) volume remains an indispensable reference to the most advanced thinking on poetic meter at the end of the 1980s.

Since that time, a number of important theoretical developments have taken place, which have led to new approaches to the analysis of meter. For example, Optimality Theory, developed by Prince and Smolensky (1993), suggests that speakers of a language generate a number of logically possible candidates to be pronounced, and choose the optimal one, that is, the form that best satisfies a set of possibly conflicting constraints. Languages may rank the constraints differently, so that in case of conflict, the form that satisfies the higher-ranking constraint is the one that wins out. Under this approach, the patterns of poetic meter are also seen as different ways of satisfying a set of constraints. Different rankings of constraints will produce different patterns of poetic lines.

This volume represents some of the most exciting current thinking on the theory of meter. It includes a number of papers that were presented at the conference on Formal Approaches to Poetry that took place at the University of Toronto on October 8-10, 1999, and some papers that were submitted at a later time. In terms of empirical coverage, the papers focus on a wide variety of languages, including English, Finnish, Estonian, Russian, Japanese, Somali, Old Norse, Latin, and Greek. Thus, the collection is truly international in its scope.

The volume contains diverse theoretical approaches that are brought together for the first time, including Optimality Theory (Kiparsky, Hammond), other constraint-based approaches (Friedberg, Hall, Scherr), a mora-based approach (Cole and Miyashita, Fitzgerald), a semantic-pragmatic approach (Fabb), and an alternative generative approach developed in Estonia (M. Lotman and M. K. Lotman). The volume also addresses the issue of the relationship between meter and music. In recent work by Hayes and MacEachern (1998), the metrical form of a verse is equated with the way the text is aligned with the musical beats in performance. Kiparsky advocates a greater division between meter and music, and argues that a quatrain of English folk verse has an intrinsic metrical form that is independent of how it is set to music (Hanson and Kiparsky 1996). The quatrain structure is also examined by Árnason, who focuses on quatrains in Germanic verse. Finally, the volume includes papers employing the Quantitative approach to verse (Tarlinskaja,

Friedberg, Hall, Scherr, Youmans) associated with the Russian school of metrics (Bely 1910, Tomashevsky 1929, Taranovsky 1953, Gasparov 1974, Bailey 1975, Tarlinskaja 1976). This approach describes the grammars of poets in terms of their statistical preferences in constructing certain types of lines (for example, lines with stresses omitted in certain positions). Statistical preferences allow us to distinguish the styles of different poets as well as to differentiate literary periods.

The volume is intended for two types of audiences. The first are linguists, including those with a specific interest in poetry, as well as those who work on stress and speech rhythm, phrasing, and the phonology-syntax and phonetics-phonology interfaces. This volume will also be relevant to those concerned with constraint systems and linguistic theory in a general way.

The second, much larger, audience consists of students of poetry and the connection between language and literature. It is only a matter of time before students of literature rediscover metrical analysis. We hope that the presence of scholars whose interests are as much literary as linguistic (Fabb, Youmans), and the wide array of languages covered, will help to make this book of interest to this audience, and will serve to create renewed interest in this area among students of literature.

References

Bailey, James
    1975. *Toward a Statistical Analysis of English Verse*. Lisse/Netherlands: Peter de Ridder Press.

Bely, Andrei
    1910 *Simvolizm: Kniga statei* [Symbolism: A Book of Essays]. Moscow: Musaget.

Gasparov, Mikhail Leonovich
    1974 *Sovremennyi russkii stix: Metrika i ritmika*. [Modern Russian Verse: Meter and Rhythm]. Moscow: Nauka.

Kiparsky, Paul, and Gilbert Youmans
    1989 *Rhythm and Meter*. San Diego: Academic Press.

Hanson, Kristin, and Paul Kiparsky
    1992 A parametric theory of poetic meter. *Language* 72: 287–335.

Hayes, Bruce, and Margaret MacEachern
    1998 Quatrain form in English folk verse. *Language* 64: 473–507.

Prince, Alan, and Paul Smolensky
    1993   Optimality Theory: Constraint interaction in Generative Grammar. Manuscript, Rutgers University and University of Colorado at Boulder.

Taranovsky, Kiril
    1953   *Russki dvodelni ritmovi*. Beograd: Srpska Akademija Nauka.

Tarlinskaja, Marina
    1976   *English Verse: Theory and History*. The Hague: Mouton.

Tomashevsky, Boris
    1929   *O stixe*. [On Verse]. Munich: Wilhelm Fink Verlag.

1. Music and meter

A modular metrics for folk verse*

Paul Kiparsky

1. Introduction

Hayes & MacEachern's (1998) study of quatrain stanzas in English folk songs was the first application of stochastic Optimality Theory to a large corpus of data. It remains the most extensive study of versification that OT has to offer, and the most careful and perceptive formal analysis of folk song meter in any framework. In a follow-up study, Hayes (in press) concludes that stress and meter – or more generally, the prosodic structure of language and verse – are governed by separate constraint systems which must be jointly satisfied by well-formed verse. Apart from its convincing arguments for a modular approach to metrics, it is notable for successfully implementing the analysis in OT, a framework whose parallelist commitments might seem philosophically at odds with modularity.[1]

Taking modularity a step further, I argue here that the composer and performer of a song constructs a match between *three* tiers of rhythmic structure: linguistic prominence, poetic meter, and musical rhythm. They are organized along similar principles, as hierarchies of alternating prominence representable by trees or grids. But they are autonomous, in the sense that a text has an intrinsic prosodic form independently of how it is versified (Liberman and Prince 1979, Hayes 1995), a stanza has an intrinsic metrical form independently of how it is set to music (Hanson and Kiparsky 1996), and a tune has an intrinsic musical rhythm independently of the words that may be sung to it (Jackendoff and Lehrdahl 1983). Moreover, each rhythmic tier is subject to its own constraints. The stress pattern (or other linguistic prominence relation) which determines the intrinsic linguistic rhythm of a song's text is assigned by the language's prosodic system. The meter of its stanzas and the rhythm of its tune are normally drawn from a traditional repertoire of rhythmic patterns. How the tiers correspond to each other, and in what ways they can be mismatched and mutually accommodated, is regulated by conventions that evolve historically, though within limits grounded in the faculty of language.

These are familiar and heretofore uncontroversial ideas, but Hayes' work questions one aspect of them. It equates the metrical form of a verse with the way its text is aligned with the musical beats in performance. I present three arguments against this identification and in support of the traditional division of labor between meter and music. The first argument demonstrates the autonomy of metrical form by showing that constraints on the form of stanzas are invariant across musical performance and melodic variation. The second shows that the modular approach allows major simplifications in the metrical constraint system, and, more importantly, makes them entirely grounded in elementary principles of poetic form. The third argument is that the simplified constraints not only define the occurring stanza forms, but also predict the relative frequencies with which they are used in folk songs. These results vindicate a fully modular view of the metrics/music interface.

Following H&M's lead, I will be using Optimality Theory, which is well suited to model the groundedness of metrical preferences and constraints and their competition within a metrical system. But I argue that variation is better treated by partial constraint ranking (Anttila 1997, 2003) than by stochastic OT.

The core data are also the same as H&M's, namely the ballads and other songs from England and Appalachia collected and transcribed by Sharp & Karpeles (1932) and by Ritchie (1965). For a fuller picture of the variation within this tradition I have complemented the corpus with the versions of the same songs from Niles (1961) and especially from Bronson (1959–72), and with the early 20th century American ballad recordings in the Folkways Anthology (Smith 1952/1997). I also drew on Isaac Watts' collection of hymns, a body of popular verse which differs minimally from folk songs in a way which provides an empirical test of a central prediction of my theory.

While delving a little deeper than H&M into the folk song tradition itself, I also narrowed my focus by excluding two more peripheral sets of data, namely H&M's judgments about the well-formedness of their own made-up pieces of verse, and the nursery rhymes with which they sometimes supplement their folk song corpus. H&M introduce their intuitions about constructed verses in order to assess the metricality of quatrain types which their theory predicts but which don't occur, and of those which their theory excludes but which do occur. I simply decided to treat all unattested quatrain types as unmetrical, except where the gap can plausibly be considered accidental,[2] and quatrain types attested more than once as metrical, letting the theory adjudicate the status of the singletons. Hugging the empirical ground this way turned out to pay off because the simplest analysis draws the line in almost exactly the right place. This is not to deny that wellformedness judgments have a place in the study of meter. However, in the case of a complex and sophisticated traditional genre of oral literature with its own metrical conventions the intuitions themselves require validation, e.g., by showing that they converge with usage in the clear cases.[3]

My reason for setting nursery rhymes aside are somewhat different. Their meters are simply too diverse to be entirely covered in the same constraint system as folk song quatrains. A corpus such as Opie & Opie (1997) contains a mixture of almost every popular conventional verse form with simple rhythms similar to those of sports cheers and chanted slogans (Gil 1978, Kopiez & Brink 1998). Selecting from this material without some independent criterion runs the risk of circularity, so the better course is to stick to a homogeneous corpus.

2. The structure of folk song quatrains

2.1. The core generalizations

Hayes and McEachern classify lines into four types on the basis of their rhythmic CADENCE, which they define in terms of the grid placement of the final two syllables (p. 476). The four types are **4**, **3**, **Green O** (abbreviated **G**), and **3-feminine** (abbreviated 3_f). (In the appendix to their paper they recognize other types, such as 4_f, **5**, 5_f, **6**; I return to the first of these briefly below.) The following stanza (Sharp & Karpeles 1932, #272A), also cited by H&M, illustrates three of the four types.

(1)   a. I wóuld | not már|ry a bláck|–smíth,   (Type **G**)
        b. He smúts | his nóse | and chín; | Ø   (Type **3**)
        c. I'd rá|ther már|ry a sól|dier bóy   (Type **4**)
        d. That már|ches thróugh | the wínd. | Ø   (Type **3**)

The meter is iambic tetrameter in the odd lines, alternating with trimeter in the even lines. Accents mark syllables in the metrically strong positions, which in this simple children's song exactly coincide with the strongest beats of the tune; the dash and Ø are H&M's conventions for marking empty beats.

Here is how Sharp & Karpeles transcribe the song as Mr. Bridges sang it for them in Franklin County, Virginia, in 1918:

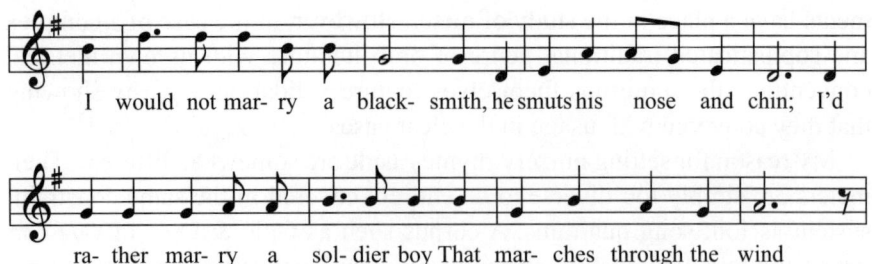

Type **4** lines have a syllable in the fourth strong position, separated from the third strong position by another syllable (*-dier* in (1c)). In the grid representation employed by H&M, such a line looks like this:

(2) Type **4**

```
                x                       x
                x           x           x           x
    x           x   x       x   x       x   x       x
    x   x   x   x   x   x   x   x   x   x   x   x   x   x   x   x
    I'd     ra-     ther    mar-    ry  a sol-    dier    boy
```

Type **3** lines (the even-numbered lines in (1)) terminate in the third strong position; the fourth strong beat remains empty (marked Ø by H&M):

(3) Type **3**

```
                x                       x
                x           x           x           x
    x           x   x       x   x       x   x
    x   x   x   x   x   x   x   x   x   x   x   x   x   x   x   x
    He      smuts   his     nose    and     chin
```

Type **G** lines (line (1a)) have a single syllable after the third strong position in the verse, which falls on the fourth strong beat in the song; H&M's dash in (1) signifies the empty beat before it (often filled by a prolongation of the preceding syllable).

(4) Type **G**

```
                            x                       x
        x               x           x           x
x       x       x       x   x       x       x   x
x   x   x   x   x   x   x   x   x   x   x   x   x   x   x   x
I   would   not   mar-ry   a   black-          smith
```

(1) is an instance of a quatrain type whose prototypical form is **4343** – known as the BALLAD STANZA (sometimes referred to as COMMON METER). H&M point out that the odd-numbered lines in such stanzas sometimes vary freely between **4** and **G**, as in (1). Indeed, this turned out to be by far the most important type of free variation among line types in the folk songs they studied.[4] H&M introduce a fifth line type, **F**, defined as the disjunction of **4** and **G**, to represent this variation.

The schema for (1) would be **F3F3**, standing for $\left\{{4\atop G}\right\}3\left\{{4\atop G}\right\}3$.[5] They further note that the choice between **4** and **G** depends on the wording of the verse. In type **4** lines, the final syllable bears at least as strong a stress as the penult. In type **G** lines it is weaker: in traditional terms, they have a feminine ending.

Lines with a feminine ending have another rendition, H&M's type 3_f. In this type of line, the lone monosyllable after the third beat is initiated *before* the fourth strong beat, typically on the intervening weak beat (beat $3\frac{1}{2}$). Depending on the tune and in part on the singer's preferences, the very same line of verse may be sung either as 3_f or as **G**, as illustrated by the following line from *The Gypsy Laddie* (Child #200). In order to make the distinction between **G** and 3_f as clear as possible I reproduce the corresponding transcription of Sharp & Karpeles 1932 in (5).

(5) a. Type 3_f: She's góne | with the gýp|sen Dá|vy Ø (S&K #33A)

She's gone with the gyp- sen Da- vy.

b. Type **G**: She's góne | with the gíp|sy Dá|-vý (S&K #33J)

She's gone with the gip- sy Da- vy.

12 Paul Kiparsky

Here are the corresponding grid representations according to H&M's conventions in (6).

```
                    x                           x
                    x           x               x               x
        x   x   x   x   x   x   x   x   x   x   x   x   x   x   x   x
        x   x   x   x   x   x   x   x   x   x   x   x   x   x   x   x
(6)a.  She's  gone  with the gyp-   sen    Da-       vy      Ø


            x                       x
            x           x           x           x
        x   x   x   x   x   x   x   x   x   x   x   x   x   x   x
        x   x   x   x   x   x   x   x   x   x   x   x   x   x   x
   b.  She's  gone  with the gip-   sy     Da-              vy
```

Thus, with respect to metrical form, type **G** lines are indistinguishable from type 3_f lines, but with respect to musical performance they are more like type **4** lines. Here comes the first gain of our modular strategy. By separating the constraints on musical performance from constraints on the metrical form of stanzas, we can unify H&M's categories 3_f and **G** at the metrical level without positing a composite category **F**, while at the same time relating **G** and **4** at the level of musical performance (four strong beats). Metrically, we can consider all three as a single type characterized by a monosyllabic last foot; let us call this metrical type **3′**. A **3′** line is of "type **G**" if its final syllable is placed on the fourth strong beat, and of "type 3_f" if its final syllable comes before it. Variation between **G** and **4**, then, is a consequence of exercising in the final foot of its four-foot lines the option which allows a foot to be monosyllabic. The *musical* implementation of such a final monosyllabic foot is appropriate to the tune to which it is sung: rendition **G** supplies four strong beats when the melody requires it, rendition 3_f supplies three; within the limits imposed by that constraint the singer is free to decide and variation is free to occur.

The unification of 3_f, **G**, and **F** as **3′** is made possible by the separation of metrical constraints on stanzas from musical constraints and text-to-tune alignment. It is not just a simplification but has the benefit of straightforwardly excluding rare or non-occurring types of free variation, such as **G**/3_f, or **4**/3_f, or **G**/**3**, as gratuitous violations of musical parallelism: they introduce a rhythmic inconsistency by mixing three-beat and four-beat lines in corresponding positions of stanzas. Some of them do occur in exceptional circumstances. For example, 3_f corresponds to **4** in the four-line refrain stanza of the song in (1). This correspondence is allowed because of the different melody to which that stanza is sung.

(7) a. Sól|dier bóy, |sól|dier bóy,   (Type **4**)
     b. Sól|dier bóy | for mé; | Ø   (Type **3**)
     c. If é|ver Íget márried   (Type **3_f**)
     d. A só|ldier's wífe | I'll bé. | Ø   (Type **3**)

Another reason why the modularization is desirable is that it correctly predicts an additional type of interstanza variation, namely between feminine and masculine lines. Among the lines considered here, these would be **3/3_f** in H&M's terms.[6] (The parallel variation **4/4_f** is even more common.) For the same reason that we expect **3'** to be performed as "**G**" when it alternates in the verse with **4** (for example, in the odd-numbered lines of a **4343** quatrain, i.e., a so-called ballad stanza), we expect it to be performed as "**3_f**" when it alternates in the verse with **3** (as in the even-numbered lines of a ballad stanza). Ordinarily this variation can't happen *within* a single ballad stanza, because the even-numbered lines must rhyme, and a **3_f** line cannot rhyme with a **3** line. *Across* stanzas, though, rhyme is not an obstacle to this variation, and there it is in fact not uncommon, as in the following ballad stanzas.

(8) Oh, she took him by the bridle rein,   **4**
     And she led him to the stable.   **3'** realized as **3_f**
     "Here's fodder and hay for your horse, young man, **4**
     And me to bed if you're able,   **3'** realized as **3_f**
     And me to bed if you're able." (v. 1)

     "I'll have to sheathe my dagger,   **3'** realized as **G**
     My codpiece is withdrawn.   **3**
     I'll don my bugle britches,   **3'** realized as **G**
     I hear the merry horn,   **3**
     I hear the merry horn." (v. 8)

(*Bugle Britches*, Niles 65A, Child #299)

Note how **3'** is realized as **G** in odd positions, where it matches **4** in other stanzas, and as **3_f** in even positions, where it matches **3** in other stanzas. Note also that the theory correctly predicts another type of variation, between **4′** (realized as **4_f**) and **4**, as seen in (9):

(9) Oh, it's down, down, down went that ivory comb,   **4**
    And wild her hair did toss,   **3**
    For none did know as well as Margot   **4′** realized as **4_f**
    How much she suffered loss. (v. 4)   **3**

    Lady Margot died like hit might be at night,   **4**
    Sweet Willie, he died of the morrow.   **3′** realized as **3_f**
    Lady Margot, she died of a pure heart,   **3′** realized as **G**
    Sweet Willie, he died of his sorrow. (v. 13)   **3′** realized as **3_f**

    (*Lady Margot and Sweet William*, Niles 29A, Child #74)

A more general argument for separating stanza form from text-to-tune mapping is that the same words are commonly sung to different musical measures, yet maintain certain invariant constraints on stanza form. For example, one version of the song cited in (9) begins like this:

(10) Sweet Wíl|liam aróse | one mór|ning in Máy,
    And dréssed | himsélf | in blúe
    Pray téll | us this lóng, | long, lóve, | said théy,
    Betwéen | lady Már|garet and yóu.

This song is in iambic/anapestic ballad stanzas, with the line pattern **4343** and ABAB rhyme. It was traditionally sung both in triple measure ($\frac{3}{2}$, S&K #20P, p. 145) and in duple measure ($\frac{2}{2}$, S&K #20A, p. 132, #20D, p. 137, or $\frac{4}{4}$, S&K #20J, p. 143). For H&M these would be different stanza forms: the former would be **5454** (see their Web Appendix), the latter would be **4343**. Let us compare it with another famous ballad, *Lord Bateman* (a.k.a. *Young Beichan*, Child #53):

(11) Lord Báte|man wás | a nó|ble Lórd,
    A nó|ble Lórd | of hígh | degrée
    He shípped | himsélf | on bóard | a shíp
    Some fó|reign cóun|try fór | to sée.

This song is in strict iambic LONG METER stanzas **(4444)**, again rhyming ABAB – another common metrical form in folk song quatrains. Traditionally it was sung to three different measures: $\frac{3}{4}$ time (#37 in Bronson 1959, 413 ff.), $\frac{4}{4}$ time (*ibid.* #2), and $\frac{5}{4}$ time (*ibid.* #25). These all correspond to different grids, *and therefore to different stanza forms according to H&M*. But the fact is that the stanza shape in each of these songs, however performed, is fixed: iambic/anapestic ballad stanzas in (10), and iambic long meter in (11). These meters are well-established traditional verse forms that folk poets work with. In the H&M scheme, they dissolve into a multiplicity of formally unrelated grid patterns.

The heart of the matter is how text and tune are related in a song tradition. Obviously they must be reasonably well matched to each other, and they have a more or less firm conventional association. Yet they are to some degree independent. They can originate and develop separately, and lines, couplets, and entire quatrains can float from one song to another. A newly composed song can be sung to an old melody, and an old song can get a new melody (Hayes in press, fn. 11). This means that the relation of verse form to musical performance is not so close as H&M claim. Therefore, instead of defining a stanza form in terms of the grid alignment of positions in musical performance, I treat stanza form and melody as separate structures between which an orderly correspondence must hold. According to this view, the meter of a song, including its stanza form, is subject to its own constraints and has its own independent existence which does not change with the tune.

One does not have to listen to folk songs for very long to realize that that correspondence between the strong beats in meter and music can be extremely indirect. Some singers achieve exciting effects by playing with the timing, drawing out some syllables over many beats and crowding others into a single beat.[7]

A further argument for separating constraints on musical performance from metrical constraints on stanza form is that the metrical constraints are applicable also to literary verse that was never meant to be sung or chanted. This holds true not only for imitations of folk genres, but also for purely literary stanza forms which have no counterpart in songs. In general, literary inventions obey the same laws of stanza construction as folk poetry, namely parallelism and closure, merely in a less stereotypical, and sometimes experimental way. For example, the ballad stanza can be expanded by doubling the odd-numbered lines (**443443** with AABCCB rhyme, sometimes called common particular meter, e.g., Dylan Thomas' *A Process in the Weather of the Heart*), by adding a third couplet (**434343**, ABCBDB, e.g., Longfellow' *The*

Slave's Dream). Doubling the quatrain and tying the two quatrains together by putting B=C yields the Romance *ballade* stanza (ABABBCBC), which does of course originate in songs. Other literary modifications for closure are ABABBCC (rhyme royal), ABABBCBCC (the Spenser stanza), and ABABCCB (the Thompson stanza, where CC is feminine), and ABABABCC *(Ottava rima)*. These stanza forms are simply more ornate manifestations of the same organizing principles that we see at their simplest in folk song quatrains.

To summarize, the modular approach unifies the treatment of meter in songs and spoken verse, and accounts for the fact that metrical form remains invariant across different musical measures. At a more technical level, it makes for a simpler metrical inventory, and correctly predicts why some line types alternate with each other, and why others do not occur at all. The particulars follow.

2.2. Deriving the quatrain typology

Returning to folk verse, let's review where we stand. Classifying lines by their final cadence, like H&M, but simplifying the typology by folding their line types **G, 3$_f$,** and **F** into a single metrical type **3'**, we are left with three types of lines in all, **4, 3'**, and **3**, which are distinguished by whether the last foot is binary (call it **F**), unary (**f**), or empty (**Ø**). What types of quatrains could be built from these lines, and which of those quatrains are in actual use? We'll answer this question in two steps, by considering first the subclass of RHYMING QUATRAINS, which are of the form ABCB, where at least the even-numbered (B) lines rhyme. (The odd-numbered lines A and C may also rhyme, but more often they do not.) That includes the great bulk of the folk song material under study. The second subclass comprises quatrains in which closure is achieved by another structural device, the refrain.

By unifying **G, 3$_f$,** and **F** as **3'**, we have reduced H&M's 625 theoretically possible rhyming quatrains to 3^4=81, of which nine are reliably attested. In table (12) they are laid out as combinations of two couplets (distichs), the first given by the row and the second by the column. The figures in parentheses give the number of examples of each type that H&M report from their corpus.[8]

This reduced table is an improvement in that all the combinations now at least fit on a page, but even so it is still rather daunting. It can be further pared down by noting that, of the nine theoretically possible types of couplets, only six occur, namely **44, 43', 43, 3'3', 3'3,** and **33**. The other three types, **3'4, 34,** and **33'**, are absent from both halves of quatrains (with the exception of one occurrence of **3′3′3′4**). The missing types of couplets are not a random class: they are just those in which *the second line is longer than the first.* The generalization, then, is that the lines of a couplet must not increase in length. Adopting H&M's concept of SALIENCY as measured by the inverse of length (shorter lines are more salient than longer lines), one way of formulating the descriptive generalization would be (13).

(12)	44	43′	43	3′4	3′3′	3′3	34	33′	33
44	4444 *(203)*	4443′ *(0)*	4443 *(35)*	443′4 *(0)*	443′3′ *(0)*	443′3 *(0)*	4434 *(0)*	4433′ *(0)*	4433 *(1)*
43′	43′44 *(0)*	43′43′ *(64)*	43′43 *(0)*	43′3′4 *(0)*	43′3′3′ *(0)*	43′3′3 *(1)*	43′34 *(0)*	43′33′ *(0)*	43′33 *(0)*
43	4344 *(1)*	4343′ *(1)*	4343 *(188)*	433′4 *(0)*	433′3′ *(0)*	433′3 *(0)*	4334 *(0)*	4333′ *(0)*	4333 *(0)*
3′4	3′444 *(0)*	3′443′ *(0)*	3′443 *(0)*	3′43′4 *(0)*	3′43′3′ *(0)*	3′43′3 *(0)*	3′434 *(0)*	3′433′ *(0)*	3′433 *(0)*
3′3′	3′3′44 *(0)*	3′3′43′ *(0)*	3′3′43 *(0)*	3′3′3′4 *(1)*	3′3′3′3′ *(5)*	3′3′3′3 *(3)*	3′3′34 *(0)*	3′3′33′ *(0)*	3′3′33 *(0)*
3′3	3′344 *(0)*	3′343′ *(0)*	3′343 *(8)*	3′33′4 *(0)*	3′33′3′ *(0)*	3′33′3 *(84)*	3′334 *(0)*	3′333′ *(0)*	3′333 *(1)*
34	3444 *(0)*	3443′ *(0)*	3443 *(0)*	343′4 *(0)*	343′3′ *(0)*	343′3 *(0)*	3434 *(0)*	3433′ *(0)*	3433 *(0)*
33′	33′44 *(0)*	33′43′ *(0)*	33′43 *(0)*	33′3′4 *(0)*	33′3′3′ *(0)*	33′3′3 *(0)*	33′34 *(0)*	33′33′ *(0)*	33′33 *(0)*
33	3344 *(0)*	3343′ *(0)*	3343 *(6)*	333′4 *(0)*	333′3′ *(0)*	333′3 *(1)*	3334 *(0)*	3333′ *(0)*	3333 *(1)*

(13) A couplet must not have decreasing saliency.

Alternatively, we can define a couplet as PARALLEL if its lines are equally salient (i.e., of the same length) and SALIENT if its lines are decreasing in length, and rephrase the descriptive generalization as (14).

(14) A couplet must either be parallel or salient.

In a framework where constraints are inviolable, (13) might seem preferable to the disjunctive formulation in (14). In OT, however, (14) can be thought of naturally in terms of competition between two constraints, which cannot both be obeyed at the same time:

(15) a. SALIENCY: A couplet is salient.
b. PARALLELISM: A couplet is parallel.

Of these different ways of formulating the generalization, (15) is most like H&M's (although they do not define saliency and parallelism exactly like this), and we shall see that it indeed turns out to work out best for the full system. To the extent that we can derive stanza form from the competition between saliency and parallelism, we have support for an OT model in which such constraint competition can be treated by free ranking.

Taking into account the generalization just obtained (whether expressed as (13), (14), or (15)), we can erase the rows and columns corresponding to the three systematically missing couplet types from the chart. Doing so gives us the more manageable display in (16). I have reversed the order of **43** and **43'** to make the following exposition more perspicuous, and numbered the rows from (1) to (6) and the columns from (a) to (e) for easy reference, so that e.g., (3c) refers to the quatrain form **43'43'**.

(16)

	a. 44	b. 43	c. 43'	d. 3'3'	e. 3'3	f. 33
1. 44	4444 *(203)*	4443 *(35)*	4443'	443'3'	443'3	4433 *(1)*
2. 43	4344 *(1)*	4343 *(188)*	4343' *(1)*	433'3'	433'3	4333
3. 43'	43'44	43'43	43'43' *(64)*	43'3'3'	43'3'3 *(1)*	43'33
4. 3'3'	3'3'44	3'3'43	3'3'43'	3'3'3'3' *(5)*	3'3'3'3	3'3'33
5. 3'3	3'344	3'343 *(8)*	3'343'	3'33'3'	3'33'3 *(84)*	3'333 *(1)*
6. 33	3344	3343 *(6)*	3343'	333'3'	333'3 *(1)*	3333 *(1)*

Inspection of the new chart reveals that most of the occurring quatrain types are lined up along the NW/SE diagonal, in roughly descending frequency, with a smaller group down the second column (column b), but skipping two of the cells (3b and 4b). So to a first approximation we can say that the two couplets of a rhyming quatrain must either be identical in form (the diagonal), or the second of them must be a maximally salient couplet **43** (column b). This suggests that, at a higher level, quatrains are organized by a similar principle as couplets: quatrains must be composed of parallel couplets, or their second couplet must be maximally salient, which is to say **43**. To make this visually clear let us shade all cells in the chart which do *not* conform to the conditions just stated.

(17)   Rhyming Quatrains

	a. 44	b. 43	c. 43′	d. 3′3′	e. 3′3	f. 33
1. **44**	4444 (203)	4443 (35)	4443′	443′3′	443′3	4433 (1)
2. **43**	4344 (1)	4343 (188)	4343′ (1)	433′3′	433′3	4333
3. **43′**	43′44	43′43	43′43′ (64)	43′3′3′	43′3′3 (1)	43′33
4. **3′3′**	3′3′44	3′3′43	3′3′43′	3′3′3′3′ (5)	3′3′3′3	3′3′33
5. **3′3**	3′344	3′343 (8)	3′343′	3′33′3′	3′33′3 (84)	3′333 (1)
6. **33**	3344	3343 (6)	3343′	333′3′	333′3 (1)	3333 (1)

The unshaded area now contains all the attested rhymed quatrain types (except for the unique instances in the shaded cells, which I assume are not part of the core system), but there is still overgeneration in two cells: types (3b) **43′43** and (4b) **3′3′43** do not occur. (H&M's constraint system precludes the former and admits the latter, but neither is attested in their corpus.) The reason for this gap is obvious when we recall that in rhymed folksong quatrains the second line must rhyme with the fourth.[9] Simply because of the phonological equivalence that rhyme requires, a masculine line can only rhyme with a masculine line, and a feminine line can only rhyme with a feminine line. For example, in folk songs we find no "rhymes" between stressed and unstressed syllables, such as those between *Davy* and *see* and between *morning* and *ring* in the following constructed couplets:[10]

(18) a. Lady Márgot has pút on her sílken gówn
         To gó with the gípsy Dávy.
         She's ríding with hím on a mílk-white stéed
         Some fóreign lánd to sée.   (construct)
     b. Lady Márgot díed like it míght be at níght,
        Sweet Wílliam, he díed in the mórning.
        Lady Márgot was búried in her sílken gówn,
        Sweet Wílliam was búried with her ríng.   (construct)

The even lines do not rhyme *even if performed as **G** lines*. Therefore, since a line of type **3′** cannot rhyme with a line of type **4** or **3**, both couplets of a rhymed quatrain must end the same way, either in a masculine line (types **44, 43, 3′3, 33**) or in a feminine line (types **43′, 33′**). This excludes the two unshaded but unattested quatrain types **43′43** and (4b) **3′3′43** in (17), as well as fourteen others which have already fallen by the wayside because they are neither parallel nor salient. Blocking out these sixteen rhyme-incompatible types with a darker shading leaves nine white cells, and they correspond to the nine attested types of rhyming quatrains.

(19) Rhyming Quatrains

	a. **44**	b. **43**	c. **43′**	d. **3′3′**	e. **3′3**	f. **33**
1. **44**	4444 *(203)*	4443 *(35)*	4443′	443′3′	443′3	4433 *(1)*
2. **43**	4344 *(1)*	4343 *(188)*	4343′ *(1)*	433′3′	433′3	4333
3. **43′**	43′44	43′43	43′43′ *(64)*	43′3′3′	43′3′3 *(1)*	43′33
4. **3′3′**	3′3′44	3′3′43	3′3′43′	3′3′3′3′ *(5)*	3′3′3′3	3′3′33
5. **3′3**	3′344	3′343 *(8)*	3′343′	3′33′3′	3′33′3 *(84)*	3′333 *(1)*
6. **33**	3344	3343 *(6)*	3343′	333′3′	333′3 *(1)*	3333 *(1)*

Having mapped out the terrain provisionally, let's proceed to the analysis.

2.3. The constraints

Like H&M, I understand saliency to be a gradient property and define it *relationally*: a line or other unit is salient in relation to another similar unit. But I take saliency to be a *syntagmatic* relation between sister constituents. A couplet whose second line is **3** is salient if its first line is **4** or **3′**, but not if its first line is **3**. And just as saliency is a matter of contrast between sister constituents, so degree of saliency is a matter of the degree of that contrast.

Assume, uncontroversially, the following hierarchy of verse constituents (cf. H&M 475).

(20)

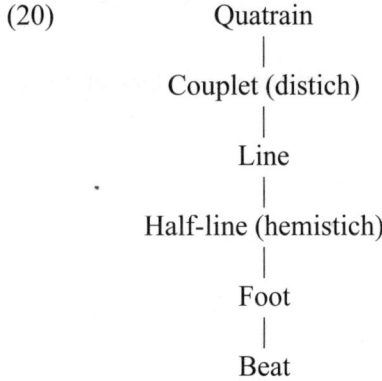

Quatrain
|
Couplet (distich)
|
Line
|
Half-line (hemistich)
|
Foot
|
Beat

Each unit but the lowest is made up of exactly two units of the next lower level (except possibly for the special case of refrain quatrains, if my above conjecture about their constituency is right). It is because of this highly regimented binary metrical hierarchy that a type **3** line is perceived as ending in a null (empty) foot (Ø), and a type **3′** line is perceived as ending in a unary (degenerate) foot (**f**).[11]

We define saliency as a primitive at the lowest level, the foot, and define the saliency of larger constituents recursively. A line consists of four feet, each having two metrical positions, or BEATS, of which one or both may remain empty. Descriptively, saliency is the inverse of length, measured in beats: a full foot (**F**) is NONSALIENT, a reduced foot (**f**, Ø) is SALIENT. Theoretically, we take saliency to be unfaithfulness, specifically mismatches between metrical positions and the linguistic elements that correspond to them. In English verse, saliency results from an unfilled position in the metrical grid, definable as a violation of the faithfulness constraint MAXBEAT:

(21) MAXBEAT: Beats are realized.

Assume that each unrealized beat incurs a violation of (21). Then **F** is the maximally faithful foot type, and Ø, with both its empty beats, is maximally unfaithful. By putting saliency = unfaithfulness, we obtain the hierarchy:

(22) a. Full foot **(F)**: [σ σ] (perfect match, nonsalient)
 b. Degenerate foot **(f)**: [σ] (mismatch, salient)
 c. Null foot **(Ø)**: [ ] (maximum mismatch, maximally salient)

Diverging from H&M, we then define saliency and parallelism at higher levels of metrical structure in recursive fashion.

(23) *Definitions*:
 a. A constituent is SALIENT if its last immediate constituent is the most salient.
 b. A constituent is PARALLEL if its immediate constituents are equally salient.

At the quatrain level, the couplet type **43** has a privileged status in that it is the only type of couplet that can close a nonparallel quatrain. There are two plausible ways to distinguish **43** formally from the other salient couplet types **43'** and **3'3**. One way is to view **43** as the MAXIMALLY SALIENT couplet type. Another characterization of **43** is as a salient couplet which contains only unmarked (binary) feet. The latter means formally that it obeys the constraint FOOTBIN, which is standard in metrics and metrical phonology.

(24) FOOTBIN: Feet are binary.

With the present data, at any rate, these two ways of singling out **43** are empirically indistinguishable. Conceptually, the second is perhaps preferable because FOOTBIN is needed anyway to pick out meters which prohibit degenerate feet (**3'** lines), that is, meters which allow only **4343**, **4444**, **3343**, and **3333** quatrains. (We will encounter one such meter in section 4 below.)

The constraints on folk song stanzas, then, are these:

(25) *Constraints*:
  a. SALIENCY: A constituent is salient.
  b. PARALLELISM: A constituent is parallel.
  c. CLOSURE: The salient couplet of a salient quatrain contains no marked feet.

No metrical constituent at any level can be both salient and parallel. Therefore, if both (25a) and (25b) are visible in a metrical system, they must be able to dominate each other, i.e., they are crucially freely ranked with respect to each other. Except for this, the constraints can be arbitrarily ranked, or unranked.

Application of (23a) at each level of the metrical hierarchy yields the following:

(26) a. A half-line (hemistich) is salient if its second foot is more salient than the first. Hence, the salient hemistichs are **F Ø**, **f Ø**, and **F f**.
  b. A line is salient if its second hemistich is more salient than the first. Hence, the salient lines are those of type **3'** and **3** (in terms of hemistichs, **21'** and **21**).
  c. A couplet is salient if its second line is more salient than the first. Hence, the salient couplets are **43**, **43'**, and **3'3**.[12]
  d. By (25c), the final couplet of a salient quatrain is not only salient, but unmarked, i.e., it is of the form **43**.

The following summary table shows how saliency and parallelism at different levels of the metrical hierarchy combine to derive the observed typology.

(27)

	Nonsalient (parallel)	Salient
Feet	F (ss)	f (s), Ø
Hemistichs	2 (=FF)	1' (=Ff), 1 (=FØ)
Lines	4 (=22)	3' (=21'), 3 (=21)
Couplets	44, 3'3', 33	43', 3'3, 43
Quatrains	4444..., 3333	*4443'..., **333'3, 4443..., 3343

2.4. Refrain quatrains

Refrain quatrains are much less common. Unlike the type discussed so far, they do not have to rhyme, probably because the closure function of rhyme is served by the refrain constituent. In fact, in the limiting case, the repeated element of the refrain is just the last word of the last line, effectively functioning as a cross-stanza rhyme. For example, this song has ten stanzas, each consisting of three rhyming **4** lines plus a refrain line which ends in *Shiloh*:

(28) All you Southerners now draw near,   **4**
      Unto my story approach you here,   **4**
      Each loyal Southerner's heart to cheer   **4**
      With the victory gained at Shi – loh.   **3'**
                          The Battle of Shiloh (Sharp & Karpeles #136)

As far as I can tell, refrain quatrains allow all metrical types in (19), plus a few additional ones: **4443'** (8x), **3'3'3'3** (3x), **4433** (5x), **43'43** (2x), in addition to a sprinkling of entirely unique quatrains (Hayes and McEachern 1998:496 ff.).

The occurrence of the new type **43'43** in refrain quatrains fills a gap in the typology of (19); remember that our metrical constraints predict this type, and the reason is doesn't occur in rhyming quatrains is that the even-numbered lines **3'** and **3** cannot rhyme. In refrain quatrains rhyme is not a factor, so this type is expected.

To fit refrain quatrains into our constraint system we must make some assumptions about their constituent structure. They do not seem to consist of two couplets, but simply of four coordinated lines (**[4443']**), or in some cases even three lines capped by a refrain (**[444][3']**), as in this children's song (Sharp & Karpeles #264):

(29) This is the way we go to church,   **4**
      Go to church, go to church,   **4**
      This is the way we go to church,   **4**
      Early Sunday mor – ning.   **3'**
      This is the way we wash our clothes,   **4**
      Wash our clothes, wash our clothes,   **4**
      This is the way we wash our clothes,   **4**
      Early Monday mor – ning.   **3'**
      (and so on for each day of the week)

In either case, constraint (25c) is not applicable as formulated, so that refrain quatrains of types **4443'** and **3'3'3'3** satisfy all constraints in (25). Moreover, since the refrain need not rhyme, the masculine/feminine mismatch between the even-numbered lines is not an inhibiting factor. The occurrence of these additional quatrain types in such refrain quatrains is then expected.[13] As for quatrains of type **4433** (unmetrical by H&M's constraints but attested 5 times in refrain quatrains in their corpus, in addition to the single non-refrain occurrence in (19)), I have no firm analysis to propose. They could arise from **43** couplets by doubling of both lines. Alternatively, if they have the structure **[443][3]**, they would literally satisfy our definition of parallelism, since in such a structure both the tercet **443** and the refrain **3** (= **21**) are maximally salient.

2.5. Restrictiveness and locality

Besides being simpler than H&M's, and using very general off-the-shelf constraints rather than custom-made ones, this analysis has some other empirical and conceptual advantages. It is more accurate in that it successfully rules out several non-occurring rhyme quatrain types that H&M's system admits: ***3$_f$3$_f$43$_f$** and ***GG4G** (our ***3'3'43'**, type 4c in (19)), ***33F3** and ***33G3**[14] (our ***333'3**, 6e in (19)), and **3$_f$3$_f$F3$_f$** (excluded for the same reason as ***3'3'43'**). This OVERGENERATION PROBLEM is a direct consequence of H&M's failure to separate meter from text-to-tune alignment.

SALIENCY and PARALLELISM apply at each level to determine how a unit combines into a unit of the next higher level: feet into half-lines, half-lines into lines, lines into couplets, and couplets into quatrains (where the last combination is subject to an additional restriction, (25c)). That is why the properties of units at different levels of the metrical hierarchy are substantially the same. This cross-level generalization was noted by Hayes & MacEachern in the Web appendix to their article, but not formally built into their theory. The present approach exploits it to obtain a substantial simplification of the constraint system and along with it a more explanatory analysis.

The modular approach advocated here leads us to expect certain locality effects in the evaluation of metrical constraints. The acceptability of a given type of constituent is assessed locally and its distribution depends on saliency and parallelism at the next higher level. The well-formedness of a quatrain depends on the properties of the couplets that it consists of, the well-formedness of a couplet depends on the properties of the lines that it consists of, and so on.

The data provide some evidence for this kind of "metrical subjacency." For example, no quatrain type requires a special type of foot, and no type of foot is restricted to just one place in a quatrain. Because of this, the reduced foot types Ø and **f** are in principle available not only at the end of a line or hemistich (in the line types **3** and **3′**), but anywhere in the line:

(30) a. Green | grow | the rush|es O   type **4**
     b. Lang, | lang | may their la|dies sit   *Sir Patrick Spens*, type **4**
     c. Fírst | níght | when Í | got hóme
                          Drunkard's Special (Folkways Anthology), type **4**
     d. Háir | ón | a cábbage | héad   *ibid.*, type **3f**

However, in non-final positions they are not motivated by saliency, hence much rarer.

Still, the data does clearly reveal two types of global dependencies, both involving constraints on foot structure imposed at higher levels. First, saliency in final position is inherited upward from lower to higher constituents – a cornerstone of our analysis. Secondly, constraint (25c) as formulated prohibits marked feet anywhere in the closing couplets of salient quatrains, which requires universal quantification at the quatrain level over the smallest constituents. Although the limited nature of this globality is encouraging, the question whether a restrictive metrical typology can be developed must be left to future research.

3. Hayes and MacEachern: the details

3.1. OT metrics

Formal approaches to metrics were constraint-based long before OT. Many operated with two kinds of constraints, INVIOLABLE constraints, which must be satisfied by all and only well-formed verse, and PREFERENCES, which are violable but at the cost of complexity. A metrical system or subsystem, such as a rhyme scheme or a stanza form, is defined by the designated subset of constraints that it must satisfy obligatorily. The preferences among the permissible realizations of that form are defined by some selection of the remaining universal constraints. In one or another way, every theory must have something that corresponds to this distinction between inviolable constraints and preferences. Among currently available theoretical architectures, OT is the theory of choice for this, because it models competing constraints and preferences, predicts that preferences in one system typically correspond to obligatory constraints of another, and makes strong testable typological predictions. But it is important to understand that OT is just a formal theory of constraint interaction and does not by itself have anything to say about metrics. For that we need an actual set of metrical constraints, and there are many different ideas about what these look like (see Golston 1998 and Friedberg 2002 for two recent proposals).

H&M's theory has the form of a set of markedness constraints analogous to those used in phonology. Each markedness constraint imposes some metrical well-formedness condition. Every well-formed quatrain pattern is not only good enough – it is the *best* under some ranking of the markedness constraints. H&M deal with preferences by augmenting their markedness constraints with a quantitative component, for which they use stochastic OT. Each constraint is assigned a place on a scale of real numbers, which governs its likelihood of outranking other constraints and being ouranked by them.

One problem with this approach is that it does not relate frequency intrinsically to unmarkedness. Much traditional work shows that the most frequent metrical structures tend to be those which are the simplest. For H&M, the question of differences in relative complexity simply does not arise. Each quatrain type is simply the best under some constraint ranking. It is the numerical part of the metrical grammar that models the patterns of relative preference among the competing optima. Small or large adjustments of the numbers, even keeping the ranking invariant, change these patterns in delicate or radical ways. Let's call this the MARKEDNESS PROBLEM.

Another general problem with characterizing a stanza form as the optimal output of a set of ranked markedness constraints is the HARMONIC BOUNDING PROBLEM: how to distinguish two stanza forms that differ only in strictness. The looser of them, requiring satisfaction of fewer constraints, cannot be characterized by any ranking of independently motivated markedness constraints. For example, consider the two commonest rhyming patterns found in folk song quatrains, ABCB and ABAB. They share the requirement that the even-numbered lines must rhyme, but the ABAB scheme in addition requires that the odd-numbered lines must rhyme. A stanza where both line pairs rhyme, such as (10), obviously satisfies both these constraints. How to define formally a verse form, normal in folk songs, that requires only odd-numbered lines to rhyme? The problem is that the ABAB stanza type satisfies all the markedness constraints that ABCB does and then some – in OT terms, ABCB is HARMONICALLY BOUNDED by ABAB. In order to characterize the looser rhyme scheme ABCB as the optimal output to some system of ranked markedness constraints, we would have to find some respect in which it is more harmonic than ABAB. We would need something like an "anti-rhyme" constraint, but that will not do because ABAB stanzas like (10) are not *prohibited* in ABCB verse, they are just not *required*. For example, (10) is an ABAB stanza in an otherwise ABCB song, see (9).[15]

To anticipate the following discussion: the analysis proposed below eliminates the harmonic bounding problem by positing a FAITHFULNESS constraint which may be ranked among the markedness constraints. (Hayes (in press) himself uses this device to solve the problem of optionality in prosodic correspondence.) FAITHFULNESS dictates that the wording of the input be retained in the output, even if that leads to violations of lower-ranked constraints. On this assumption, the difference between the ABAB and ABCB rhyme schemes could be characterized by alternative rankings of the following constraints:[16]

(31) a. CLOSING RHYME: The even-numbered lines of a quatrain must rhyme.
      b. FULL RHYME: Alternate even-numbered and odd-numbered lines of a quatrain must rhyme.
      c. FAITHFULNESS: Keep the input wording.

The ranking (31b) >> (31c) defines a verse form with an ABAB rhyme scheme. The ranking (31a) >> (31c) >> (31b) defines a verse form with an ABCB rhyme scheme, in which the even-numbered lines of a quatrain must rhyme (and the odd-numbered lines may rhyme). Thus, although the traditional idea of a meter being "subject to" or "not subject to" that constraint makes no sense within OT, it can be adequetely simulated by the ranking of FAITHFULNESS with respect to that constraint.

The harmonic bounding problem is not the only infelicitous consequence of the notion that each stanza type is optimal under some ranking of universal markedness constraints. It leads directly to gaps in coverage and unnecessary complications. I develop this point in sections 3.2–3.4, and then show how my proposed alternative avoids them, without losing any of the real insights of the H&M theory.

We can divide H&M's constraints roughly into three classes, which deal respectively with saliency, parallelism, and correspondence between metrical position and musical beats. These are taken up in turn in 3.2–3.4.

3.2. Saliency

H&M define saliency by means of the auxiliary concepts of a CADENCE and CADENTIALITY. A (rhythmic) cadence is the grid placement of the final two syllables of the line (p. 476). The cadentiality of a line type is measured by the number of beats assigned to its cadence. The more grid positions the cadence occupies in the song, the more cadential the line. More precisely, cadentiality depends primarily on the number of grid positions assigned to its final syllable; when this yields a tie, it is resolved by the number of grid positions assigned to the penultimate syllable. The following hierarchy of cadentiality results (p. 484–485):

(32) $3 \gg 3_f \gg G \gg 4$

As explained above, I view the distinction between 3_f and **G** as a choice between two musical settings of a **3'** line of verse. I adopt the rest of the hierarchy unchanged, but as explained in (22)–(25) I don't stipulate it but rather derive it from faithfulness. The following discussion demonstrates the virtues of this approach.

In H&M's OT system, saliency must be both a categorical property and a gradient property. Categorical saliency is defined in (33).

(33)   A metrical constituent is (categorically) SALIENT if
   a. its final rhythmic cadence is more cadential than all of its nonfinal cadences,
   b. all of its nonfinal cadences are uniform.

The (b) part of H&M's definition of saliency is satisfied if all cadences in question are of the same type. Thus, the salient quatrains are **444G, 4443$_f$, 4443, GGG3$_f$, GGG3, 3$_f$3$_f$3$_f$3**, the salient couplets are just the second halves of the salient quatrains, namely **4G, 43$_f$, 43, G3$_f$, G3, 3$_f$3**, and each line type is trivially salient. The *degree* of saliency of a constituent is assessed by the cadentiality of its final cadence according to the hierarchy (32). As an illustration, consider the quatrain **3$_f$343**. By (33), the whole quatrain is nonsalient, both its couplets are salient, and each line is salient in proportion to its cadentiality: the second and fourth lines are maximally salient, the third line is minimally salient, and the first has an intermediate degree of saliency.

The notion of saliency plays a key role in most of H&M's constraints, most directly in (34)–(36):

(34) LINES ARE SALIENT (H&M (38)): Assess violations for any nonsalient line, according to its degree of nonsaliency.

(35) COUPLETS ARE SALIENT (H&M (39)): Assess violations for any nonsalient couplet, according to its degree of nonsaliency.

(36) QUATRAINS ARE SALIENT (H&M (40)): Assess violations to the extent that the quatrain is nonsalient.

This brings out another difference between the two approaches: for H&M, a constraint such as (34) LINES ARE SALIENT plays a direct role in the evaluation of quatrains; in fact, if this constraint is ranked first, a quatrain **3333** results. For me, the relevant property of **3333** for quatrain structure is parallelism.

A subtlety of the H&M system is that, in the gradient evaluation of (34) LINES ARE SALIENT and (35) COUPLETS ARE SALIENT, quality trumps quantity: for example, the quatrain **3343** is a worse violation of (34) than the quatrain $3_f 3_f 3_f 3_f$ is, because even one minimally salient line of the form **4** is worse than four medium-salient lines of the form 3_f. My solution needs no counterpart to this stipulation.

Both gradient and categorical saliency play a role in three further constraints which deal with the category of a LONG-LAST CONSTRUCTION, defined in (37) (H&M (29)):

(37) A quatrain is a LONG-LAST CONSTRUCTION if:
 a. its second couplet is salient by the all-or-nothing definition (33) (= H&M (22));
 b. both its [the couplet's] first and second lines are more salient than the third line (by the gradient definition [of H&M (23), essentially according to the hierarchy in (32) above]).

Although the definition covers a number of quatrain types, the only long-last stanza form that is actually used is **3343** (so-called SHORT METER). Long-last stanzas are derived when the following constraint is undominated:

(38) PREFER LONG-LAST (H&M (41)): Avoid any quatrain that is not a long-last construction.

The next two constraints form a hierarchy. (39a) is subsumed by (39b), but (39b) is inviolable (undominated) whereas (39a) can be ranked differently to give different quatrain types.

(39) a. TOTAL LONG-LAST COHESIVENESS (H&M (42a)): Avoid long-last constructions whose third line is not 4.
b. PARTIAL LONG-LAST COHESIVENESS (H&M (42b)): Avoid long-last constructions whose third line is not 4 or G.

The treatment of this stanza type reveals another difference between the approaches. The "long-last construction" is simply a type of salient quatrain, which requires no special definitions or constraints.[17] The concept of "long-last construction" and the constraints that refer to it are probably artifacts of H&M's OT approach.[18] It needs them because the quatrain type **3343** must not only be good enough – it must be the *best* under some constraint ranking. If we don't adopt this framework, we can get rid of (37)–(39), which certainly is a welcome move because just this part of the system is responsible for the above-mentioned overgeneration of the unattested quatrain types ***3$_f$3$_f$43$_f$, *GG4G, *3$_f$3$_f$F3$_f$, *33G3** and ***33F3**.

3.3. Parallelism

H&M define PARALLELISM by means of the auxiliary concept of a MAXIMAL ANALYSIS. A maximal analysis is the largest sequence of salient constituents comprising a quatrain (H&M: 488), formally defined like this (H&M's (24)):

(40) **Def:** Let $C_1, C_2, \ldots C_n$ be a sequence of adjacent metrical constituents exhausting the material of a quatrain Q.
If for each **C** of $C_1, C_2, \ldots C_n$
a. **C** is salient by the all-or-nothing definition (33) [H&M's (22)]; and
b. there is no salient constituent **C'** dominating **C**;
then $C_1, C_2, \ldots C_n$ is the MAXIMAL ANALYSIS of Q.

The following two constraints are undominated.

(41) PARALLELISM (H&M (25)): The cadences ending the units of the maximal analysis of a quatrain must be identical.

For example, the quatrain type 3_f343 satisfies parallelism in virtue of its maximal analysis **[3_f3][43]**.

(42) STANZA CORRESPONDENCE (H&M (37)): In a song, the set of salient domains must be invariant across stanzas.

This constraint crucially employs the categorical version of saliency defined in (33).

Recall that for H&M, saliency requires nonfinal cadences to be uniform, which is just what PARALLELISM requires of maximal analyses (see (41)) – a redundancy. Note also that H&M's definition of saliency contains a parallelism condition (33b), and the definition of parallelism in turn relies on saliency (via (40)). Both the redundancy and the whiff of circularity are eliminated in the alternative I proposed through the recursive application of the parallelism and saliency constraint at each level.

3.4. Metrical Constraints

In H&M's OT system, 3_f and **G** must each be optimal under some constraint ranking, a result achieved by positing the following two constraints, which roughly correspond to MAXBEAT but are split into two antagonistic constraints, one requiring **G**, the other requiring 3_f, and allowing them to rank freely with respect to each other.

(43) FILL STRONG POSITIONS (H&M (31)): Fill the four strongest positions in the line.

High-ranked FILL STRONG POSITIONS forces **G** instead of 3_f. High ranking of the next constraint has the opposite effect, of forcing 3_f instead of **G**.

(44) AVOID LAPSE (H&M (32)): Avoid sequences in which no syllable is placed in the interval between any two of the four strongest positions of the line.

Any theory needs something like (43), but (44) is more surprising. The configuration in question – an empty weak beat – is not a "lapse" in the traditional sense of metrical phonology (nor is it exactly a "clash" either). For us, the work of this constraint is done in the text-to-tune system: **3'** is implemented as **3$_f$** when the melody has a rest in the fourth strong beat.[19]

The realization of a line as type **G** or type **4** is governed by MATCHSTRESS. Instead of H&M's version, I reproduce that of Hayes (in press), which supersedes it, as in (45). In effect, a lexical stress is matched to the strongest available position. I would assume an equivalent constraint as part of the metrical theory.

(45) MATCH STRESS
Assess a violation if:
- σ_i and σ_j (in either order) are linked to grid positions G_i and G_j respectively;
- σ_i is more stressed than σ_j;
- G_i is stronger than G_j; and
- σ_i and σ_j occupy the same simplex word.

In sum: the notion that each attested line type is the best under some constraint ranking forces H&M to posit a number of complex and otherwise unmotivated constraints plus additional conventions on their interpretation. Some of them have no other purpose than to single out directly a particular line type. This proliferation of constraints compromises the factorial typology of metrical systems.

4. Relative frequency

4.1. Stochastic OT versus partial ranking

Quantitative metrical data provide a novel proving ground for OT theories of variation and for OT itself. The challenge here is to make sense of the massive disparities in relative frequency among the different quatrain types.

An interesting and empirically well-supported studied theory of variation in the OT framework holds that variation arises when the grammar specifies a partial ranking (Anttila 1997, 2003). A form F is grammatical if there is a fully ranked tableau consistent with that partial ranking in which F is the optimal candidate. The probability of a form F is predicted from the proportion of those tableaux relative to all tableaux that are consistent with the partial ranking. For example, in a grammar with three unranked constraints, there are six tableaux for any given input. Suppose that for a certain input A, two of these tableaux select output A$_1$ and four select output A$_2$. Then A$_2$ is predicted to be twice as frequent as A$_1$ is, as a realization of A. In practice, of course, the number of constraints, rankings, and tableaux is much larger, the options more numerous, and the gradations of relative frequency are correspondingly more delicate.

H&M's analysis is clearly incompatible with this perspective on variation. The frequency of the different quatrain types bears no orderly relation to the number of constraint rankings on which they are derived. For example, the rarest well-formed quatrain type **3333** is obtained by any ranking in which (34) LINES ARE SALIENT is undominated. Since there are seven other constraints whose ranking can vary, that makes a total of 7!=5,040 tableaux. On the other hand, one of the commonest line types, **4343**, requires the rather particular ranking (35) COUPLETS ARE SALIENT >> (43) FILL STRONG POSITIONS >> (44) AVOID LAPSE, which is consistent with a mere 5!=120 tableaux. The prediction is completely off course.

Instead, H&M assume a stochastic OT theory of variation which posits that each constraint has a range of fixed width, within which it can freely vary. Constraints may outrank each other to the extent that their ranges overlap. (The theory proposed by Boersma, and adopted in later work also by Hayes, posits a probabilistic distribution within the range; the center of the range represents its most likely place in the ranking, with probability decreasing towards the margins.) To discover the range of a constraint on the continuous scale, the learner must gather, store, and process frequency data about the output variants. This contrasts with Anttila's theory, which derives variation patterns from the *absence* of information about the mutual ranking of constraints, in effect claiming that they can be acquired without frequency information.

The folk song data is actually somewhat awkward for stochastic OT as well, under H&M's constraints. The problem again lies with the constraints (35) COUPLETS ARE SALIENT, (43) FILL STRONG POSITIONS, and (44) AVOID LAPSE. Ranked as in (46a), they give the output **4343**. Full demotion of COUPLETS ARE SALIENT as in (46b) gives **4444**. These are the two most frequent quatrain types of all. By the logic of the stochastic OT model, the intermediate ranking of COUPLETS ARE SALIENT in (46c) should produce an even more frequent output than at least one of the other rankings. But, disconcertingly, it gives a type which is substantially *less* common than either, namely **4G4G** (see H&M's fn. 42 for discussion).

(46) a. COUPLETS ARE SALIENT >> FILL STRONG POSITIONS >> AVOID LAPSE:
Output **4343** (very frequent)
b. FILL STRONG POSITIONS >> AVOID LAPSE >> COUPLETS ARE SALIENT:
Output **4444** (very frequent)
c. FILL STRONG POSITIONS >> COUPLETS ARE SALIENT >> AVOID LAPSE:
Output **4G4G** (less frequent)

This is an instance of what we called the MARKEDNESS PROBLEM.

One of the most appealing ideas behind Anttila's theory is that variation is *more* easily learned than non-variation, because it comes about when some constraint ranking is not learned and the learner remains, in that respect, in the initial state of entertaining alternative rankings. Remarkably, Anttila-style analyses, in spite of their discrete and minimalist character, tend to match the observed frequencies reasonably well, sometimes as accurately as the stochastic approach, which places a much greater burden on acquisition, and extends the power of the theory by bringing in the real numbers.

While the stochastic model is less restrictive than Anttila's in this respect, it is more restrictive in another. It predicts that the constraints are strictly stratified along the scale; the width of a constraint's range is fixed, and only its place on the continuous scale relative to the other constraints determines the probability of the rankings. In Anttila's partial ranking model, and in H&M's version of the stochastic model, the range of a constraint can overlap with the range of a set of ranked constraints. Here is a simple example. Suppose we have two ranked constraints $C_1 >> C_2$, and a constraint C_0 which is unranked with respect to them. Assume the candidates $Cand_0$, $Cand_1$, and $Cand_2$, which satisfy only C_0, C_1, and C_2 respectively. Then there are three fully ranked tableaux:

(47) a. $C_0 >> C_1 >> C_2$ optimal output: $Cand_0$
b. $C_1 >> C_0 >> C_2$ optimal output: $Cand_1$
c. $C_1 >> C_2 >> C_0$ optimal output: $Cand_1$

Anttila's theory entails that $Cand_1$ is twice as frequent as $Cand_0$, and that $Cand_2$ has zero frequency. The unordered constraint in this partial ranking is C_0. $Cand_1$ and $Cand_2$ each violate this constraint once. But $Cand_1$ and $Cand_2$ do not have the same frequency. In such cases, the frequency of a form is not simply proportional to the number of its violations of unordered constraints in a partial ordering. Quantitative studies of variation have turned up several instances of this type (Anttila 1997 Ch. 3,4, 2002, 2003). We shall see that the metrical system under investigation is another such case.

4.2. Formalizing the constraint system

The correlation between the frequencies of the quatrains tabulated in (16) with the markedness of their lines and couplets is a promising starting point for an explanatory quantitative analysis. The constraints needed for the categorical data, given above in (21), (24), and (25), are repeated below in (48).

(48) a. SALIENCY: Constituents are salient.
      b. PARALLELISM: Constituents are parallel.
      c. MAXBEAT: Beats are realized.
      d. FOOTBIN: Feet are binary.

With some additional assumptions, we can derive from these constraints a quantitative model of the actual frequency distribution.

First, we have to spell out how the constraints in (48) are assessed and how they interact in the metrical grammar to distinguish metrical from unmetrical lines.

Recall that lines composed of four full binary feet (type **4** lines) violate neither MAXBEAT nor FOOTBIN. All other lines have one or more missing beats; they violate the constraint MAXBEAT. Lines containing unary or 'degenerate' feet (type **3′**) violate, in addition, the constraint FOOTBIN. Couplets and quatrains obviously violate a constraint if they contain any line that violates it. In addition they may violate SALIENCY or PARALLELISM at the couplet and/or quatrain level. Of the nine theoretically possible couplet types, two (namely **3′4** and **33′**) never have a chance because they are rejected by all four constraints; the others satisfy one or more of them as follows:

(49) a. PARALLELISM : **44, 3′3′, 33**
      b. SALIENCY: **43, 43′, 3′3**
      c. MAXBEAT: **44**
      d. FOOTBIN: **44, 43, 33, 34**

There are 4!=24 possible rankings of the constraints in (49). Each ranking defines a type of metrical structure, either a stanza, a couplet, a line, a hemistich, or a foot, according to the level of analysis. Let us suppose that lines shorter than **3** and lines longer than **4** are categorically excluded by other, undominated constraints, which leaves us with **3, 3′**, and **4**. These can combine with each other into nine kinds of couplets, of which six are metrical, as we have seen. Each type of metrical couplet can be paired with another of the same type to make a parallel quatrain. Thus, the problem of characterizing the types and relative frequency of parallel quatrains (the ones that appear on the diagonal in table (16), which form the vast majority of all quatrains) can be reduced to that of characterizing the types and relative frequency of couplets.

Of the nine theoretically possible couplet types, only **43** satisfies both SALIENCY and FOOTBIN. Therefore, when both of these constraints outrank PARALLELISM and MAXBEAT, **43** is selected as the optimal couplet. And **44** is the only couplet type that satisfies MAXBEAT. So, when MAXBEAT outranks the other constraints (or even whenever it outranks just SALIENCY), **44** is the optimal couplet. In fact, all 24 possible rankings of (48a–d) yield either **43** or **44**. Therefore, to derive the four other couplet types (namely **43′, 3′3′, 3′3, 33**), and the parallel quatrains containing them, something must be added to the system.

H&M solve the analogous problem by adding constraints that favor all the other couplet and quatrain types, so that each of them gets to be the optimal output of at least one constraint ranking. The problems we identified above are traceable to this strategy: *(1)* the OVERGENERATION PROBLEM (too many quatrain types are predicted), *(2)* the HARMONIC BOUNDING PROBLEM (how to characterize metrical forms which differ merely in strictness), and *(3)* the MARKEDNESS PROBLEM (the frequency distribution of the quatrain types is not systematically related to complexity or markedness).

A better method is to complement the four constraints in (48) with just one other constraint, FAITHFULNESS. By Richness of the Base, the input to the constraint system is any metrical form whatever. FAITHFULNESS dictates that the input is realized as such (rather than being replaced by something else, or suppressed). The effect of FAITHFULNESS is to license any candidate not excluded by higher-ranked constraints as metrical. Constraints ranked above this cutoff-point restrict metricality, while constraints ranked below it are inactive. We shall say that M is METRICAL with respect to a constraint system if it is the optimal output for some input. Tableau (50) shows how **43′** is metrical under the constraint ranking shown, when **43′** itself is taken as the input.[20] The reader can verify that **43** and **3′3** are also metrical on the same ranking, for they are the optimal outputs corresponding to the inputs **43** and **3′3** respectively. However, **44** is unmetrical under this ranking, for it never is the optimal output. As tableau (51) shows, it is bested by three other candidates even in the most propitious case where it is the most faithful candidate, i.e., when the input is **44** itself.[21] Similarly, **3'3'** and **33** are unmetrical on this ranking, for any input. And it should be clear that moving FAITHFULNESS to any lower rank cuts down the inventory generated to just **43**, for any input.

(50)

Input: **43'**	SAL	PAR	FAITH	FTBIN	MAX
1. 44	*		*		
2. ☞ 43'		*		*	*
3. 43		*	*		*
4. 3'3'	*		*	*	*
5. 3'3		*	*	*	*
6. 33	*		*		*
7. 34	*	*	*		*
8. 33'	*	*	*	*	*
9. 3'4	*	*	*	*	*

(51)

Input: **44**	SAL	PAR	FAITH	FTBIN	MAX
1. ✗ 44	*				
2. 43'		*	*	*	*
3. ☞ 43		*	*		*
4. 3'3'	*		*	*	*
5. 3'3		*	*	*	*
6. 33	*		*		*
7. 34	*	*	*		*
8. 33'	*	*	*	*	*
9. 3'4	*	*	*	*	*

This approach escapes the three above-mentioned objections. The overgeneration problem does not arise because regardless of input, the constraints generate all and only the attested types of lines, couplets, and quatrains. The harmonic bounding problem does not arise because the invariant metrical form of a poem or song is defined by a specific ranking of the constraints in (48) with each other and with FAITHFULNESS. One limiting case is where FAITHFULNESS ranks at the bottom, so that the only quatrains generated are **4343, 4443,** and **4444,** depending on the ranking of (48a–d). As FAITHFULNESS is promoted over the metrical markedness constraints, the system becomes more permissive. Finally, in the other limiting case, where FAITHFULNESS outranks *all* the metrical constraints, any input is accepted, which is to say the output is prose. When at least one metrical markedness constraint is visible (dominates FAITHFULNESS), the system defines a meter.

The markedness problem is solved in the best possible way: we can derive the frequency differences among metrical types by using Anttila's partial ranking theory of variation. The free ranking of markedness constraints generates a limited number of preference patterns, among them those which are instantiated in the folk song corpus under study. This is shown in the next subsection.

4.3. A partial ranking account

Rankings can be either free or fixed. If each permissible ranking is assigned the same probability, then the more constraint rankings generate a metrical type, the more frequent it is. Therefore, we complete our definition of metricality by adding the quantitative aspect:

(52)   a. M is metrical if is the optimal output in some tableau.
       b. The frequency of M is proportional to the number of tableaux in which it is optimal.

In the simplest partial ranking, all four metrical constraints in (25) would be freely ranked among each other. But as mentioned, FAITHFULNESS must be dominated by at least one markedness constraint (otherwise we would have prose). Which markedness constraint dominates FAITHFULNESS? Certainly not MAXBEAT, for if it were to rank above FAITHFULNESS, only **44** would be derivable, which is too strict. On the other hand, FOOTBIN >> FAITHFULNESS would be too loose, because it admits the unmetrical ***34**. The remaining possibilities, namely SALIENCY >> FAITHFULNESS and PARALLELISM >> FAITHFULNESS, have exactly the desired effect. Either one of these rankings, or both, exclude the unmetrical couplet types ***34, *3′4, *3′3** (and of course all quatrains that contain them) while still admitting all the metrical ones (as the reader can check). Thus, the possible metrical grammars for this system are:

40 Paul Kiparsky

(53) a. SALIENCY >> FAITHFULNESS
 b. PARALLELISM >> FAITHFULNESS
 c. SALIENCY, PARALLELISM >> FAITHFULNESS

While the categorical restrictions on couplets (and on parallel quatrains) can be modeled by any of these three fixed constraint rankings, one of them, (53a), also predicts the observed frequencies quite well. To see this, consider the effect of eliminating all tableaux where FAITHFULNESS dominates SALIENCY. It halves the total number of admissible tableaux from 5!=120 to 60. These 60 tableaux are displayed compactly in table (54).

(54) Couplet outputs of rankings consistent with SAL >> FAITH (unshaded cells)

Ranking of markedness constraints				Ranking of FAITHFULNESS			
				2nd	3rd	4th	5th
SAL	MAX	FTBIN	PAR	43 43' 3'3	43 43' 3'3	43	43
SAL	MAX	PAR	FTBIN	43 43' 3'3	43 43' 3'3	43 43' 3'3	43
SAL	FTBIN	MAX	PAR	43 43' 3'3	43	43	43
SAL	FTBIN	PAR	MAX	43 43' 3'3	43	43	43
SAL	PAR	MAX	FTBIN	43 43' 3'3	43 43' 3'3	43 43' 3'3	43
SAL	PAR	FTBIN	MAX	43 43' 3'3	43 43' 3'3	43	43
MAX	SAL	FTBIN	PAR	44	44	44	44
MAX	SAL	PAR	FTBIN	44	44	44	44
FTBIN	SAL	PAR	MAX	44 43	43	43	43
FTBIN	SAL	MAX	PAR	44 43	43	43	43
PAR	SAL	MAX	FTBIN	44 3'3' 33	44 3'3' 33	44	44
PAR	SAL	FTBIN	MAX	44 3'3' 33	44 3'3' 33	44 43	44
MAX	FTBIN	SAL	PAR	44	44	44	44
MAX	PAR	SAL	FTBIN	44	44	44	44
FTBIN	MAX	SAL	PAR	44	44	44	44
FTBIN	PAR	SAL	MAX	44 43 33	44 33	44 33	44
PAR	MAX	SAL	FTBIN	44 3'3' 33	44	44	44
PAR	FTBIN	SAL	MAX	44 3'3' 33	44 33	44 33	44
MAX	FTBIN	PAR	SAL	44	44	44	44
MAX	PAR	FTBIN	SAL	44	44	44	44
FTBIN	MAX	PAR	SAL	44	44	44	44
FTBIN	PAR	MAX	SAL	44 43	44	44	44
PAR	MAX	FTBIN	SAL	44 3'3' 33	44	44	44
PAR	FTBIN	MAX	SAL	44 3'3' 33	44 33	44	44

(54) lists all 24 rankings of the four constraints in (48), followed by four columns representing the ranking of FAITHFULNESS among them in second, third, fourth, and fifth position, respectively. (Of course, it cannot be ranked in first position because that would violate (53a).) The cells show the possible outputs of the corresponding tableaux (for the totality of inputs). The cells representing the subset of 60 permissible tableaux are unshaded.

The prediction is that the relative frequency of each couplet type should be proportional to the total number of times it appears in the unshaded cells of (54). The table in (55) compares the expected frequencies of each couplet type with its corpus frequency.[22]

(55) Couplets in H&M corpus

Type	frequency in tableaux		frequency in corpus	
44	33%	(30 tableaux)	37%	(461 couplets)
43	33%	(30 tableaux)	35%	(433 couplets)
43'	13%	(12 tableaux)	12%	(144 couplets)
3'3	13%	(12 tableaux)	15%	(183 couplets)
3'3'	4%	(4 tableaux)	1%	(14 couplets)
33	4%	(4 tableaux)	1%	(16 couplets)
other	0%	(0 tableaux)	0%	(3 couplets)
Total	100%	(92 tableaux)	100%	(1254 couplets)

The three-way split **44, 33** (most frequent), **43', 3'3** (medium), **3'3', 33** (rare) comes out cleanly, and even the actual corpus percentages are reasonably close to the predicted percentages. This means that, with a minimum of extra assumptions, the constraint ranking needed for the categorical data also makes sense of the observed frequency profile.

To summarize, the single additional restriction that SALIENCY is more important than FAITHFULNESS does two things: it excludes the prohibited couplet types, and it generates the pattern of preferences among the remaining permissible couplet types.

4.4. Testing the theory: Isaac Watt's hymns

Now let us consider what the theory predicts about a metrical system which imposes the further constraint that feet must be rigorously binary (iambic), so that degenerate feet (or "extrametrical syllables") are disallowed. It has no lines of the form **3'**, hence no couplets that contain such lines (namely of the form **43'**, **3'3**, and **3'3'**).

This stricter meter exists. Not surprisingly, it arose in the 18th century by the superimposition of neoclassical metrical norms on the popular quatrain forms of folk poetry and song. The prolific 18th-century hymn composer Isaac Watts follows it rigorously. Most of his hymns are in quatrains of common meter (**4343**), long meter (**4444**), and short meter (**3343**), in that order of frequency.[23] Formally, the couplet typology of this more restrictive system can be derived from the previous one by promoting FOOTBINARITY over FAITHFULNESS. In other words, we add to SAL >> FAITH a second fixed constraint ranking, FTBIN >> FAITH. There are again three ways to do that:

(56) a. SAL >> FTBIN >> FAITH
 b. SAL, FTBIN >> FAITH
 c. FTBIN >> SAL >> FAITH

And again it turns out that one of these rankings, (56a) SAL >> FTBIN >> FAITH, approximates the actual *quantitative* profile of the corpus. The outputs of the twenty tableaux permitted by (56a) are displayed in the unshaded portions of the table.

The theoretical frequencies of the couplets predicted by (57) compared with their actual frequencies in Isaac Watts' hymns follow in (58).[24] The predictions are even more accurate for the hymns than for the folk songs. This was perhaps to be expected, for Watts' hymns are about as homogeneous a corpus as could be imagined, whereas the folk songs have been created and reshaped by many people in different periods and places.

What the folk songs and Watts' hymns have in common is the overall preference for saliency over parallelism at the couplet level. The other metrical grammars consistent with the same categorical facts for the folk songs and hymns, namely (53b,c) and (56b,c), predict different frequency profiles. In all of them, type **44** is more common than type **43**. In other words, these hypothetical verse forms are like the ones studied here except that their frequency distributions favor parallelism over saliency. These predicted alternative metrical practices do not seem to occur in English folk songs, and the question is why not. I conjecture that the rationale for the observed preference for saliency over parallelism lies on the musical side: it is a feature of stanzas intended to be sung. The most likely place to find parallelism dominant would then be in literary verse designed for reading rather than singing.[25]

A modular metrics for folk verse 43

(57) Outputs of rankings consistent with S<small>AL</small> >> F<small>T</small>B<small>IN</small> >> F<small>AITH</small> (unshaded cells)

Ranking of markedness constraints				Ranking of F<small>AITHFULNESS</small>			
				2nd	3rd	4th	5th
S<small>AL</small>	M<small>AX</small>	F<small>T</small>B<small>IN</small>	P<small>AR</small>	43 43' 3'3	43 43' 3'3	43	43
S<small>AL</small>	M<small>AX</small>	P<small>AR</small>	F<small>T</small>B<small>IN</small>	43 43' 3'3	43 43' 3'3	43 43' 3'3	43
S<small>AL</small>	F<small>T</small>B<small>IN</small>	M<small>AX</small>	P<small>AR</small>	43 43' 3'3	43	43	43
S<small>AL</small>	F<small>T</small>B<small>IN</small>	P<small>AR</small>	M<small>AX</small>	43 43' 3'3	43	43	43
S<small>AL</small>	P<small>AR</small>	M<small>AX</small>	F<small>T</small>B<small>IN</small>	43 43' 3'3	43 43' 3'3	43 43' 3'3	43
S<small>AL</small>	P<small>AR</small>	F<small>T</small>B<small>IN</small>	M<small>AX</small>	43 43' 3'3	43 43' 3'3	43	43
M<small>AX</small>	S<small>AL</small>	F<small>T</small>B<small>IN</small>	P<small>AR</small>	44	44	44	44
M<small>AX</small>	S<small>AL</small>	P<small>AR</small>	F<small>T</small>B<small>IN</small>	44	44	44	44
F<small>T</small>B<small>IN</small>	S<small>AL</small>	P<small>AR</small>	M<small>AX</small>	44 43	43	43	43
F<small>T</small>B<small>IN</small>	S<small>AL</small>	M<small>AX</small>	P<small>AR</small>	44 43	43	43	43
P<small>AR</small>	S<small>AL</small>	M<small>AX</small>	F<small>T</small>B<small>IN</small>	44 3'3' 33	44 3'3' 33	44	44
P<small>AR</small>	S<small>AL</small>	F<small>T</small>B<small>IN</small>	M<small>AX</small>	44 3'3' 33	44 3'3' 33	44 43	44
M<small>AX</small>	F<small>T</small>B<small>IN</small>	S<small>AL</small>	P<small>AR</small>	44	44	44	44
M<small>AX</small>	P<small>AR</small>	S<small>AL</small>	F<small>T</small>B<small>IN</small>	44	44	44	44
F<small>T</small>B<small>IN</small>	M<small>AX</small>	S<small>AL</small>	P<small>AR</small>	44	44	44	44
F<small>T</small>B<small>IN</small>	P<small>AR</small>	S<small>AL</small>	M<small>AX</small>	44 43 33	44 33	44 33	44
P<small>AR</small>	M<small>AX</small>	S<small>AL</small>	F<small>T</small>B<small>IN</small>	44 3'3' 33	44	44	44
P<small>AR</small>	F<small>T</small>B<small>IN</small>	S<small>AL</small>	M<small>AX</small>	44 3'3' 33	44 33	44 33	44
M<small>AX</small>	F<small>T</small>B<small>IN</small>	P<small>AR</small>	S<small>AL</small>	44	44	44	44
M<small>AX</small>	P<small>AR</small>	F<small>T</small>B<small>IN</small>	S<small>AL</small>	44	44	44	44
F<small>T</small>B<small>IN</small>	M<small>AX</small>	P<small>AR</small>	S<small>AL</small>	44	44	44	44
F<small>T</small>B<small>IN</small>	P<small>AR</small>	M<small>AX</small>	S<small>AL</small>	44 43	44	44	44
P<small>AR</small>	M<small>AX</small>	F<small>T</small>B<small>IN</small>	S<small>AL</small>	44 3'3' 33	44	44	44
P<small>AR</small>	F<small>T</small>B<small>IN</small>	M<small>AX</small>	S<small>AL</small>	44 3'3' 33	44 33	44	44

(58) Couplets in Isaac Watts' hymns

Type	frequency in tableaux		frequency in corpus	
44	38%	(8 tableaux)	40%	(3140 couplets)
43	57%	(12 tableaux)	57%	(4538 couplets)
43'	0%	(no tableaux)	0%	(no couplets)
3'3	0%	(no tableaux)	0%	(no couplets)
3'3'	0%	(no tableaux)	0%	(no couplets)
33	5%	(1 tableau)	3%	(258 couplets)
Total	100%	(21 tableaux)	100%	(7936 couplets)

4.5. Parallelism versus saliency at the quatrain level

The constraint systems developed above distinguish the well-formed lines, couplets, and quatrains from the ill-formed lines, couplets, and quatrains in two related but distinct traditions of popular songs. They also model the relative frequencies of the six kinds of well-formed couplets, which are of course identical to the relative frequencies of the corresponding six kinds of parallel quatrains (making up over 90 per cent of the total number of quatrains). The three well-formed types of salient quatrains are infrequent in comparison, but the available data shows the same overall statistical preferences. What we have not yet done is to explain *why* parallel quatrains are so much more frequent than salient quatrains. The constraint rankings (53a) and (56a) which give the right results at the couplet level would predict just the opposite at the quatrain level. Either different levels at the metrical hierarchy can have different partial constraint rankings, or there are as yet unformulated level-specific constraints.[26]

Perhaps the generalization is that at the higher end of the metrical hierarchy (20), parallelism supersedes saliency as the dominant organizing principle. Indeed, above the level of the stanza, parallelism is almost completely dominant: this is the generalization behind H&M's STANZA CORRESPONDENCE constraint (see (42)). Once we understand the nature of the generalization and the principle or causal factors behind it, we can formulate the appropriate constraint and incorporate it into the metrical system. This will make another set of statistical predictions which can then be tested against the corpus data.

5. Conclusion

The form of a song is determined jointly by the meter of its stanzas and the way they are set to the rhythm of the tune. A small number of constraints applying at each level in the metrical hierarchy characterize the form of quatrains in two English song traditions. Coupled with the idea that statistical preferences arise from the partial ranking of constraints, these constraint systems also account for the frequency profiles of the quatrain types.

Notes

* I am grateful to Bruce Hayes for his detailed comments and criticisms of an earlier version of this paper. I take full responsibility for any errors.
1. The tension between empirically motivated modularity and OT's parallelist program arises in other domains as well: a counterpart in phonology is stratal OT (Kiparsky 2000, to appear).
2. This is only the case for refrain quatrains, which are so infrequent as a whole that the data is unlikely to be a full sample (section 2.4).
3. Especially judgments about relative acceptability, if H&M are right that they arise from a probabilistic component of the metrical grammar which could only be acquired by exposure to a very large body of songs.
4. The same is true of literary verse; Macaulay's *Horatius* is probably the best-known example. However, variation between 3_f and **4** is not uncommon. Examples in the Folkways Anthology include *Bandit Cole Younger* (Edward Crain) and *Engine 143* (Carter Family).
5. Hayes (in press) reformulates the constraints in such a way that they apply directly to **4** and **G**, doing away with the need for the category **F**.
6. Of course, in that case the extra final syllables cannot be considered degenerate feet of their own because that would destroy the metrical form of the stanza. Rather, at the metrical level, this variation corresponds to the familiar option of extrametricality in iambic lines.
7. Many examples can be heard on the Folkways Anthology (Smith 1952): *The Butcher's Boy* (Buell Kazee), *John Hardy was a Desperate Little Man* (Carter Family), *Stackalee* (Frank Hutchison), *White House Blues* (Charlie Poole and the North Carolina Ramblers).
8. I have tried to separate non-rhyming refrain quatrains, which are treated separately in 2.4 below. Some of the figures in (12) are inflated because H&M don't consistently separate the statistics for the two types. This is not important for now, but it will potentially be a consideration later when we turn to the relative frequencies of the types. Note also that, for the reasons stated in the text, I have classified H&M's type **F** as **3'**.
9. Quatrains composed of rhymed couplets (rhyme scheme ABAB) also occur, but almost all of them seem to be of the **4444** type.
10. Apparent exceptions result from the fact that the folk tradition allows some types of trochaic words, especially those in *-y*, to be actually pronounced iambically in line-final position, usually under stress clash (see Hayes (in press) for a formal account). I think this stress inversion would not occur in (18), but it would be normal in a (constructed) line such as *She's góne with yóung Davý*, turning it into a regular **3** line, which of course *can* rhyme with another **3** line or **4** line.

11. To be consistent with our notation for lines, the reduced foot types should really be labeled Ø and ', and the full foot **1**, but I will continue to use the Ø, **f**, and **F** for clarity.
12. Grossly speaking, the effect is to put short hemistichs at the end of lines and short lines at the ends of couplets. (See Friedberg 2002 for a related generalization about Russian tetrameter.) This might seem to contradict the well-known tendency to put heavy elements last. But according to the proposal in the text, it is an entirely separate principle, based on putting salient (marked) elements last. The former is grounded in parsing efficiency, the latter is a poetic closure effect.
13. Such types as ***433'3**, ***33'43**, and ***333'3** are still unmetrical because they have a gratuitous parallelism violation. The first three lines are neither parallel nor salient and therefore the quatrain is unmetrical.
14. H&M (p. 481) discuss a possible example of *****33G3**, rightly pointing out that it could be a **44** couplet, as indeed Sharp & Karpeles treat it in their edition.
15. Such examples can be easily multiplied. The rhyming requirement of Skaldic verse is satisfied every bit as well by half rhyme (assonance) as by full rhyme. Systems where alliterating words must have the same C- also allow CV-alliteration. Fully binary (iambic/trochaic) lines are permitted in *dolnik* verse.
16. These constraints are merely illustrative. Other characterizations of the rhyme patterns are conceivable, but the point should be independent of which of them is correct.
17. A caveat: singling out **3343** stanzas as a special type, if such a thing proves to be necessary, is not easy in my approach. It would probably require specifying maximal saliency at both the quatrain and line levels.
18. This would *not* be the case if (38) were truly unifiable with the literal "long-last" constraint, as it appears in natural language (irreversible binomials, Heavy NP-Shift) and in verse (placement of caesuras). At the moment this seems rather a stretch, given the very specific form of (37).
19. In H&M's analysis, AVOID LAPSE also serves to limit the distribution of empty weak beats in lines like (30).
20. For simplicity, I mark violations of these constraints categorically rather than gradiently in the tableaux that follow. This should make no difference to the result.
21. It is immaterial which of those three is the actual winner in this case. If FAITHFULNESS is gradiently evaluated, it would be the one which is "closest" to the input.
22. One might expect the frequency of couplets to be determined in part by saliency at the quatrain level. If that were the case, then a better gauge of the "intrinsic" markedness of a couplet type would be the frequency with which it occurs in in parallel quatrains. But this factor turns out to be insignificant. The relative frequencies of couplet types in parallel quatrains are practically the same as the overall couplet frequencies given here (within one percentage point in each case).

23. The type **4443** is quite absent. It must be excluded by some quatrain-level constraint, perhaps requiring the even-numbered lines to be parallel. (This would jibe with the fact that in the overwhelming majority of quatrains, the even-numbered lines rhyme with each other).
24. The data is from Watts' Hymns and Spiritual Songs [1707] together with his Psalms of David [1719] according to the text in http://www.ccel.org/w/watts/psalmshymns/TOC.htm. The site identifies the meter of each hymn, which I have checked against the text, and corrected in a few cases. I have only counted quatrains, which are by far the most frequent stanza type in Watts' hymns. However, counting the other stanza types (sextets and octets) would not materially change the picture. There are also a few hymns in iambic pentameter.
25. Shape-note hymns, of which the best-loved collection is probably *The Sacred Harp*, have been hugely popular in Southern Appalachia, where much of the H&M folk song corpus originated. Niles (1961 *passim*) testifies to the influence that shape-note singing had on secular singing style. Metrically they are intermediate between the folk songs and Isaac Watts' hymns. This is not surprising, for as Bruce Hayes *(in litt. el.)* points out to me, the *Sacred Harp* is a heterogeneous compilation, which contains, in addition to folk-like material that resembles the Sharp corpus, also a layer of older hymns influenced by Western classical music, plus 19th and 20th century additions of varying quality.
26. Both these formal options are well-motivated in phonology (Kiparsky to appear).

References

Anttila, Arto
    1997   Variation in Finnish phonology and morphology. Ph.D. Dissertation, Stanford University.
    2002   Morphologically conditioned phonological alternations. *Natural Language and Linguistic Theory* 20: 1–42.
    2003   Finnish vowel coalescence and the derived environment problem. In *The Nature of the Word*, Kristin Hanson and Sharon Inkelas (eds.), Cambridge, Mass.: MIT Press.

Boersma, Paul
    1997   How we learn variation, optionality, and probability. *IFA Proceedings* 21: 43–58.

Bronson, Bertrand Harris
    1959–72   *The Traditional Tunes of the Child Ballads; with their Texts, According to the Extant Records of Great Britain and America. Vol. 1–4.* Princeton, N. J., Princeton University Press.

Friedberg, Nila
 2002 Metrical complexity in Russian iambic verse: A study of form and meaning. Ph.D. Dissertation, University of Toronto.

Gil, David
 1978 Hasofet Ben Zona: Israeli soccer cheers and jeers. *Maledicta* 2: 129–45.

Golston, Chris
 1998 Constraint-based metrics. *Natural Language and Linguistic Theory* 16: 719–770.

Hanson, Kristin, and Paul Kiparsky
 1996 A parametric theory of poetic meter. *Language* 72: 287–335.

Hayes, Bruce
 1995 *Metrical Stress Theory*. Chicago: University of Chicago Press.
 in press In *The Nature of the Word*, Kristin Hanson and Sharon Inkelas (eds.), Cambridge, Mass.: MIT Press.
 to appear Faithfulness and componentiality in metrics. In: *The Nature of the Word: Essays in Honor of Paul Kiparsky,* Kristin Hanson and Sharon Inkelas (eds.). Cambridge, Mass.: MIT Press.

Hayes, Bruce, and Margaret MacEachern
 1998 Quatrain form in English folk verse. *Language* 74: 473–507. With appendices in http://www.humnet.ucla.edu/humnet/linguistics/people/hayes/metrics.htm.

Jackendoff, Ray, and Fred Lehrdahl
 1983 *A Generative Theory of Tonal Music*. Cambridge, Mass.: MIT Press.

Kiparsky, Paul
 2000 Opacity and cyclicity. *The Linguistic Review* 17: 351–367.
 to appear Opacity and paradigm effects.

Kopiez, Reinhard, and Guido Brink
 1998 *Fußball-Fangesänge*. Würzburg: Königshausen & Neumann.

Liberman, Mark, and Alan Prince
 1979 On stress and linguistic rhythm. *Linguistic Inquiry* 8: 249–336.

Niles, John Jacob
 1961 *The Ballad Book*. Boston, Houghton Mifflin.

Opie, Iona, and Peter Opie
 1997 *The Oxford Dictionary of Nursery Rhymes*. 2nd ed. Oxford, New York: Oxford University Press.

Ritchie, Jean
 1965 *Folk Songs from the Southern Appalachians as Sung by Jean Ritchie*. New York: Oak Publications.

Sharp, Cecil, and Maud Karpeles
 1932 *English Folk Songs from the Southern Appalachians*. London: Oxford University Press.

Smith, Harry (ed.)
    1952   *Anthology of American Folk Music.* Folkways Records. Reissued by Smithsonian Folkways Recordings, 1997.

Watts, Isaac
    [1707]   Hymns and spiritual songs. http://www.ccel.org/w/watts/psalmshymns/TOC.htm
    [1719]   Psalms of David. http://www.ccel.org/w/watts/psalmshymns/TOC.htm

2. Metricality

What is "metricality"?
English iambic pentameter

Marina Tarlinskaja

1. Introduction: Metricality of texts and lines

Let us look at the segment "But forgot to put the leaf back in closing". Is this an iambic pentameter line? It seems unlikely; and yet the line comes from Robert Frost's iambic poem *Maple* (line 67). This is how it begins:

(1)   Her teacher's certainty it must be Mabel
      Made Maple first take notice of her name.
      She asked her father and he told her, "Maple –
      Maple is right." "But teacher told the school
      There's no such name." "Teachers don't know as much
      As fathers about children, you tell teacher <...>"

How do we evaluate line 67? To answer this question, we need to approach the problem of metricality from two angles: metricality of a text, and metricality of a line.

Metricality of an iambic text arises, first, from an objective, statistically relevant contrast in the mean stressing of even and odd syllabic positions in the whole text, and, secondly, from what was subjectively accepted as "good verse" by the audience of a particular literary tradition during a specific epoch. A poetic form acceptable to the English audience of Shakespeare's times was considered barbarous by the 18th c. English Classicism.

To see if a text is "objectively" iambic we need to check whether there is a contrast in the mean stressing of its even and odd syllabic positions. Even syllabic positions (2, 4, 6...) called strong, or S, only tend to be filled with stressed syllables in English iambs, while odd positions (1, 3, 5...) called weak, or W, only tend to bear no stresses. Different poetic traditions and different periods of a tradition accept a dissimilar number of syllables stressed in a way uncharacteristic of the positions they occupy. The contrast in stressing needs to be strong enough to be recognized by the audience. How strong should the contrast be? Analyses of large portions of texts by many authors working in different genres might give us a clue. The poet's own opinion of the verse form does not always serve as an indicator. Coleridge declared that in *Christabel* he had created a new form of verse that depended only on the number of stresses in the line; and yet the form turned out to be loose iambic tetrameter; and what Frost called "loose iambic" (as did Halle and Keyser in 1998) turned out to be a strict stress-meter, the so-called "dolnik" (Tarlinskaja 1993).

Having established overall metricality of a text, we turn to metricality of individual lines. Metricality of a line is best viewed historically and empirically: what types of lines were accepted as metrical by poets of a particular literary tradition and epoch? In other words, which types of lines were used regularly, and which are exceptions? If we establish that, on the whole, Frost's long poems *The Generation of Men*, or *Maple*, or *Wild Grapes*, are in iambic pentameter, and then discover that lines of the type "With a swish in the grass. What if the others <...>" (*The Generation of Men* 23) appear in his texts infrequently but consistently (75 times, or in 2.5% of the 3,000 lines examined) they must have been metrical for Frost, but not for Pope: in Pope's iambs such lines never occur. If lines like "But forgot to put the leaf back in closing" appear only six times in Frost's 3,000 lines (0.2% of lines) then they should probably be considered anomalous. Should the number of such lines go up, the text might become transitional, from iambic to syllabic (Tarlinskaja and Teterina 1974), and with more anomalous lines, purely syllabic.

The meter of a poem becomes clear to the reader or listener from the context. Our experience as readers is often believed to create an intuition that tells the difference between "metrical" and "unmetrical". But do all readers of all epochs have the same intuition? What do we know of intuitions of Shakespeare's audience? Only analyses of verse texts rather than interpretations of present-day informants or declamators can give us reliable clues. To find out whether a text has a tendency towards an "iambic" alternation of stresses, we calculate the mean percent of stresses that fall on all even and all odd syllabic positions. At this point we disregard what rhythmical types of lines occur in the text, and which positions accept more or fewer "deviations". We merely assume that, if the text is iambic, there will be a contrast in stressing of its "evens" and "odds", though the contrast varies in different epochs and poetic traditions.

Table 1 shows the percent of stresses (calculated from the total number of lines) that fill each syllabic position of excerpts, each 600 lines long, from poetic texts of five authors: Shakespeare's *Hamlet*, Donne's *Satyres*, Pope's *The Rape of the Lock*, Byron's *Don Juan*, and three poems by Frost (*The Death of a Hired Man, Maple*, and *Wild Grapes*). Next, we calculate the mean number of stresses on all evens[1] and on all odds, and substract the figures characterizing the "odds" from those of the "evens". The results show us the contrast between the evens and the odds. The data in Table 1 are arranged in the order of a decreasing contrast. To compare with actual verse, Lilya Teterina and I constructed a prose model of English syllabic verse. The model was built from Donne's *Sermons* (Tarlinskaja and Teterina 1974, Tarlinskaja 1976 Chapter 8). The model was a quasi-text consisting of 500 decasyllabic segments from prose that satisfied two conditions: they had to begin with the beginning of a phrase, the way verse lines usually do, and they had to have stresses on the 10th syllabic position in the proportion of Donne's actual poetry, about 80%.

Table 1. Stressing of S and W in English iambic pentameter and a prose model of decasyllabic verse (in percent from the number of lines)

	Strong positions					Mean	Weak positions					Means	
	2	4	6	8	10	2–8	1	3	5	7	9	1–9	S–W
Pope	78	98	74	86	99	84	32	12	3	2	1	10	**74**
Byron	71	80	76	70	94	74	16	13	7	7	9	10	**64**
Shakesp.	61	82	73	69	93	71	25	9	9	12	8	13	**59**
Frost	61	79	75	74	94	72	28	21	12	14	7	17	**56**
Donne	61	80	67	71	78	70	39	27	20	25	15	25	**44**
Model	38	40	48	38	80	42	22	34	33	38	15	27	**14**

Let us consider the mean difference between evens and odds (mean S minus mean W). In an "ideal" iamb the difference should be 100%, in an "ideal" syllabic verse (a "text" consisting of decasyllabic segments randomly picked out from prose) it should be close to zero. In our samples of the actual English iambic pentameter, the highest difference was found in Pope's *The Rape of the Lock*: 74%, and the lowest in Donne's *Satyres*: only 44%. The stressing of Robert Frost's verse is close to Byron's and Shakespeare's; it is well above Donne's *Satyres*. Frost's poems are, without any doubt, iambic pentameter.

Why is the index of our prose model of syllabic verse above zero? Recall that we selected the segments from prose with some features of actual verse: the segments began after a phrase boundary, and their tenth syllable was to be stressed in about 80% of all cases. English phrases often begin with an unstressed grammatical word, so the first syllable of a phrase is often unstressed, while the second syllable is frequently stressed ("The Soule...", "When God...."). The stressed ends of the model "lines", working backwards, create some accentual dissimilation: if the final syllable is stressed, the penultimate syllable tends to be unstressed (two consecutive stresses in English are less frequent than unstressed monosyllabic intervals between stresses). Thus, our model of syllabic verse has a hint of an iamb-like alternation of stresses. However, the difference between its evens and odds does not begin to approach even Donne's *Satyres*, our loosest iamb. The *Satyres* are still iambic pentameter, though on its way to syllabic verse. Even in French syllabic verse there is a vague "iambic" cadence, felt in particular by non-native speakers of French used to syllabo-tonic verse (the Germans or the Russians). But the probability of this "iambic" trend in French verse is the same as in prose (Gasparov 1996). French verse is syllabic, while even Donne's *Satyres* are iambic, but with some features of syllabic verse. And Frost's verse of the poems analyzed is unquestionably iambic: it is definitely not a purely syllabic form, and it is opposed to his own strict stress-meter (Tarlinskaja 1993).

Now we may turn to Frost's "deviating" lines and see whether some of them are still metrical, or anomalous even for this poet. The problem of metricality is more complicated for English iambs than for their European counterparts, such as German or Russian. First, the most common iambic meter in English is not tetrameter (as in Russian) but pentameter, with its more numerous accentual line variations. Secondly, the creators of the English iamb, first Chaucer, and later Wyatt, learned from French and Italian syllabic poetry and incorporated some of its features, as in Wyatt's earlier translations of Petrarch's sonnets. Finally, words in English are short, and there are many stressed monosyllables that often fall on W syllabic positions. Consequently, the English iamb allows a wide range of licenses.

2. Theories of iambic meter

American scholars have been discussing for forty years now how to define a "well-formed" iambic pentameter line. The debate was started by Halle and Keyser (1966, 1971); several other scholars contributed to the discussion, for example, Magnuson and Ryder (1971), and Kiparsky (1975, 1977). Halle and Keyser assumed that at the basis of iambic poetry lies an abstract model, a sequence of alternating syllabic positions W S W S W S..., and that actual lines are generated from the model according to a set of rules. (A similar approach was outlined by Russian "formalists" during the first quarter of the 20th century (Zhirmunsky 1925, Tomashevsky 1929, cf. Halle's review of Zhirmunsky's works in Halle 1968)). Lines that do not comply with the rules were called ill-formed. The formulation of the rules was modified several times to account for a wider range of actual lines.

2.1. Stress maxima

The earliest theory disallowed "stress maxima" on W (Halle and Keyser 1966, 1971) making a good proportion of actual iambic verse unmetrical. Here are some random examples from Byron where the stress maxima on W are formed by monosyllables:

(2) In the sign of the Scorpion <...>   (*Sardanapalus* 3.1: 278)
     From the sky to preserve <...>   (*Sardanapalus* 3.1: 281)
     Like a ship on the ocean <...>   (*The Two Foscari* 3.1: 129)
     I have sued to accompany <...>   (*The Two Foscari* 3.1: 139)

Donne, and later Shelley, Browning, Swinburne, and Frost all disregarded the rule. Here are some random examples from Frost:

(3) And the back of the gig they stood beside   (*The Fear* 6)
     With his pipe in his mouth and his brown jug (*The Generation of Men* 105)
     When they made her related to the maples   (*Maple* 139)

2.2. Monosyllables

Later it was suggested that a stress maximum on W is acceptable if it is constituted by monosyllables, but unmetrical if it is created by polysyllabic lexical words, unless such a word occurs at the beginning of a line, of the second hemistich, or a phrase (Kiparsky 1975, 1977). This constraint, though more permissive, still made numerous actual lines ill-formed. Here are examples from Frost's iambic pentameter where a stress maximum on W is generated by a disyllabic initially-stressed noun that does not occur at the beginning of a phrase or hemistich:

(4)   And the sawyer had slammed the carriage back   (*Paul's Wife* 63)
      With a lawyer at hand to find you out   (*The Self-seeker* 134)
      With an income in cash of, say, a thousand   (*New Hampshire* 409)

2.3. Initially-stressed disyllables

Later still, initially-stressed disyllables ("bowing", "sudden") matched against positions WS were accepted as metrical, while end-stressed disyllables such as "intend" and "obscure" matched against positions SW were disallowed, at least for Shakespeare's verse (Hanson and Kiparsky 1996: 297). However, such cases occur even in Shakespeare's verse, especially in his dramas (though Shakespeare might have used the initially-stressed variant of these words, cf. Kökeritz 1974: 332–339):

(5)   He deserved prison <...>   (*The Winter's Tale* 2.1: 120)
      Less appear so, in comforting your evils   (*The Winter's Tale* 2.2: 101)
      And begin, "Why to me? <...>   (*The Winter's Tale* 5.1: 47)
      This compelled fortune! – have your mouth filled up
                                   (*Henry VIII* 2.4: 87)

In Donne's verse such deviations are a regular occurrence (6), as they are in later poetry, such as that of Shelley (7):

(6)   Of refined manners, yet ceremonial man   (*Satyre I*: 28)
      All demands, fees, and duties <...>   (*Satyre V*: 39)
      Time enough to have beene interpreter   (*Satyre IV*: 64)
      Who, in the other extreme, only doth <...>   (*Satyre IV*: 220)
(7)   Who sees and permits evil <...>   (*The Cenci* 3.1: 101)
      A gulf of obscure hatered <...>   (*The Cenci* 4.4: 100)
      Yet you would say, 'I confess anything'   (*The Cenci* 5.2: 55)

In Frost's iambs, where end-stressed disyllables on positions SW are a common occurrence, the disyllabic end-stressed word on SW is sometimes followed by an unstressed monosyllable on S; thus a stress-maximum on positions SWS is generated:

(8) And <u>declare to</u> the cliffs too far for echo (*The Census-Taker* 56)
I <u>refuse to</u> adapt myself a mite (*New Hampshire* 234)
Long <u>enough for</u> recording all our names on (*Snow* 10).

2.4. End-stressed disyllables on SW

A modified theory accepted end-stressed disyllabic words on SW, provided such words were not at the end of a phrase (Hayes 1989). Hayes claimed that "She <u>replied</u> earnestly..." is iambic (and occurs in Shelley's *The Revolt of Islam*), while "She <u>replied</u>, 'Ernest...'" (a construct) is not. However, though the latter cases do not occur in the poetry of Classicism, they are regularly found at the end of a phrase and a clause in looser iambic poetry; here are some examples from Frost:

(9) She <u>withdrew</u>, // shrinking, from beneath his arm (*Home Burial* 31)
I <u>suppose</u> // she deserves some pity too (*The Housekeeper* 192)
Is <u>extreme</u>, // where they shrink to none at all (*The Census-Taker* 63)
You <u>forget</u> // where we are <...> (*The Fear* 25)

Such lines occur even in Shakespeare: "And <u>begin</u>, // "Why to me?"

True, SW positions in the English iamb are sensitive (Magnuson and Ryder 1971, Tarlinskaja 1976, Bjorklund 1978). First, a string characterized by "a loss of stress on S followed by a stress on W" causes two adjacent strong stresses, as in (10):

(10)   S   W   S
And <u>the church fell</u>, and crushed him to a mummy
(Shelley *The Cenci* 1.3: 60)

These might disrupt the "iambic momentum" of the rhythm. Secondly, disyllabic end-stressed words ("suppose", "withdraw") are infrequent in English. And finally, English poets might have been conscious of foot boundaries (Tarlinskaja 1984). "Stress plus non-stress" on positions WS (instead of "non-stress plus stress") occur within a foot, and are frequent, while "non-stress plus stress" on positions SW (instead of "stress plus non-stress") occur across a foot boundary, and are relatively rare.

Strings of stress deviations on adjacent two, three, or more metrical positions were termed "rhythmical figures" (Bailey 1975: 34). We will use symbols of metrical positions to refer to various types of rhythmical figures. Thus, stress deviations on positions WS ("Swift to the Lock <...>", "Sudden he viewed <...>") are called "rhythmical figure WS"; deviations on WSW ("Shake the red cloak <...>") are rhythmical figure WSW, and so on.

Morphology (parts of speech) and syntax (their syntactic combinations in phrases) have some link with stressing, and, consequently, with metricality. For instance, English poets of all epochs prefer the figure SW in mid-phrase where a loss of stress on S is followed by a stressed word on W which is syntactically linked to the next word with a stress on S:

(11)   W S W   S   W S W   S W S
        And his head swam, and he sank down to earth
                                          (Arnold *Sohrab and Rustum* 693)

This helps to straighten the disrupted iambic rhythm in the same phrase. As we shall see below, the figure SW is particularly often coupled with attributive phrases ("And the pale Ghosts <...>", "And the high mountains <...>"); probably because the stressing of prepositional attributes tends to be subordinate to the stress of the following modified noun. Even in Frost's iambs, where the figure SW is more frequent than WS, and may occur at the end of a phrase or clause, it does not occur at the end of a sentence: "And like the actress exclaim // 'Oh, my God <...>'" (*New Hampshire* 207) is possible, but *"And like an actress exclaimed. /// Then she left" (a construct) is not. The strong syntactic break between sentences must make it harder to straighten out the disrupted iambic rhythm.

2.5. Other verse traditions

The definition of "iambic meter" was finally stretched so far that it was claimed to incorporate Italian and French syllabic verse: by applying a succession of rules to the basic iambic model one can generate texts far removed from the model (Biggs 1996, 1999, Saltarelli 1999). According to such an all-encompassing approach, not just syllabic but also accentual verse and ternary meters ("I galloped, he galloped, we galloped all three") can all be generated from one basic model: iambic. However, many poetic traditions in European literatures are based on different principles. Systems of verse in modern Romance literatures have been traditionally syllabic; they rely not so much on locations of stresses as on the number of syllables in lines. Modern iambic verse, however (English, German, or Russian) is syllabo-tonic; it relies on both the number of syllables and on the number and location of stresses in the line. The classical Italian *hendecasillabo* has only two obligatory stresses, at the ends of hemistichs (positions 4 or 6, and 10), while other stresses shift almost freely. And in French verse the probability of an iambic rhythm is the same as in prose (Gasparov 1996: 123, 125–134, 311–313). Some forms have a common ancestor and are typologically similar; but accentual verse, syllabic verse, binary meters and ternary meters do not have to be reduced to one general form – iambic. It may be beneficial to look for language universals in the multitude of human languages; but a verse universal effaces the differences between literatures, poetries, and poets.

"Metricality" means different things when applied to different iambic traditions. Because the Russian iamb is stricter than the English, the only feature that has been discussed in relation to metricality is the so-called shift of stress from the first S onto the preceding W. The shift is considered metrical only if it occurs across a word boundary. According to Jakobson (1922, in Jakobson 1979: 28–29), "Gost' izbezhal..." [The guest escaped] is metrical for the 19th c. Russian iamb, while "Gosti sbezhali..." [The guests ran away] is not. Jakobson argued that the metrical scheme is present in the reader's mind and requires a potential mental "re-accentuation" of the disyllabic word on positions WS, which is phonologically disallowed. English rhythmical equivalents of the Russian examples are "Fall from his hands <...>" and "Falling for France <...>" (Byron *Childe Harold's Pilgrimage* 4.16: 7 and 1.56: 9). Both are metrical for the English iamb.

Interestingly, in Pope's *The Rape of the Lock* and in Frost's analyzed[2] poems the total frequency of WS and WSW is identical: they occur in 14% of the lines. The figure SW, however, displays period differences. In Pope's poem, the figure SW appears in only 4.2% of all lines, as in the examples in (12).

(12) On the rich Quilt <...>   (4: 35)
      While the Fops envy <...>   (4: 104)

In Frost's poetry, this figure appears in 14.5% of the lines – three and a half times more often. In Frost's poems we also find the figure SWS, as in "And the back of the gig they stood beside" (*The Fear* 6): 44 times in 1770 lines (2.5%). If we assume that Pope's verse illustrates the most regular English iamb, then lines with the figure SW are metrical even for Pope. Frost's metrical style is very different from Pope's: the figure SWS, for example, never occurs in Pope's verse, while Frost uses SW and SWS more frequently than WS and WSW. The figure SW is metrical for all English iambs, while SWS is metrical only for periods of looser verse.

Lines containing longer strings of deviating syllables, especially figures that start with an SW, are rare. The tetrasyllabic SWSW, as in "You had stood the spade up against the wall" (Frost *Home Burial* 87) occur only 17 times in 1770 lines (1%). Lines with longer figures, e.g., SWSWSW containing polysyllables, as in "But forgot to put the leaf back in closing" (*Maple* 67), and "And accommodate her young life to his" (*A Servant to Servant* 128) appeared only six times in 3,000 lines: 0.2% of the lines. These anomalous lines were composed for semantic purposes. Here is the context of the second example (a young bride discovers that she has to take care of a raving-mad brother of her husband):

(13)   Father and mother married, and mother came
       A bride, to help take care of such a creature,
       And accommodate her young life to his.
       That was what marrying father meant to her.
       She had to lie and and hear love things made dreadful
       By his shouts in the night. He'd shout and shout
       Until the strength was shouted out of him <...>
                                    (*A Servant to Servant* 126–132)

(Notice the semantic link between the micro-texts of the two rhythmical figures in the excerpt: "And accommodate her young life" to "his shouts in the night".)

Metricality of lines may be viewed as concentric circles. The most frequent types of lines, called "meter-fixing" (Chatman 1965: 133), are in the center. Deviating and less frequent types (Chatman called them "meter-fixed") are progressively farther from the center; they disrupt the iambic momentum and make the meter harder and harder to recognize. Let us arrange the "meter-fixed" types of lines in an approximately increasing degree of complexity (the order is only tentative and arguable).

(A)   A stress maximum on W generated by monosyllables, as in "In the sign of a Scorpion <...>"
(B)   A stress maximum on W incorporating a disyllabic end-stressed word: "With a lawyer at hand <....>"
(C)   A syntactic break after WS, WSW or SW:

(14)   See the Queen! /// Norbert – this one more last word <...>
                                     (Browning *Saul* 880)
       Dead! The sweet bond broken! /// They come! Let me <....>
                                     (Shelley *The Cenci* 5...4: 137)
       To affirm /// there is such a thing as evil
                                     (Frost *Build Soil* 50)

(D)   Tetrasyllabic WSWS generated by monosyllables or incorporating a disyllabic word:

(15)   One by one he subdued his father's trees   (Frost *Birches* 28)
       After a while picking peas in his garden   (Frost *The Code* 108)
       How many bards gild the lapses of time!   (Keats *Sonnet IV*: 1)

(E)   Tetrasyllabic SWSW generated by monosyllables: "Though I found your hand full of wilted fern" (Frost *The Exposed Nest* 11).
(F)   Tetrasyllabic SWSW incorporating a disyllabic end-stressed word: "I prefer to sing safely in the realm" (Frost *Build Soil* 48).
(G)   Pentasyllabic WSWSW generated by monosyllables: "One by one I lost off my hat and shoes" (Frost *Wild Grapes* 72).
(H)   Pentasyllabic WSWSW incorporating a polysyllabic word: "Guaranteed to come safely off with you" (Frost *How Hard It Is To Keep From Being King...* 125).
(I)   Hectasyllabic SWSWSW incorporating a disyllabic end-stressed word: "But forgot to put the leaf back in closing."
(J)   Polysyllabic figures incorporating a polysyllabic word: "And accommodate her young life to his."

3. Reasons for deviations from the metrical scheme

Why do English poets deviate from the metrical scheme? Hanson and Kiparsky (1997) feel that poets do so to incorporate an optimal amount of vocabulary. Indeed, the language material that the poet has to work with does influence certain properties of verse. For example, the abundance of strongly-stressed monosyllables on W positions of the English iamb is to a certain extent explained by their high proportion in the English language; and frequent missing stresses on S in Russian iambs are the consequence of the numerous polysyllabic words in Russian.

But the relationship between the poetic form and language givens is not straightforward, and poets frequently choose a form that is not optimal for the language givens. Poets may have other considerations, for example, following a prestigious foreign model. Czech poets chose the iambic form imitating the German pattern, though Czech is a language with an obligatory initial word stress, and the iamb is inconvenient for Czech (Jakobson 1979). "Deviations" in the English iamb come not from the poets' desire to incorporate a maximum amount of vocabulary, but from the roots of the English iambic convention and its wave-like evolution, alternating periods of stricter and looser verse. The early Renaissance poet Thomas Wyatt learned to write poetry by translating Petrarch's sonnets, and the syllabic verse of Italian *hendecasyllabo* allows various kinds of licenses in stressing.

Poets of an established canon comply with the tastes and expectations of their epoch. There are more deviations in Donne's iambs than in Dryden's because Donne worked during the period of the Baroque, and Dryden during the time of Classicism. Shakespeare has more deviations than Pope not because Shakespeare's vocabulary is larger than Pope's, but because Shakespeare's audience expected and tolerated the kind of "deviations" that Pope's audience would not. "Deviations" are part of the canon. Almost every line with "deviations" can be modified to eliminate them:

(16) Colors that change whene'er they wave their Wings   (Pope)
      Their colors change whene'er they wave their wings   (construct)
      Gained but one Trump and one Plebeian Card   (Pope)
      She gained a trump and one plebeian card.   (construct)

English poets could compose verse without rhythmical figures, and their rhythmical vocabulary, already strongly constrained by the iambic form, would hardly change.

Thus, "deviations" from the iambic scheme stem, first, from the historical roots of the form and, secondly, from the requirements of the canon of a particular epoch. And thirdly, the use of deviations is explained by the semantic potential of rhythmical figures: they stand out, attract the reader's or listener's attention, and may serve as rhythmical italics, to emphasize certain semantic categories. Almost as soon as rhythmical figures became part of the English iambic verse, already in the poetry of Surrey (see examples below), they began to be used as an expressive device.

Consider the semantic functions of the most frequent figures: WS, WSW, and SW. The figures seem to be experienced differently depending on the parts of speech of the constituents and the syntactic pattern coupled with the figure. For example, poets seem to feel that attributive phrases mapped against positions SW(S) are less disruptive than subject and predicate; phrases like (17) are more numerous than (18):

(17)   With <u>a mild</u> look of courage <....>
    (Shelley *The Revolt of Islam* 2420)
(18)   Where <u>the waves</u> rolled like mountains <...>
    (*The Revolt of Islam* 4792)

The former pattern occurs in the iambic verse of all periods, while the latter mostly during periods of looser verse, and even then sparingly. In Shelley's *The Revolt of Islam* attributive phrases accompany 84% of all figures SW(S) formed by monosyllables, while "subject plus predicate" are coupled with less than 5%. The frequency of these two syntactic patterns in verse outside rhythmical figures and in prose does not display such a striking difference. Though there is no direct correlation between syntax and stress, some syntactic structures are more likely to be highlighted by intonation than others (Bolinger 1972: 644). Subject and predicate are probably more likely to be both strongly stressed, while a modifier on W is more likely to be subordinate to the stress of the modified noun. Thus, as we shall see below, the subject-and-predicate patterns coupled with SW are more frequently used for semantic purposes than attributive patterns.

Different rhythmical figures attract different parts of speech. Thus, WS and WSW containing monosyllables or a disyllabic word with an initial stress are usually coupled with a verb (Tarlinskaja 1984), while SW prefers adjectives. In the verse text outside rhythmical figures, as in prose, the most frequent lexical part of speech is the noun. The proportion of the four lexical parts of speech in the rhythmical figures and outside the figures in Shelley's *The Revolt of Islam* is shown in Table 2.

Table 2.   The proportion of nouns, verbs, adjectives and adverbs in rhythmical figures (the whole text, 4818 lines) and outside the figures (Canto VI) in Shelley's *The Revolt of Islam* (in percent from the total of the lexical parts of speech). The maxima are underlined.

	Nouns	Verbs	Adj.	Adv.	Other	Total
Outside figures	<u>46</u>	23	18	8	5	2088
In WS, WSW	20	<u>56</u>	10	8	6	714
In SW (monosyl.)	9	10	<u>77</u>	1	3	560

The figures WS and WSW attract not just verbs, but verbs of particular semantic categories (Tarlinskaja 1987). The largest grouping in *The Revolt of Islam*, for example, incorporates verbs of intense and vigorous motion (19), 175 out of the total of 400 verbs forming the figures WS and WSW, or 44%:

(19)   Waving a sword <...>
       Smote on the beach <...>
       <...> rushed through their ranks

If we also add verbs indicating "violence", and "violence leading to death" (20), as well as verbs indicating restraining by force (21), and loud sounds (22), the proportion of verbs indicating vigorous, forceful, violent action reaches 58% of all verbs accompanying WS and WSW.

(20)   Stabbed in their sleep <...>
       Kill me!' – They burned <...>
(21)   Locked in stiff rings <...>
       Clasped that bright Shape <...>
(22)   Curse and blaspheme <...>
       Shrieked the exulted Priest <...>
       Creaked with the weight of birds <...>

In contrast, verbs occurring in situations of calm or referring to a state (23) incorporate only 43 verbs (11%).

(23)   Sitting with thee <...>
       Resting at eve <...>
       Knew I what solace <...>
       Awed by the ending <...>

Obviously, Shelley found the figures WS and WSW a suitable accompaniment to vigorous activity rather than to a static state.

Even more unexpectedly, rhythmical figures are conventionally coupled with particular words. In *The Revolt of Islam* the verb "fall", for example, appears in WS nine times; some examples are given in (24).

(24)   Fell like bright Spring <...>   (56)
       Fell like a shaft <...>   (4020)

Fell on the pale opressors <...>   (114)
<...> fell on my brain   (551)
Fell to the sea <...>   (250)
Fell o'er that snowy child <...>   (4655), etc.

Other verbs appear only once. Outside rhythmical figures, "fall" is by far not the most frequent verb.

The verb "fall" regularly accompanies WS and WSW in the iambs of all English poets (i.e., poets who wrote in English), from Surrey through Frost. Here are some examples:

(25)   Fell to the ground, all ouerspred with flash
                (Surrey *Translations from the Aeneid* Book 2: 396)
       Fell to the ground, and whatso that with flame
                (*Translations from the Aeneid* Book 2: 652)
       Fell on the bedd <...>
                (*Translations from the Aeneid* Book 4: 870)
       Fall to the base earth <...>   (Shakespeare *Richard II* 2.4: 20)
       <...> fall by the side   (Shakespeare *Sonnet 151*: 12)
       Falling on Diomed <...>
                (Shakespeare *Troilus and Cressida* 5.2: 176)
       Fell from the Conduit <...>
                (Swift *A Description of a City Shower* 60)
       Fell on the ground <...>
                (Wordsworth *The Old Cumberland Beggar* 19)
       Fall to the ground <...>   (Wordsworth *The Excursion* 7: 315)
       Fell on my face <...>   (Tennyson *The Lover's Tale* 988)
       Fall on my head <...>   (Keats *Endymion* 132)
       <...> fell on her hands   (Keats *The Eve of St. Agnes* 25: 4)
       Fall from his hand <...>   (Byron *Childe Harold* 4.16: 7)
       Falls from my withered hand <...>   (Shelley *The Cenci* 1.1: 128)
       Fell from my lips <...>   (*The Cenci* 2.1: 113)
       Falling like dew <...>   (Byron *Don Juan* 3.88: 2)
       Falling in whispers <...>   (Tennyson *The Lover's Tale* 259)
       Falling for France <...>   (Byron *Childe Harold* 3.56: 9)
       Falling in love <...>   (Frost *Paul's Wife* 131)

Other verbs of the semantic group "motion downwards", such as "sink", "dip", "drop", "droop", "kneel", "bend" also often accompany WS and WSW.

68 *Marina Tarlinskaja*

Another semantic subcategory regularly emphasized by the figures WS and WSW is "vibrating motion". Here are examples of just one verb, "shake":

(26) Shakes the whole Roofe, or ruines all   (Herrick *Liberty* 5)
Shakes the thin roof, and echoes round the walls
                    (Crabbe *The Village. The Poor-house* 48)
Shake the red cloak, and poise the ready brand
                    (Byron *Childe Harold* 1: 779)
Shakes the high ticket <...>   (Milton *Arcades* 58)
Shook her weak bosom <...>   (Arnold *Tristram* 2: 133)
Shake the whole tree <...>   (Browning *By the Fire-side* 203)
Shake the loose reigns! ye slaves of God
                    (Yeats *The Wanderings of Osin* 1: 331)
Shake my fell purpose, not keep pace between <...>
                    (Shakespeare *Macbeth* 1.5: 47)
Shakes the old beldame earth <...>
                    (Shakespeare *Henry IV, 1* 3.1: 31)
Shook the pale apple blossom <...>
                    (Yeats *The Shadowy Waters* 275)
Shakes in thy fear <...>   (Tennyson *Gareth and Lynette* 940)
Shakes with decay <...>   (Shelley *Fiordispina* 19)
Shook with her agony <...>   (Keats *The Cap and Bells* 44: 8)
Shook as he stumbled <...>   (Browning *Sordello* 1: 753)
Shake the ale-horns <...>
                    (Yeats *The Old Age of Queen Maeve* 50)
Shakes its cocooning mists <...>
                    (Hopkins *I am Like a Slip of Comet* 8)
Shaking his bloody darts <...>   (Shakespeare *Henry VI 2* 3.1: 366)
Shaking his bloody fingers <...>
                    (Shakespeare *Julius Caesar* 3.1 :198)
Shaking a fist <...>   (Browning *Fra Lippo Lippi* 154)
<...> shaking of earth (Shakespeare *Troilus and Cressida* 1.3: 97)
Shaking the dust <...> (Wordsworth *Thanksgiving Ode* 125)
Shaking and waving, vapour vapour chased
                    (Yeats *The Wanderings of Oisin* 2: 164)

The verb "shake" is more frequent within rhythmical figures than outside them.

Consider briefly the figure SW(S) generated by monosyllables in the syntactic pattern "subject plus predicate". Again we notice recurring verbs, and among them, again, "fall":

(27)   As <u>his foe fell</u>; then, like a serpant, coiled <...>
              (Byron *The Island* 4.12: 56)
       And <u>the church fell</u>, and crushed him to a mummy
              (Shelley *The Cenci* 1.3: 50)
       Or <u>the dews fall</u>, or th'angry sun look down   (Shelley *Hellas* 438)
       And kiss'd him. <u>And awe fell</u> on both the hosts
              (Arnold *Sohrab and Rustum* 729)
       And <u>the crown fell</u>, and the crown jewels scattered
              (Frost *How Hard It Is To Keep From Being King...* 6)

All rhythmical figures disrupt the iambic momentum, therefore SW, similarly to WS and WSW, must be viewed as a suitable mimetic accompaniment to situations referring to a vigorous action, especially directed downwards (the "upwards" verbs are less frequent).

Nouns that refer to moving objects, such as parts of the body (head, hair, hands, arms, wings) also recur. The recurring rhythmical-grammatical-lexical patterns are particularly noticeable if they incorporate at least two identical lexical words or their close synonyms. Such patterns gravitate to a limited number of motifs: movement, especially of wings or of human head and limbs; strong emotions and their physical display (sobbing, choking, laughing, winking, turning red or pale); fighting, delivering or receiving a blow, suffering, dying and killing; natural phenomena (waves, winds).

Below is given just one illustration of a rhythmical-grammatical-lexical pattern: a selected list of recurring structures accompanying the figures WS and WSW triggered by the noun "wings". The patterns usually have the following composition: there is, typically, a monosyllabic verb on W followed by a monosyllabic grammatical word on S (a variant: a disyllabic initially-stressed verb on WS, and no grammatical word on S) followed by a monosyllabic modifier on W followed by the noun "wings" with its stress on S. The noun "wings" ("plumes, pinions") is often coupled with the verbs "spread", "bear", "flutter", "lift", "shake", "beat" and "clap". Here are some examples:

(28)   <u>Spread thy broad wings</u> over my love and me
              (Spenser *Epitalamion* 319)

Spread thy broad wings, and souze on all the kind
    (Pope *Epilogue to the Satires, Dialogue 2*: 15)
Spread her broad wings, that flutter'd with affright
    (Coleridge *To the Honourable Mr. Erskine* 2)
Spreads his black Wings, and slowly mounts to Day
    (Pope *The Rape of the Lock* 4: 88)
Spread thy soft Wings, and waft me o'er the Main
    (Pope *Sapho to Phaon* 210)
Spread thy full wings, and waft him o'er
    (Tennyson *In Memoriam* 9: 4)
Spread his light wings, and in a moment flies
    (Pope *Eloisa to Abelard* 76)
Spread his light wings of saffron and of blue
    (Byron *English Bards and Scotch Reviewers* 523)
Spreading swift wings as sails to the dim air
    (Shelley *The Revolt of Islam* 2591)
Clapp'd his glad Wings, and sate to view the fight
    (Pope *The Rape of the Lock* 5: 54)
Clapp'd her strong wings, and sought the cheerful isle
    (Wordsworth *Lines Written at a School Exercise"* 46)
Weighs his spread wings, at leisure to behold
    (Milton *Paradise Lost* 2: 1046)
Closed his dark wings, relaxed his eye
    (Walter Scott *The Lady of the Lake* 2: 524)
Plumes his wide wings and seek's sol's palace high
    (Blake *An Imitation of Spenser* 43)
Fall with soft wings, stuck with soft flowers
    (Crashaw *Temperance* 46)
Climb with swift wings after their children's souls
    (Shelley *The Cenci* 1.3: 85)
Mounts on rapt wings, and with a moment's flight
    (Wordsworth *The Source of the Danube* 7)
Lifted his wings, and stood attentive-wise
    (Keats *The Cap and Bells* 56: 2)
Bears in his wings so many a changefull token
    (Spenser *Muiopotmos* 101)
Bear on your wings and in your notes his praise
    (Milton *Paradise Lost* 5: 199)
Shaking her wings, devouring all in haste

(Shakespeare *Venus and Adonis* 57)
Flirting her wings and saying chikadee   (Frost *Snow* 231)

Such recurring rhythmical-grammatical-lexical patterns are formulaic. Formulas appear, as it turns out, not only in folk and archaic oral poetries, as was previously thought (cf. Parry 1971), but also in literary verse (Gasparov 1999, Tarlinskaja 1989). Their discovery does not compromise poets or rob them of their individuality, but helps us to understand the mechanisms of composing poetry. It also proves that poets use rhythmical figures not because they succumb to the pressure of language, but because these figures are part of the poetic convention, and serve semantic purposes.

Thus, deviations in the English iamb do not occur merely to incorporate an optimal amount of vocabulary. They originated from the influence of Italian syllabic verse on the first modern English poet Thomas Wyatt, and became part of the iambic form that developed since. Almost at once their use for stylistic and semantic purposes also became part of the poetic convention. The number of deviations in the English iambic verse, their specific position in the line, their limited patterns of structuring, their morphological, syntactic and lexical features and the narrow thematic repertoire of the micro-contexts that they accompany show that the primary cause of deviations is not the pressure from the language but the codes of the poetic convention. English poets could compose their verse without rhythmical figures, as did Anatoly Liberman (1983) in his stylized translations of the Russian poet Mikhail Lermontov, and the rhythmical vocabulary of English verse would not change; but the poetic style would.

4. Conclusion

So, what IS metrical for the English iambic pentameter?

For the *whole text*, the typical range of contrast between even and odd positions lies somewhere between 50–60%; the polar tendencies are 80% or higher, and 40% (a probable minimum: 44% in Donne's *Satyres*).

In individual lines, monosyllabic "deviations" and disyllabic and trisyllabic rhythmical figures WS, WSW and SW (composed of two monosyllables) are within the stricter canon, while SW generated by a disyllabic end-stressed word and the trisyllabic SWS are metrical for a looser canon. Among longer strings, some are felt to be less disruptive than others. Figures WSWS, especially if they do not incorporate an end-stressed disyllable, seem to be less disruptive than SWSW. A disyllabic word at the beginning of the figure seems less disruptive than at the end. Thus, "After a while picking peas in his garden" is felt to be less disruptive than "How many bards gild the lapses of time", though both contain WSWS. Polysyllabic words incorporated into longer figures and syntactic boundaries at the end of the figures make them even more disruptive and less metrical. Pentasyllabic, hectasyllabic and longer figures, particularly incorporating disyllabic and longer words may be considered anomalous; they complicate recognition of the iambic meter, and are mostly composed for semantic purposes. Too many deviations efface the iambic meter and move the form towards purely syllabic verse, as in Donne's *Satyres*. Various types of deviations and their acceptable number are signs of particular epochs in the history of the English poetic tradition. Thus, Pope's line "Make the soul dance upon a Jig to Heaven" (*Epistle IV To Richard Boyle, Earl of Burlington* 144) would be metrical for Frost, while "Made a girl's marriage and ruled in her life" (Frost *Maple* 164) is metrical for Frost but not for Pope.

Notes

1. The final position is disregarded in the calculation: the high stressing on position 10 somewhat effaces the difference in stressing within the line.
2. Figures in brackets below indicate the number of lines. Frost's poems extensively analyzed for this article include *The Death of the Hired Man* (109), *A Hundred Collars* (179), *Home Burial* (116), *A Servant to Servant* (177), *The Code* (114), *The Generation of Men* (212), *The Black Cottage* (127), *The Housekeeper* (214), *The Fear* (93), *Maple* (170), *Paul's Wife* (157), and *Wild Grapes* (102); the total is 1770 lines. Earlier, more poems were analyzed, with a total of 3000 lines.

References

Bailey, James
    1975   *Towards a Statistical Analysis of English Verse*. Lisse/Netherlands: The Peter de Ridder Press.
Biggs, Henry Parkman
    1996   A statistical analysis of the metrics of the Classical French decasyllable and the Classic French alexandrine. Manuscript of a PhD dissertation, UCLA.

1999 The Classic French decasyllable of DuBellay (16th century): A generative metrical perspective. Paper presented at the 1999 Toronto conference on generative metrics.

Bjorklund, Beth
1978 *A Study in Comparative Prosody: English and German Iambic Pentameter*. Stuttgart: Academischer Verlag Hans-Dieter Heinz.

Bolinger, Dwight
1972 Accent is predictable (if you're a mind-reader). *Language* 48.3: 633–644.

Chatman, Seymour
1965 *A Theory of Meter*. London-The Hague-Paris: Mouton & CO.

Frost, Robert
1975 *The Poetry of Robert Frost. All Eleven of his Books – Complete*. Edward Conney Latham (ed.), 6th reprint. New York: Holt, Rinehart and Winston.

Gasparov, M. L.
1996 *A History of European Versification*. Translated by G.S. Smith and Marina Tarlinskaja. G.S. Smith and L. Hotford-Strevens (eds.), Oxford: Clarendon Press.

Gasparov, Mikhail L.
1999 *Metr i smysl* [Meter and meaning]. Moskva: Rossijskij gosudarstvennyj gumanitarnyj universitet.

Halle, Morris
1968 Zirmunskij's theory of verse: A review article. *A Slavic and East European Review* 12: 213–218.

Halle, Morris, and Samuel J. Keyser
1966 Chaucer and the study of prosody. *College English* 28: 187–219.
1971 *English Stress: Its Form, Its Growth, and Its Role in Verse*. New York: Harper and Row.
1998 On meter in general and on Robert Frost's loose iambics in particular. In: *Festschrift for Professor K. Inoue,* E. Iwamoto (ed.). Japan: Kanda University of International Studies.

Hanson, Kristin, and Paul Kiparsky
1996 A parametric theory of poetic meter. *Language* 72.2: 287–335.
1997 The nature of verse and its consequences for the mixed form. In: *Prosimetrum: Cross-cultural Perspectives on Narrative in Verse and Prose*, Karl Reichi and Joseph Harris (eds.), 17–44. Cambridge: D.S Brewer.

Hayes, Bruce
1989 The prosodic hierarchy in meter. In: *Rhythm and Meter,* Paul Kiparsky and Gilbert Youmans (eds.), 201–260. Orlando: Academic Press.

Jakobson, Roman
 1979 O cheshskom stixe, preimushchestvenno v sopostavlenii s russkim [On Czech verse – mainly compared with Russian]. In: *Selected Writings V*, 3–130. The Hague: Mouton.

Kiparsky, Paul
 1975 Stress, syntax, and meter. *Language* 51: 576–616.
 1977 The rhythmic structure of English verse. *Linguistic Inquiry* 8.2: 189–247.

Kökeritz, Helge
 1974 *Shakespeare's Pronunciation*. London: Yale University Press (fourth printing).

Liberman, Anatoly
 1983 *Mikhail Lermontov. Major Poetical Works*. Translation, introduction, and commentary by Anatoly Liberman. Minneapolis: University of Minnesota Press.

Magnuson, Karl, and Frank G. Ryder
 1971 Second thoughts on English prosody. *College English* 33: 198–216.

Parry, Milman
 1971 *The Makings of Homeric Verse. The Collected Papers of Milman Parry*. Edited by Adam Parry. Oxford: Clarendon.

Saltarelli, Mario
 1999 The rhythm of Dante's *Commedia*: Iambic or trochaic? Paper presented at the 1999 Toronto conference on generative metrics.

Tarlinskaja, Marina
 1976 *English Verse. Theory and History*. The Hague: Mouton.
 1984 Rhythm-morphology-syntax-rhythm. *Style* 18.1: 1–26.
 1987 Rhythm and meaning: Rhythmical figures in English iambic pentameter, their grammar, and their links with semantics. *Style* 21.1: 1–35.
 1989 Formulas in English literary verse. *Language and Style* 22.2: 115–130.
 1993 *Strict Stress-Meter in English Poetry Compared with German and Russian*. Calgary: University of Calgary Press.

Tarlinskaja, M.G., and L.M. Teterina
 1974 Verse-prose-metre. *Linguistics* 129: 63–86.

Tomashevsky, Boris
 1929 *O stixe*. [On verse]. München: Wilhelm Fink Verlag.

Zhirmunsky, Viktor M.
 1925. *Vvedenie v metriku*. [Introduction to metrics]. Leningrad: Academia.

3. English meter

Generated metrical form and implied metrical form

Nigel Fabb

1. Introduction

Metrical verse is characterized by rules and by tendencies. In English iambic pentameter, a stressed syllable *must* be in an even-numbered position or first position if it is in a polysyllable; it will *tend* to be in an even-numbered position or first position if it is a monosyllable. This example demonstrates that there is an apparent relation between rule and tendency (they relate similar phonological characteristics to the same positions in the line), which raises the possibility that they should be explained together, and indeed this has generally been assumed. However, I will argue in this paper that rules and tendencies require completely different kinds of explanation. Rules are explained by a generative theory (specifically Bracketed Grid theory, Fabb and Halle (forthcoming)); tendencies are explained by a pragmatic theory (specifically Relevance Theory, Sperber and Wilson (1995)).

2. Form as content

There are two kinds of form. One kind of form is constitutive. Linguistic form is an example of constitutive form in the sense that phonetic form for example, is what enables us to speak; speech is made of phonetic form. The same is true of other kinds of linguistic form; without syntactic form there would be no sentences. Generative linguistics explains constitutive form by suggesting that form is created by rules which build and relate utterances and meanings. Constitutive form is a determinate fact of some part of the world (e.g., of speech) and can be discovered. This kind of form holds of something because it constitutes that thing.

The other kind of form holds of something because it is held by someone; it exists only as the content of a thought about the text. Many kinds of literary form exemplify this. Consider for example genre. Genre is clearly not a determinate fact of a text or something which constitutes it or enables it to exist; we hold a text to be in a certain genre because it has characteristics which more or less correspond to our expectations about the genre. This means that it is possible to disagree about the genre of a text; it is not a determinate fact. Furthermore, the text can be in a mixture of genres, can be indeterminate in genre, and so on. These characteristics all suggest that the genre of a text is among the meanings communicated by the text. The genre of a text is a proposition such as 'this text is a sonnet' which is implied by other propositions communicated by the text such as 'this text has fourteen lines' and 'this text has a sonnet rhyme scheme'. This kind of form is a kind of content, which we might call implied form, as opposed to constitutive form. Implied form, like any implicature of a text, is optional, can be vague or indeterminate, ambiguous and even self-contradictory. Thus genre can be manipulated in all these ways, as has been demonstrated very clearly by postmodernism; these manipulations are possible only because genre is a kind of content, implied by the text, rather than a determinate fact of the text.

The idea that form can be implied is ontologically parsimonious; in fact we get it for free, because it requires no specific mechanisms other than those already required as part of a pragmatic theory. In this it differs from constitutive form, which always requires a special theory to explain it, and is thus ontologically expensive. Most kinds of literary form can be shown to have characteristics which show that they are kinds of implied form rather than kinds of constitutive form. In Fabb (2002a) I argue that genre, some aspects of the division of a text into lines, and the organization of lines into stanzas, are all kinds of implied form and not kinds of constitutive form. The question therefore arises whether it is possible for all kinds of literary form, including metrical form, to be implied. In section 5 of this paper I explore some ways in which metrical form can be explained pragmatically, but I also suggest that some of the aspects of metrical form must be constitutive rather than implied, and thus require a special metrical theory (offered in section 3). (The discussion here is developed more fully in Fabb 2002a, 2004.)

Relevance Theory (Sperber and Wilson 1995) offers a good basis for a pragmatic account of form as implied. In order for a thought 'this text is a sonnet' to be communicated, the text must offer evidence for the thought. This might include titling the text 'sonnet' for example, but it will also include communicating the thoughts 'this text is in fourteen lines' or 'this text has a rhyme scheme ABABCDCDEFEFGG'. The question might arise, how a text communicates these latter thoughts as they are not the contents of propositions developed from the sentences from which the text is made. I suggest that we can adapt the Relevance-Theoretic notion of 'explicature' to explain how these thoughts arise. An explicature is an explicit meaning, developed by minimal inference from a logical form. For example, a logical form may include a pronoun with an external referent (i.e., whose referent cannot be established by rules of coreference). In order to develop a proposition from the logical form the referent of the pronoun must be established. This cannot be done by linguistic rules, but must involve some inferencing. Once established by inferencing, we have an explicature of the utterance, which we might call a 'literal meaning' (and not necessarily the final communicated meaning of the utterance). We might similarly say that having fourteen lines, or having a certain rhyme scheme, while not necessarily 'facts' of the text which can be derived from it by rule, nevertheless require minimal inferencing before they can be established and are fairly determinate, and are what we might call 'literal forms' of the text. These formal explicatures such as 'this text has fourteen lines' are propositions which can then be the basis of further inferencing by the usual procedures. The deduction by which the thoughts are developed would look like (1) in Relevance Theory (using the rule of *modus ponens*). Thought (A) is a formal explicature, thought (B) is a thought which might be part of general knowledge; and together these form the premises from which thought (C) is derived as a conclusion.

(1)   A   This text has fourteen lines.

       B   If a text has fourteen lines then it is a sonnet.

       therefore

       C   This text is a sonnet.

An important part of Relevance Theory relates to the extent to which a thought is held to be true (or held to be communicated by a text). Thoughts are not best characterised as fully true or fully false, but are held with a certain degree of strength corresponding to the commitment with which they are held by the thinker (as tentative hypothesis vs. certainty, for example). Thus the thought that a text is a sonnet can be strong, but it can also be weak in the case of texts which have sonnet-like characteristics but are not obviously sonnets in all respects. In the above deduction, thought B is somewhat weak on its own (not every text of fourteen lines is a sonnet), and so the conclusion will be strengthened if it can also be reached by other means (e.g., via thoughts about its rhyme scheme). The notion of strength gives us the basis for understanding tendential or approximative form; form which seems to be very strongly present is the content of strongly held thoughts, while form which seems to be weakly present is the content of weakly held thoughts. In section 4, I return to pragmatics to suggest that some aspects of metricality hold as the content of strong or weak thoughts about the text.

3. Counting as the basis of a metrical theory

In Fabb and Halle (forthcoming) we demonstrate that all kinds of metrical verse can be explained by the same theoretical apparatus, which we call Bracketed Grid theory (see also Fabb 2002a, b, Fabb and Halle in press a, b).

The meters of the world include meters which are syllable-counting with no regular rhythm (e.g., Welsh), mora-counting (e.g., Sanskrit *arya*), accentual with variable length lines (e.g., the meter of *Beowulf*), accentual-syllabic (e.g., English), quantitative (e.g., Greek), rhythmically periodic (e.g., Arabic) and rhythmically non-periodic (e.g., Classical Sanskrit), meters with 'resolution' (e.g., Somali *gabay*) and meters without (e.g., Somali *geerar*), meters with apparently flexible lengths (e.g., English loose meters, and possibly all accentual meters) and meters with fixed lengths (e.g., English strict meters). (See endnote 1 for sources relating to the meters mentioned in this section.)

We take the view that the fundamental principle of all metrical verse is counting, and that the mechanism for doing the count can also explain other regular aspects of the meter such as rhythm, word boundary rules, and sound patterning rules. Our mechanism for counting has ways of permitting a fixed number of syllables to be counted, while also permitting extra syllables in the line (as in the loose meters, or in resolution, or extra syllables at the edge of the line). In principle, metricality arises just when syllables are counted; however, we note a descriptive generalization that there is usually some additional control over the line relative to the count. Thus in rhythmically periodic meters such as English iambic pentameter (which has an underdetermined periodic rhythm), even-numbered syllables tend to be stressed and odd-numbered syllables tend to be unstressed, and thus the rhythm is relative to the counting of syllables in the line. In rhythmically aperiodic meters such as Classical Sanskrit, specific syllables have specific weights; in the meter which defines the first half of the *mahāmālikā* line there are ten syllables, all light except for the seventh, ninth and tenth which are heavy. Again, the weights are defined in terms of the count. In the Welsh *englyn penfyr* the first line has ten syllables, of which the seventh, eighth, or ninth syllable must rhyme with the final syllable of the next two lines; again a metrical constraint defined in terms of the count. In Dyirbal *gama* the eleven-syllable line must have a word boundary before the sixth and eighth syllables, and may also have a word boundary before the third syllable; another regularity defined in terms of the count.

Bracketed grid theory thus offers a way of counting syllables by building a representation – a bracketed grid – over which conditions can be stated which explain these additional regularities. The count provides the basis for all other regularities in the line. Note that this is fundamentally different from traditional and also other generative metrical approaches, which have been based mainly on English, and which define the rhythm as fundamental and the count as secondary. Apart from the fact that this approach fails to account for syllable-counting meters and rhythmic but aperiodic meters, it also fails to explain why metrical texts are always verse (i.e., divided into lines), as argued in Fabb (2003). If rhythm is fundamental to metricality, then prose (text not divided into lines) should be able to be metrical; if counting is fundamental then the count must begin and end somewhere and hence the text must be divided into lines. As far as we know there is no systematically rhythmic prose, and this absence justifies the claim that counting is fundamental and rhythm (if present) secondary.

I now show how bracketed grid theory works by using the familiar example of iambic pentameter; this is a meter which can be satisfactorily explained by many different theories, but the advantage of our theory is that we explain it in a way which will also explain all other kinds of metrical verse.

The first task for a theory which counts elements of the line is to identify which elements are counted; these elements are projected as a line of asterisks and these asterisks are counted. But in this meter, not every syllable is actually counted; thus in general, syllables project as asterisks but some syllables do not. Typical kinds of syllables which do not project include a syllable ending in a vowel which precedes a syllable beginning in a vowel and which optionally projects (i.e., synaloepha), and there are other such options. The possibility of not projecting certain syllables means that every line has exactly ten counted syllables, but can have more than ten spoken syllables; thus it can vary in length in one sense while being rigid in length in another (a problem which much concerned eighteenth century metrists such as Walker (1781: 197)). This is one way in which counting nevertheless allows variable length lines; there are other aspects of the theory which allow other syllables selectively not to be counted, thus permitting variable length in the actual line which is generated by rules which rigidly specify length.

A line of iambic pentameter will thus have ten asterisks projected from it. Here is a line from Matthew Arnold's 'Sohrab and Rustum' (Allott and Allott 1979), projecting ten asterisks (note that there are potentially more than ten syllables in this line – those which do not project are underlined).

(2)   Of Elburz, from th_e_ Aral_i_an est_u_aries,
       * * *   *   * * * * * *

The theory must present us with rules which generate a line of exactly ten asterisks. We do this by using iterative rules which build binary or ternary feet (with non-maximal feet permitted). A foot in this theory is a sequence of asterisks ending in a right bracket or beginning in a left bracket; this is an innovation of Idsardi (1992), where there is no requirement that a foot be bounded at both ends. Thus feet are built by inserting brackets into the line of asterisks, and allowing each foot to be represented by projecting one asterisk (its head) to be a member of a higher line of asterisks. Thus we can insert right brackets into this line of asterisks from right to left skipping two asterisks at a time to get the following representation:

(3)   Of Elburz, from the Aralian estuaries,
      * *) *   *)   * *) * *) * *)

This gives us five feet; we can represent each foot by an asterisk on the next line; this is the head of the foot and in this meter the rightmost asterisk in the foot projects as the head.

(4)   Of Elburz, from the Aralian estuaries,
      * *) *   *)   * *) * *) * *)   gridline 0
       *   *   * * *   gridline 1

This gives us the first part of the grid, which must now be completed such that the last constructed gridline has just one asterisk; the requirement that the rules end up with a grid with one final asterisk is the way the rules control the number of syllables in the line. There are many scansions which are permitted by the theory for building a grid with ten terminal asterisks; the actual scansion must give a grid which enables other regular aspects of the line to be explained. Since iambic pentameter also has a regularity which differentiates even from odd syllables, the grid must likewise enable even and odd asterisks to be differentiated. The rules which build such a grid are as follows:

(5) The grid-building rules for iambic pentameter

   a. Project each syllable as an asterisk on gridline 0.

   b. Gridline 0 (feet)
   Proceeding from Right to Left, apply the following rules:
   i. Insert a Right parenthesis to the Right of the nearest asterisk
   ii. Skip the next asterisk
   iii. Return to rule i.
   The rightmost element in each foot is projected to the next gridline.

   c. Gridline 1 (metra)
   Proceeding from Right to Left, apply the following rules:
   i. Insert a Right parenthesis to the Right of the nearest asterisk
   ii. Skip the next asterisk
   iii. Skip the next asterisk
   iv. Return to rule i.
   Condition: the final foot constructed is incomplete (specifically binary).
   The rightmost element in each metron is projected to the next gridline.

   d. Gridline 2 (cola)
   Proceeding from Left to Right, apply the following rules:
   i. Insert a Left parenthesis to the Left of the nearest asterisk
   ii. Skip the next asterisk
   iii. Return to rule i.
   The leftmost element in each colon is projected to the next gridline.

The grid which these rules build is the following; it will always have exactly ten syllables at gridline 0.

(6)   Of Elburz, from the Aralian estuaries,
```
        *  *) *     *)       * *) * *) * *)           gridline 0
        *          *)         *   *    *)             gridline 1
                   (*                  *              gridline 2
                   *                                  gridline 3
```

Based on this grid we can now write a condition which is part of the metrical rules, and which exploits the fact that even-numbered syllables have a clearly distinct status in the grid.

(7)   Condition (English)
        A maximum must project to gridline 1.

(8)   Definition of maximum (English strict meters)
        A syllable which (a) carries primary stress in a polysyllabic word, and (b) is preceded and followed in the same line by a syllable which does not carry lexical stress, is a maximum.

   Bracketed grid theory seeks to explain fully consistent or rigid aspects of the meter. Thus in iambic pentameter, there are ten (counted) syllables and a stressed syllable in a polysyllabic word is permitted only in certain positions; these two generalizations hold of almost every iambic pentameter line. Lines where these generalizations do not hold are in our view unmetrical; nothing after all prevents a poet writing the occasionally unmetrical line (any more than speakers are prevented from producing ungrammatical sentences if they so wish). The consistency of these facts suggests that they are an instance of constitutive form; hence generative metrics makes the bold claim that there is a cognitively specific system for the generation of metrical structure. It is the consistency of these generalizations which suggests that here we are not dealing with a kind of implied form. However, as I show in the next section, it is possible to understand other characteristics of metrical lines – including tendencies – in terms of implied form.

4. Tendencies and the pragmatic use of resemblance

As Tarlinskaja (1976) has shown, and indeed as casual observation suggests, iambic pentameter lines show certain tendencies, in addition to their fixed characteristics. (Tarlinskaja probably sees even the fixed characteristics as very strong tendencies; however I propose an explanatory distinction between these.) The most striking tendency involves monosyllables. Monosyllables which have stress in the context of other words tend to fall into the same positions as stressed syllables in polysyllabic words – i.e., even-numbered positions and first position. Monosyllables which lack stress such as articles tend to fall in odd-numbered positions (see Fabb 2001 for a discussion of the placement of 'the' and 'a' in Browning's verse). These are tendencies, not rigid facts, and thus differ from the rigid control over stressed syllables within polysyllables. They can be illustrated by some more lines from 'Sohrab and Rustum'. I underline all even-numbered syllables, and double-underline all stressed syllables in polysyllables (the latter are always in even-numbered positions).

(9)   Stream over Casbin and the southern slopes
      Of Elburz, from the Aralian estuaries,
      Or some frore Caspian reed-bed, southward bound
      For the warm Persian sea-board – so they stream'd.
      The Tartars of the Oxus, the King's guard,
      First, with black sheep-skin caps and with long spears;
      Large men, large steeds; who from Bokhara come
      And Khiva, and ferment the milk of mares.
      Next, the more temperate Toorkmuns of the south,
      The Tukas, and the lances of Salore,
      And those from Attruck and the Caspian sands;

Here there is a fairly strong tendency for lexical monosyllables to be in even-numbered positions, and a rather weaker tendency for grammatical monosyllables to be in odd-numbered positions. While these tendencies also pick out the even-numbered syllables, like the condition (7) on the grid formulated in the previous section, we have no mechanism for writing a condition which holds 'to a certain extent'. Thus I will propose an alternative explanation.

Other tendencies can be found in iambic pentameter. As observed above, some types of syllable are optionally counted (projected) such as a syllable ending in a vowel before another vowel (and other cases). As was first observed by King James VI of Scotland (1584: 216), optionally projected syllables are more likely to be projected the nearer they are to the end of the line (but this is not true in all cases; it does not seem to be true of 'Sohrab and Rustum' for example). Another tendency involves weak monosyllables such as articles and resembles but is not identical to 'trochaic inversion' (as I show in Fabb 2001): if a weak monosyllable is in an even-numbered position it will tend to be the second syllable in the line. This is weakly seen in the lines from 'Sohrab and Rustum' where of three even-numbered instances of 'the', two are in second position. Tendencies are also sometimes quite localized; in Charles Lamb's sonnet 'The Gypsy's Malison' (Fuller 2000:121) every line ends on an eleventh syllable, a possibility always present for iambic pentameter lines which is here realized as a strong tendency in a particular text.

These kinds of tendential form can all be seen as tendencies towards conformity with a pattern or template. They are not well suited to generative rules, which allow for optionality of rule application but are unable to apply 'to a certain extent' as would be required. However, tendentiality and approximation to a pattern can be explained pragmatically, specifically in Relevance Theory, as instances of resemblance. Relevance Theory distinguishes descriptive from interpretive dimensions of language use (Sperber and Wilson 1995: 224–231). 'Descriptive use' is the use of a proposition to represent an eventuality, while 'interpretive use' is the use of a proposition to represent another proposition which it resembles. Irony, metaphor and other kinds of 'loose talk' are instances of interpretive use, where the utterance can be decoded as a logical form whose propositional content does not directly represent a state of affairs; instead the proposition resembles another proposition, and it may be this latter proposition which is actually being communicated by the speaker and which thereby enters into further implicatures.

I argued in section 3 that metricality can be a kind of constitutive form. I suggest now that it can *also* be a kind of implied form. That is, a text can warrant the thought 'this text is in iambic pentameter'. As a kind of implied form, this thought can hold strongly or weakly; this variability in strength corresponds to the kinds of metricality which vary in how regular they are.

Consider for example the fact that lexical monosyllables, tending to carry stress, tend also to be in even-numbered positions. If every even-numbered syllable in an iambic pentameter line carries stress then a formal explicature of this line will be 'this line has a rhythmic pattern x/x/x/x/x/'. I suggest that this formal explicature combines with a thought with the following content, which constitutes part of our general knowledge of iambic pentameter and can be manipulated in inferencing: 'if a line has a rhythmic pattern x/x/x/x/x/ then it is in iambic pentameter'. Thus a line can be in iambic pentameter in two fundamentally different ways; this can be its constitutive form, generated by metrical rules, and it can also be its implied form, derived by inferential processes from a formal explicature of its actual rhythm. If this was all we could say then only lines which had a fully periodic actual rhythm of x/x/x/x/x/ would be able to imply that they were in iambic pentameter. But interpretive use enables lines which have a rhythm resembling this rhythm also to imply, more weakly, that they are in iambic pentameter. Consider for example the line, quoted earlier:

(10)   Stream o̲ver Ca̲s̲bin an̲d̲ the so̲u̲thern slo̲p̲es

The actual rhythm of this line in performance might (depending on the performance) for example be x/x/xxx/x/, without stress on 'and'. The formal explicature is 'this line has a rhythm x/x/xxx/x/', which cannot itself imply iambic pentameter, but it resembles a proposition which can imply iambic pentameter, which is the proposition 'this line has a rhythm x/x/x/x/x/'. Because the resemblance is not exact, the implicature is weakened somewhat; but by interpretive use the line can nevertheless imply a rhythm which in turn implies iambic pentameter. This is the full derivation:

(11)   A   This line has a rhythm x/x/xxx/x/

by interpretive use

B   This line has a rhythm x/x/x/x/x/

C   If this line has a rhythm x/x/x/x/x/ then it is in iambic pentameter

therefore

D   This line is in iambic pentameter

This kind of approach enables us to explain why monosyllables tend to be organized so that the line approximates to a certain rhythmic template. Approximation to a template is a kind of interpretive use by which a specific rhythm is implied. Thus the rhythmic organization of monosyllables in iambic pentameter is not a kind of constitutive form (unlike the organization of polysyllables); instead it is a kind of implied form. The organization of the monosyllables is not driven by generative metrical rules but by the communicative need to imply metrical form. We might ask what motivates such a need to imply form; the answer might repeat Jakobson's (1960) and Bauman's (1975) claim that verbal art must draw attention to its own form.

Other kinds of tendential form can be explained in similar ways; note further that once form is explained as a kind of content, in principle it can be motivated by any functional requirement and can integrate with any kind of knowledge. In iambic pentameter lines an eleventh unstressed syllable is permitted (by the projection rules), but the fact that every line in the Lamb sonnet mentioned above has eleven syllables cannot be explained by metrical rules, which are unable to look beyond the individual line (each line is treated independently). Instead, this can be understood as a kind of parallelism whereby each line resembles the preceding line. This again suggests interpretive use and implied form. As another example, the fact that syllables are more likely to be projected towards the end of the line than towards the beginning may be reinterpreted in terms of some functional demand on implicature of metrical form, such that lines need to imply their form more strongly towards the end than towards the beginning. This seems to be true in general of iambic pentameter lines (which have final rhyme rather than initial alliteration and where iambicity seems also to be strongest in the final foot). I have suggested elsewhere (Fabb 2002a) that the division into lines might have an implied as well as a constitutive aspect, paralleling the division of metricality into implied and constitutive aspects. Hence we might understand the asymmetrical regularity of implied metrical form (cf. Hayes (1989)) as contributing to the implicature of lineation.

We can thus show that it is possible for metrical tendencies to be explained pragmatically. This enables us to dispense with any attempt to attach 'variable conditions' to the metrical grid rules; instead we can allow the generative rules to generate fully metrical lines (where the metricality is underspecified, controlling only polysyllables in the example under discussion), rather than approximately metrical lines.

5. Conclusion

In this paper I have suggested that two completely different explanations are required for the fully regular vs. the tendential or approximative aspects of metricality. Where metrical form is fully consistent it can be understood as constitutive, analogous to linguistic form more generally, and generated by rules and conditions. I outlined a generative theory which counts the elements of the line in a manner which explains other metrical regularities such as rhythm, word boundary placement and sound patterning. Where metrical form is approximative or tendential, it is explained by appealing to a theory of pragmatics, like most other kinds of literary form which also hold approximately or tendentially. These kinds of form hold of the text solely by virtue of being the content of thoughts about the text and are implied, either by deductive processes like *modus ponens*, by the development of formal explicatures, or by interpretive use.

Notes

1. A note on sources. Welsh (Williams 1953), *Beowulf* (Russom 1987), Greek (West 1987), Arabic (Stoetzer 1998), Sanskrit *arya* and Classical Sanskrit (Keith 1920), Vedic Sanskrit (Arnold 1905), Somali (Johnson 1996), English loose meters (Halle and Keyser 1999), Dyirbal (Dixon and Koch 1996). All these metrical traditions are discussed in Fabb and Halle (forthcoming); see also Fabb (1997) for examples of most of these. Thanks to Morris Halle for comments on an earlier draft of this paper, and to participants at the Toronto conference.

References

Allott, K., and M. Allott
    1979   *The Poems of Matthew Arnold.* 2nd edition. London: Longman.
Arnold, E. Vernon
    1905   *Vedic Metre in Its Historical Development.* Cambridge: Cambridge University Press.
Bauman, R.
    1975   Verbal art as performance. *American Anthropologist* 77: 290–311.
Dixon, R. M. W., and G. Koch
    1996   *Dyirbal Song Poetry. The Oral Literature of an Australian Rainforest People.* St Lucia: University of Queensland Press.
Fabb, Nigel
    1997   *Linguistics and Literature: Language in the Verbal Arts of the World.* Oxford: Blackwell.
    2001   Weak monosyllables in iambic verse and the communication of metrical form. *Lingua* 111: 771–790.
    2002a   *Language and Literary Structure: The Linguistic Analysis of Form In Verse and Narrative.* Cambridge: Cambridge University Press.
    2002b   The metres of Dover Beach. *Language and Literature*: 99–117.
    2002c   Metrical rules and the notion of 'maximum', A reply to Derek Attridge. *Language and Literature* 12: 73–80.

2003 Metrical form in poetry requires lineation but metrical form in music does not. Words and Music Conference, University of Missouri-Columbia

2004 Form as fiction. *Belgian Journal of English Language and Literature* New series 2: 63–73.

Fabb, Nigel, and Morris Halle
in press a Metrical complexity in Christina Rossetti's verse. *College Literature*.

Fabb, Nigel, and Morris Halle
in press b Telling the numbers: a unified account of syllabo-tonic English and syllabic Polish and French verse. *Research in Language*.

Fabb, Nigel, and Morris Halle
in prep. *A Treatise on Meter.*

Fuller, J.
2000 *The Oxford Book of Sonnets*. London: Oxford University Press.

Halle, Morris, and Samuel Jay Keyser
1971 *English Stress. Its Form, Its Growth and Its Role in Verse*. New York: Harper and Row.

Halle, Morris, and Samuel Jay Keyser
1999 On meter in general and on Robert Frost's loose iambics in particular. In *Linguistics: In Search of the Human Mind. A Festschrift for Kazuko Inoue,* M. Muraki and E. Iwamoto (eds.), 130–153. Tokyo: Kaitakusha.

Hayes, Bruce
1989 The prosodic hierarchy in meter. In *Phonetics and Phonology 1: Rhythm and Meter*, Paul Kiparsky and G. Youmans (eds.), 201–160. San Diego: Academic Press.

Idsardi, W.
1992 The computation of stress. PhD dissertation, MIT.

Jakobson, R.
1960 Concluding statement: linguistics and poetics. In *Style in Language*, T.A. Sebeok (ed.), Cambridge, MA: MIT Press.

Johnson, John W.
1996 Musico-moro-syllabic relationships in the scansion of Somali oral poetry. In *Voice and Power. The Culture of Language in North-East Africa,* R. J. Hayward and I. M. Lewis (eds.), 73–82. London: School of Oriental and African Studies.

Keith, A. B.
1920 *A History of Sanskrit Literature*. London: Oxford University Press.

King James VI
    1584   Ane Schort Treatise Conteining some Reulis and Cautelis to be Obseruit and Eschewit in Scottis Poesie. In *Elizabethan Critical Essays*, G. Gregory Smith (ed.), volume I: 208–225. London: Oxford University Press, 1904.

Russom, G.
    1987   *Old English Meter and Linguistic Theory*. Cambridge University Press.

Sperber, Dan, and Deirdre Wilson
    1995   *Relevance: Communication and Cognition*. 2nd edition. Oxford, Blackwell.

Stoetzer, W.
    1998   Prosody. In *Encyclopedia of Arabic Literature,* Julie Scott Meisami and Paul Starkey (eds), 619–622. London: Routledge.

Tarlinskaja, Marina
    1976   *English Verse. Theory and History.* The Hague: Mouton.

Walker, John
    1781   *Elements of Elocution. Being the Substance of a Course of Lectures on the Art of Reading.* London.

West, M.L.
    1987   *Introduction to Greek Metre*. London: Oxford University Press.

Williams, G.
    1953   *An Introduction to Welsh Poetry. From the Beginnings to the Sixteenth Century*. London: Faber.

Anapests and anti-resolution*

Michael Hammond

1. Introduction

In this paper I describe one of the meters of Robert Service (1874–1958). The particular meter I consider is anapestic-iambic, where each strong position is separated by one or two weak positions. I detail the distribution of lexical stresses in this meter and demonstrate a number of rather interesting regularities. I provide an analysis of these facts in terms of Optimality Theory (henceforth OT; Prince and Smolensky, 1993; McCarthy and Prince, 1993), showing how the mechanism of *local conjunction* (Smolensky, 1993) finds some utility.

The organization of this paper is as follows. First I outline the general character of metrical theory. Next, I outline the structure of Service's meter, focusing on the distribution of stresses. Third, I present an analysis of Service's meter using OT.

2. Generative meter

Generative metrics finds its origin in the work of Halle and Keyser (1971). The basic idea explored there and continued in subsequent work is that of a template and constraints on the alignment of linguistic material with that template.[1]

The metrical style most often treated is iambic pentameter.[2] In this style, lines are typically composed of ten syllables. Following Halle and Keyser, we can characterize the line as a string of ten positions, alternately labelled 'w' (weak) and 's' (strong).

(1)   w s w s w s w s w s

These positions are then matched with the syllables of a line.

94 *Michael Hammond*

In the generative tradition, most restrictions concern the distribution of lexically stressed syllables in w-positions.[3] A lexical stress is defined as the principal stress in a lexical item, e.g., a noun, adjective, or verb.

3. The meter of Robert Service

Let's now consider the meter of Robert Service. Service actually composed poetry in a variety of meters. The meter I analyze is exemplified in a number of his more well-known poems, e.g., "The Cremation of Sam McGee", "The Black Fox Skin", "The Northern Lights", and "The Shooting of Dan Mc-Grew". The corpus thus defined comprises 447 lines. Here are the first few lines of "Sam McGee" to get a sense of it.[4]

(2)
    w w s w s w w s w s
    There are stránge thíngs dóne in the mídníght sún [sm1]
    w w s w s w s
    By the mén who móil for góld; [sm2]
    w s w s w w s w s
    The Árctic tráils háve their sécret táles [sm3]
    w w s w s w s
    That would máke your blóod rún cóld; [sm4]
    w s w s w s w s
    The Nórthern Líghts have séen quéer síghts, [sm5]
    w w s w w s w w s
    But the quéerest they ever did sée [sm6]
    w w s w w s w s w s
    Was that níght on the márge of Láke Lebárge [sm7]
    w s w w s w s
    I crémated Sám McGée. [sm8]

This exerpt is fairly typical in terms of content, language, and meter.

I propose that each *true* line is composed of seven beats, though sometimes these lines are split on the page at the caesura – or break – that occurs after the fourth beat.[5] For example, the superficial punctuated lines cited in (2) above each contain alternately three and four beats. If we characterize these beats as strong positions, and nonbeats as weak positions, and group the lines in pairs, then we find the following patterns.

(3) w w s w s w w s w s - w w s w s w s
     w s w s w w s w s - w w s w s w s
     w s w s w s w s - w w s w w s w w s
     w w s w w s w s w s - w s w w s w s

This pattern holds generally thoughout the corpus. All punctuated lines contain three, four, or seven beats. Moreover, all the three- and four-beat lines occur in alternation so that they can be paired as illustrated into seven-beat units. Factoring in the other line types that occur in the corpus, we reach the following schema, where parentheses enclose optional positions.

(4)   (w)(w)s (w)ws (w)ws (w)ws (w)(w)s (w)ws (w)ws

4. Stresses

Let's now consider the distribution of stresses. We will see that they are sharply curtailed by the template in (4). First, a stressed monosyllable can occur in weak position when it precedes a phrase-final stress in strong position. Second, a stressed monosyllable can occur in weak position when it is immediately surrounded by stresses in strong positions. Third, a stressed monosyllable can occur in weak position when it is adjacent to a stress in strong position on one side and a stressless beat adjacent to precisely one stressless syllable on the other.

Let's now consider the cases where a lexical stress occurs in weak position. In general, only monosyllabic stresses can occur out of place, but there are a very few examples of lexical stresses in polysyllabic words that appear to be out of place. One very salient example is the repeated scansion of *Claw-fingered Kitty*, a character in "The Black Fox Skin".

(5) 　　　　　w　w　s　w　w　s w　w　s w　s　s w　w　s　w
     There was Cláw-fíngered Kítty and Wíndy Íke líving the lífe of
     　　s
     sháme; [bf1]

     　　　w　　s　w　w　　s w　w　　s w　s　　s w　w　　s　　w　　s
     Now Cláw-fíngered Kítty and Wíndy Íke, bád as the wórst were they;
     [bf46]

>   w   s   w w   s w w   s w s   s   w w   s w s
>   That Cláw-fíngered Kítty and Wíndy Íke fánged up like dógs at báy.
>   [bf68]

There are a few other examples as well, however. For example:

(6)
>   w   s w w   s   w   s w   w s
>   While hígh òverhéad, gréen, yéllow and réd, [dm33]
>   s   w w s w   s w s   w   s w w   s   w   s
>   Slóuching along in smélly rágs, a bléary-èyed, nó-góod búm; [nl5]

The polysyllabic examples are all of a specific sort: there is always more than one stress in the word and the strongest stress of the word occurs in strong position. Thus there appears to be a limit on the number of stresses that count in a single lexical domain. Examples like *cláw-fìngered*, *òverhéad*, and *bléary-èyed* can be eliminated if we only count their strongest stresses.[6]

There are also a few examples where a stressed syllable occurs in nonbeat position and there is no adjacent lexical stress. All of these examples are monosyllabic. These fall into several distinct classes; I go through each below. The first set of examples are cases where the misplaced stress precedes a particle or particlelike item in phrase-final position.

(7)
>   w   s w   s   w   s w   s   w s   w   s
>   They sée its líghts a bláze o' níghts and hárshly they lóok down;
>   [bf80]
>   w   s   w s   w w s   w   s   w w s   w   w   s w
>   The tráil was bád, and I félt hálf mád, but I swóre I would not gíve
>   s
>   in; [sm39]
>   w w s w   s   w w s   w   s   w   s   w   s w w s
>   It was ícy cóld, but the hót swéat rólled down my chéeks, and I don't
>   w   s
>   knów why; [sm51]
>   w   s w s   w w   s w   s   w   s   w   s
>   Gó on, gó on while the tráil is góod, and léave me down to díe."
>   [nl123]

The phrase-final elements are not lexical, but typically do bear strong stress in phrasal contexts. It's not unreasonable to suppose that this strong phrasal stress is sufficient to license the misplaced stress. A lexical stress adjacent to another stress can occur in weak position in many metrical styles.

There is another class of cases as well. Here the misplaced monosyllabic word occurs immediately before a word participating in a midline rhyme.

(8)   w w s   w s w w s   w s w s w w

Well, he séemed so lów that I couldn't <u>sáy</u> no; then he sáys with a

   s   w   s

sórt of móan; [sm21]

 w   s   w s w w s   w   s   w w   s w s w s

Then "Here," <u>sáid</u> I with a súdden crý, "is my cré-ma-tór-eum."
[sm44]

  w   s   w   s   w s   w   s w   s w w   s w

And "Bóys," <u>sáys</u> he, "you don't <u>knów</u> me, and none of you cáre a

  s

dámn; [dm61]

I propose that rhyming positions also count as strongly stressed. As seen in the examples above, the second and fourth beats are potential rhyming positions.[7]

Other stresses in weak positions all occur adjacent to another stressed beat. What's quite striking about Service's meter is that a huge percentage of these actually occur next to *two* other stressed beats. Of the remaining cases, there is a preponderance of examples where the adjacent stress precedes the nonbeat stress. The following chart shows all cases of medial stressed nonbeats in terms of whether the adjacent syllables are stressed.

(9)

to the left	to the right	count
stress	stress	109
stressless	stress	21
stress	stressless	50

So far the distribution of stresses in Service's meter is fairly typical of the English tradition, notwithstanding the relatively flexible template in (4). Lexical stresses in polysyllabic words cannot occur in weak position at all, and lexical monosyllables can occur in weak position only when adjacent to another stress. As noted above, cases where the mismatched monosyllable is surrounded by stresses in strong position are quite common. (This will be characterized as the "double-sided" case in subsequent discussion.)

(10)   s w w s w w s w s s w w s w s
Béaring his príze of a bláck <u>fóx</u> pélt, out of the Wíld he cáme. [bf3]
w s w s w w s w s w s w s w w
They knéw him far for the fítful mán who spát <u>fórth</u> blóod on the
s
snów. [bf7]

w s w s w s w s w s w s w s
The fóul <u>fíend</u> fóx might scáthless gó, for I would húnt no more; [bf36]

w s w s w s w s s w w s w s
A mán <u>dránk</u> déep and sánk to sléep never to wáke again; [bf61]

Let's now look at the cases where a stressed syllable in nonbeat position is adjacent to only one stressless syllable. It turns out that these are rather restricted in their distribution. First, there are a number of cases where the stress in weak position is preceded by a clear lexical stress, but where the stressless syllable following the misplaced monosyllable is actually a stressed particle or rhyming word. Here are a few examples of this sort.

(11)   w s w s w w s w s w s w s
For there be those who would rób your clóthes ere yet the dáwn
w s
<u>cómes</u> in; [bf54]
w w s w s w w s w s w s w s
And the mán <u>stóod</u> by with a bróoding éye, and gnáshed his téeth
w s
and swóre. [bf65]

w s w s w s w s w s w s w s
And hárd she préssed it to her bréast – then Wíndy Íke <u>dréw</u> near. [bf87]

w s w s w s w s w s w w s w s
He túrned to me, and "Cáp," <u>sáys</u> he, "I'll cásh in this tríp, I guéss; [sm19]

These are clearly reduceable to instances of the preceding sort: a stress in weak position followed by a strongly stressed particle or rhyming syllable.

There are also a few examples that are probably misanalyses. These are cases where the stressless syllable should probably be counted as stressed.

(12)   w   s w   s ww s w s   w w s w w s w

Now a prómise máde is a débt unpáid, and the tráil has its own stérn

  s

códe. [sm33]

 w s w w s   w   s

of all that it once héld déar; [dm46]

If we treat *own* and *once* as bearing stress, these can also be assimilated to the previous case.

There is also a class of cases built on what I will refer to as "light" verbs. Here is an exhaustive list.

(13)   w w s w s ww   s w s   w s   w w   s w

And we stárted on at the stréak of dáwn; but Gód! He lóoked ghástly

  s

pále. [sm26]

 w   s w   s ww   s   w   s   w w s   w s w

When unto them in the Lóng, Lóng Níght cáme the mán-who-hád-no-

  s

náme; [bf2]

 w w s w   s w w s w   s   w w s w s w

He was always cóld, but the lánd of góld séemed to hóld him like a

  s

spéll; [sm11]

 w s w   s w   sw s   w   w s w   w s ww   s

And every dáy that quíet cláy séemed to héavy and héavier grów;
[sm37]

 w   s w   s   w   w s w

The Árctic tráils háve their sécret táles[sm3]

 w w s w   s   w   w   s w s   w   w s   w   s w

And to every mán who could hóld a pán cáme the méssage, "Up and

  s

híke". [nl19]

The relevant verbs are all forms of *look, have, come,* and *seem*. I will treat these as nonlexical – that is unstressed – verbs.

The cases that remain are quite striking, however. The stressed syllable in weak position is always adjoined by a stressed syllable in s-position on one side and *two* stressless syllables, the closer of which is in s-position on the other side. Let's first look at the examples and then consider their import. Following are cases where the stressless syllables follow the stressed syllable in weak position.

(14)
    w w s w   s w   s   w s w   s   w   s w s
And the Yúkon swállowed through a hóle the cóld <u>córpse</u> of the sláin. [bf62]

w s   w   s w s w   s   w   s w s
A hóle <u>gáped</u> in the ríver íce; the spráy <u>fláshed</u> – that was all. [bf93]

w s   w   s w   s   s   w   s   w   s   w   s
A bírd <u>sáng</u> for the jóy of spríng, so píercing swéet and fráil; [bf94]

w s   w   s   w s w   s   w   s w w s   w
We guéssed and gróped, <u>Nórth</u>, ever Nórth, with many a twíst and

s
túrn; [nl70]

w w s   w   s   w   s   w   s
And the réindeer móss <u>gléamed</u> here and there [nl99]

Here are cases where the stressless syllables precede the stressed syllable in weak position.

(15)
    w   w   s   w   s   w   s   w s   w   w   s   w   s w
Till we wént cléan mád, it séems to me, and we squándered our <u>lást</u>

s
póke, [nl46]

w   s   w   s w   s w   s   w   s   w   s w s
Through the <u>bláck</u> cányon's ángry fóam we húrled to dréamy bárs, [nl76]

These latter cases are extremely rare; in fact, the two examples cited are the only clear cases.

In all the cases above, the stressed syllable is adjacent to a stressless syllable in beat position. However, that stressless beat is adjoined by at most one stressless syllable. What's ruled out are configurations like the following.

(16)   w w s w   w   s   w s w   s   w w   s   w s w
       *As he wátered the gréen stúff in his gláss, and the dróps <u>féll</u> after
       w   s
       the one.
       w w s   w   s   w   s   w s   w w   s   w w s
       *Till we wént cléan mád, it séems to me, and we squándered it our
       w   s
       <u>lást</u> póke,

It appears that a stressed syllable can occur in a weak position only under specific circumstances. First, a lexical monosyllable can occur in weak position when it occurs immediately between two stresses. Second, it can scan in weak position when it immediately precedes a rhyming word or particle with strong phrasal stress. The third case is where the lexical monosyllable is adjoined on one side by a stress in strong position and on the other by a stressless syllable in strong position adjoined by *one* stressless syllable.

5. Analysis

Let's now consider how to analyze this pattern in terms of OT. Let us assume that the input to a derivation is the template (4) and some string of linguistic material. The candidates are various alignments of the material with the template, along with the option of *no* alignment with the template—equivalent to the orthodox phonological "null parse".[8]

There are some basic steps that have to be taken to get this to work. First, we must posit a constraint that says it is better to align linguistic material with a template than not to align it.

(17)   PARSE-LINE (PL)
       Linguistic material should be aligned with the template.

We also need constraints that govern the precise level of the alignment. First, all syllables need to be aligned.

(18)   PARSE-SYLLABLE (Pσ)
       Each syllable must be aligned with a templatic position.

Since not all positions are obligatory, the converse statement is a little weaker.

(19) PARSE-POSITION (PP)
Each obligatory position must be aligned with a syllable.

These latter two constraints are top-ranked. The PARSE-LINE constraint, on the other hand, is outranked by the constraints that govern the overall well-formedness of the line.

(20) $\left\{ \begin{array}{c} \text{PARSE-SYLLABLE} \\ \text{PARSE-POSITION} \end{array} \right\} \gg \text{PARSE-LINE}$

Let's consider some simple examples to see the system outlined so far at work. Consider the first line from "Sam McGee", repeated from (2) above.

(21) By the mén who móil for góld; [sm2]
      w w s w s w s

The following tableau shows the application of PARSE-LINE. The "Ø" stands for the null parse.

(22)	(w)(w)s (w)ws (w)ws By the mén who móil for góld	PARSE-LINE
☞	w w s w s w s By the mén who móil for góld	
	Ø	*!

Ranking PARSE-POSITION above PARSE-LINE accounts for the fact that if there are an insufficient number of syllables in the line, the line is ill-formed.

(23)	(w)(w)s (w)ws (w)ws Mén móil for góld	PARSE-POSITION	PARSE-LINE
	s w s w s Mén Ø móil for góld	*!	
☞	Ø		*

Finally, the fact that a line with too many syllables is ill-formed is a consequence of ranking PARSE-SYLLABLE above PARSE-LINE.

(24)	(w)(w)s (w)ws (w)ws By the mén who can móil for their own góld	Pσ	PL
	w w s w w s w w s ? By the mén who can móil for their own góld	*!	
☞	Ø		*

Let's now consider the distribution of stresses within the line. The fact that stressed syllables are generally associated with strong positions is a consequence of the following constraint.

(25) STRESS-TO-STRONG (SS; preliminary)
    Stresses are aligned with strong positions.

The STRESS-TO-STRONG constraint outranks the PARSE-LINE constraint. This ranking expresses the generalization that if there is no way to align some bit of linguistic material with a template without placing a stressed syllable in weak position, then the line is ill-formed for Service. This is exemplified in the following tableau. The line given has a full complement of syllables for a three-beat line, but the lexical stress *móil* is ill-placed for the template. Hence the line is ill-formed.

(26)	(w)(w)s (w)ws (w)ws By the mén who móil for their own góld	SS	PL
	w w s w w s w w s By the mén who móil for their own góld	*!	
☞	Ø		*

Another possibility might be to scan *móil* in a strong position, but this would entail that one of the following syllables go unparsed, violating PARSE-SYLLABLE.

The next step is to allow a stressed syllable in weak position just in case it is surrounded by stressed syllables. Specifically, let us say that a stressed syllable cannot occur in weak position if it is adjacent to a stressless syllable.

104 *Michael Hammond*

(27) UPBEAT-DOWNBEAT (UD)

A stressed syllable cannot occur in weak position if it is adjacent to a stressless syllable.

This constraint *replaces* the STRESS-TO-STRONG constraint. The derivation just above goes through the same way; the stress on *móil* is adjacent to two stressless syllables and subject to the UPBEAT-DOWNBEAT constraint.

To see the difference between the STRESS-TO-STRONG constraint and the UPBEAT-DOWNBEAT constraint above we must consider a case with three adjacent stresses.

(28)   w w s w s w s
       when the brówn spríng fréshets flów; [bf5]

The following tableau shows how UPBEAT-DOWNBEAT works with these cases.

(29)	(w)(w)s (w)ws (w)ws when the brówn spríng fréshets flów	UD	PL
☞	w w s w s w s when the brówn spríng fréshets flów		
	Ø		*!

When the stresses are adjacent, no violation of UPBEAT-DOWNBEAT occurs, but when only two stresses are adjacent, a violation does occur, as in the following constructed three-beat line.

(30)	(w)(w)s (w)ws (w)ws when the brówn áutumn fréshets flów	UD	PL
	w w s w w s w s when the brówn áutumn fréshets flów	*!	
☞	Ø		*

Let's now consider the "one-sided" structure. Recall that the pattern is one where two lexical stresses are adjacent and are abutted by precisely two stressless syllables on one side. This excludes lines of the following two types.

(31) *Béaring his prízes of his fóx pélts, out of the Wíld he cáme.
       s w w s w w s w s   s w w s w s

      *The tráil was bád, and I félt hálf mád, but I swóre I would not téll
       w s w s w w s w s w w s w w s w

      Jóe;
      s

One possible treatment would be that the template can be altered under restricted circumstances. We would need constraints that limit the available template manipulations to *permutations*. Moreover, these permutations would only be allowed under the conditions discussed in the previous section. This approach seems rather brute force and the idea of templatic manipulation to accomodate this pattern is unprecedented in generative metrical theory.

Another possibility would be to simply stipulate that a lexical stress can occur in weak position next to a single stress just in case there are precisely two stressless syllables on the other side. While this would work fairly directly, it is ad hoc and unexplanatory. It offers no explanation for why such a restriction should hold.

I take a different tack here. It turns out that the ruled-out configuration can be seen as the intersection of two statistically quite infrequent "sub-configurations". Thus, the following patterns do not occur (where +/– indicates whether the relevant syllable bears lexical stress):

(32)   w w s w s   s w s w w
          – – – + + and + + – – –

We've already seen that the single-sided stress configurations are relatively rare. It turns out that putting a stressless syllable in strong position next to two stressless syllables (on the same side) is also rare, e.g.:

(33)   w w s   s w w
          – – – and – – –

If we consider the occurrence of w w s scansions over stressless syllables, we find that compared to w s scansions of stressless syllables, they are extremely rare. There are sixty lines in "The Cremation of Sam McGee", which entails that there are 420 s-positions. Of these, twenty-five are occupied by stressless monosyllables. Of those, only two occur in w w s spans. When we compare these to stressed monosyllables in the same spans, the numbers are very different. There are 158 stressed monosyllables in w s spans, but 106 stressed monosyllables in w w s spans. Thus, there is clearly a statistical skewing away from stressless monosyllables in the last position of w w s spans.

(34)

span	stressed	stressless
w s	158	25
w w s	106	2

This correlation between the absence of the more complex pattern and the rarity of the component sub-configurations can be handled straightforwardly using the device of *local conjunction* (Smolensky, 1993). The basic idea is that there is a constraint against a stress in w-position adjacent to a stressless syllable and another constraint against a stressless syllable in s-position adjacent to two stressless syllables in a row. Each of these constraints is too low-ranked on its own to have much effect. However, the local conjunction of these constraints is high enough ranked to rule out the specific pattern in question.

(35) UPBEAT-DOWNBEAT (UD)
A stressed syllable cannot occur in weak position if it is adjacent to a stressless syllable.

(36) ANTI-RESOLUTION (AR)
A stressless syllable cannot occur in s-position if it is adjoined by two weak positions on the same side.

(37)

	(w)(w)s (w)ws (w)ws But I swóre I would not téll Jóe.	[UD&AR]
	w w s w w s w s But I swóre I would not téll Jóe.	*!
☞	∅	

Here, both constraints are violated by the scansion given. Hence, the locally conjoined constraint is violated and the scansion is ruled out as shown. On this approach, the "double-sided" case is allowed because it cannot violate the UPBEAT-DOWNBEAT constraint. The "single-sided" case is only ruled out when it also violates ANTI-RESOLUTION.

There is one last case to treat: rhyming words and phrase-final particles. Recall that a lexical item can occur out of place if it occurs immediately before one of these. The analysis of these is relatively straightforward, but doesn't really bear on the issues raised so far. The intuition behind the analysis of these is that rhyming words and phrase-final particles have strong phrasal stress. In this environment, a mere lexical stress does not constitute a stress peak. Therefore the locally conjoined constraint [UD&AR] does not apply. This general idea is adopted from Hayes (1989).

6. Conclusion

In this paper I have analyzed some of the meter of Robert Service. Empirically, several results have been established. First, the general character of the meter is anapestic-iambic, with strong positions falling every two or three syllables. Moreover, the line is composed of seven strong positions with an obligatory caesura after the fourth strong.

The meter restricts the distribution of stresses in interesting ways. First, a lexical stress can occur in weak position only under two circumstances. First, it can occur in weak position if it is adjoined by a stress on one side and a strong position or stress on the other. If one of the adjacent beats is stressless, then the ANTI-RESOLUTION constraint blocks cases where that stressless beat is adjoined by two stressless syllables. Second, it can occur in a weak position if it precedes a phrasal stress.

I have provided an analysis of these generalizations in terms of OT. The treatment of the double-sided restriction is quite interesting. Empirically, the generalization appears to be that the added restrictiveness is a consequence of combining two constraints that otherwise express themselves only statistically. This suggests that it is profitable to consider statistical regularities in determining the categorical generalizations of a language.[9]

Notes

*   Thanks to Feng Wei, Colleen Fitzgerald, Heidi Harley, Terry Langendoen, and Diane Ohala for useful discussion. Thanks especially to Doug Pulleyblank for first introducing me to Robert Service's poetry. All errors are mine.

1. See Rice (1997) for a nice overview of this literature. See Fitzgerald (1998) for discussion of a plausibly templateless metrical tradition.
2. See Kiparsky (1989), Hanson (1991), and Hanson and Kiparsky (1997) for earlier treatments of anapestic-iambic meter in this paradigm.
3. Though see Hanson and Kiparsky (1997).
4. In the following, I mark all lines cited for which poem they come from and what line number they are, using line breaks as given in the Project Gutenberg editions of these poems. I abbreviate the poems as follows: sm, bf, nl, and dm.
5. Service's meter is an instance of what Oehrle (1989) has called "temporally rigid" meter. See also Cole (1999, 1998).
6. Notice that we must assume that the rhythm rule has applied in the case of *clawfingered* and *bleary-eyed*, so that the strongest stress is on the left, rather than the right. In isolation, these forms would presumably be stressed as *clàw-fíngered* and *blèary-éyed*.
7. Notice that most of the examples above involve some form of the word *say*. On the analysis here, this is an accident.
8. See McCarthy and Prince (1993) for discussion.
9. This point was made originally by Pierrehumbert (1994). See also Boersma (1998), and Hammond (1999, 2003) for more discussion.

References

Boersma, Paul
    1998   Functional phonology. Doctoral Dissertation, University of Amsterdam.
Cole, D.
    1998   The beat as a salient phonological unit. Ms, U. of Arizona.
    1999   The beat as a salient phonological unit in rigid meters. Paper presented at the LSA annual meeting.
Fitzgerald, Colleen
    1998   The meter of Tohono O'odham songs. *International Journal of American Linguistics* 64: 1–36.
Halle, Morris, and Samuel Jay Keyser
    1971   *English Stress: Its Form, Its Growth, and Its Role in Verse*. New York: Harper and Row.
Hammond, Michael
    1999   *The Phonology of English*. Oxford: Oxford University Press.
    2003   Phonotactics and probabilistic ranking. In *Formal Approaches to Function in Grammar: In Honor of Eloise Jelinek*, Andrew Carnie, Heidi Harley, and Mary Willie (eds.), 319–332. Amsterdam: Benjamins.

Hanson, Kristin
    1991   Resolution in modern meters. Doctoral Dissertation, Stanford University.

Hanson, Kristin, and Paul Kiparsky
    1997   A parametric theory of poetic meter. *Language* 72: 287–335.

Hayes, Bruce
    1989   The prosodic hierarchy in meter. In Kiparsky and Youmans (1989), 201–260.

Kiparsky, Paul
    1989   Sprung rhythm. In Kiparsky and Youmans (1989), 305–340.

Kiparsky, Paul, and Gilbert Youmans (eds.)
    1989   *Rhythm and Meter.* Orlando: Academic Press.

McCarthy, John, and Alan Prince
    1993   Prosodic morphology. Ms, U. Mass.

Oehrle, Richard T.
    1989   Temporal structures in verse design. In Kiparsky and Youmans (1989), 87–120.

Pierrehumbert, J.
    1994   Syllable structure and word structure: a study of triconsonantal clusters in English. In *Phonological Structure and Phonetic Form*, P. Keating (ed.), 168–188. Cambridge: Cambridge University Press.

Prince, Alan, and Paul Smolensky
    1993   Optimality theory. Ms, U. Mass and U. of Colorado.

Rice, Curt
    1997   Generative metrics. *Glot International* 2:3–7.

Smolensky, Paul
    1993   Harmony, markedness, and phonological activity. Paper presented at the Rutgers OptimalityWorkshop 1, [ROA].

Shakespeare's lyric and dramatic metrical styles*

Kristin Hanson

1. Introduction

Kiparsky's (1975, 1977) generative description of Shakespeare's metrical practice draws on the broadest possible range of Shakespeare's works, generalizing across genres from the lyric verse of the *Sonnets* and the narrative verse of *The Rape of Lucrece* and *Venus and Adonis* to the dramatic verse of the plays, as well as across periods of composition from the earliest of these plays, *1 Henry VI*, to the last, *The Tempest*. A strength of this broad coverage is, as Kiparsky notes, that the absence of a structure may be recognized to be systematic, at the same time that the presence of even a very rare structure may be recognized as sufficiently persistent to warrant its inclusion in a metrical description, and to suggest the form that that description should take.

This broad coverage has weaknesses as well, however. Scholars have long noted that Shakespeare's metrical practice shows significant stylistic differences across genres and periods of composition (Saintsbury 1906, Tarlinskaja 1987, Wright 1988), which Kiparsky's description does not much address. In addition, counterexamples have been shown to have as much scope to emerge as do subtle generalizations about rare structures (Youmans 1983, Golston 1988).

These latter issues have received attention especially within descriptions which emphasize frequencies over simple presences and absences as fundamental metrical facts, and express metrical practices as tendencies rather than rules as posited by Kiparsky's analysis. Here I want to suggest that this is not a necessary correlation. Rather, the two weaknesses in Kiparsky's description are related in an interesting way which points simply to the importance of recognizing that the individual works whose stylistic differences have been noted may be composed according to slightly different though related grammars. Without disputing that frequencies and tendencies are also interesting and worth modelling (much less that these texts of problematic provenance and transmission in an archaic and so only indirectly known form of the language include unassimilable data), I wish to show that some significant metrical differences in genre are differences in kinds of structures allowed, and not just their numbers. Drawing an analogy with dialect variation, Kiparsky's (1977) model of metrical description is already designed to allow the expression of differences between individual poets' practices as involving different combinations of different versions of the same basic types of conditions on metrical well-formedness, an approach supported by independent arguments in Youmans (1983). Similarly, Hayes (1989) and Hanson and Kiparsky (1996) have modeled additional differences between poets' practices through allowance of different parameter settings within common rule schemas. Hayes (1989) and Hanson (1996) have also used these resources to model chronological differences in individual poets' metrical practices, on analogy with historical variation. These resources for expressing variation extend equally naturally to expressing differences in metrical style according to genre, differences which can be seen as more analogous to register variation.

In particular, I will show that the meter of Shakespeare's *Sonnets* is distinct in its rules for all of syllable count, stress and alignment, the three basic types of rules deployed in all meters. Moreover, with respect to each of these I will show that the *Sonnets'* rules consistently keep the structure of the meter's template more foregrounded, suggesting a formal correlate of the elusive literary term "lyrical" with respect to metrical style.

The "dramatic" meter that the *Sonnets'* meter will be shown to be distinct from will be here represented primarily by the meter of *Richard II,* whose exceptional prosodic interest, Saintsbury (1906) notes, "can hardly escape any reader who has got beyond the state of thinking prosody pedantry." Although there is considerable uncertainty as to the dates of composition of the *Sonnets*, with Evans (1974, 49) giving 1593–99 as "a kind of average of critical opinion", *Richard II* is fairly securely dated to 1595, squarely within that span, partly on the basis of stylistic similarities to the *Sonnets* – "the general lyricism of the work which would put it near the sonnets, *A Midsummer Night's Dream*, and *Romeo and Juliet*" (Baker 1974, 800) – similarities also given technical substance by Tarlinskaja (1987). Furthermore, *Richard II* alone among these (and indeed among all Shakespeare's plays) is like the *Sonnets* in being composed entirely in iambic meter: there is no prose, as in *Romeo and Juliet*, and there are no other verse forms as in *A Midsummer Night's Dream*. At the same time, there are none of these plays' thematic or formal relationships to sonnets. Hence, metrical differences can be fairly confidently interpreted as related to differences in genre and in subject matter, rather than to chronological development of the poet's practice or other difficulties. This is not to say, however, that chronological changes are not relevant to the argument: some of the differences are only scantily evidenced in *Richard II,* but will be shown by additional evidence from *Hamlet* (1600– 01) and *Cymbeline* (1609–10) to be persistent, and so to merit inclusion in the metrical description. Finally, it should be noted that any contradiction in urging the appropriateness of the focus on *Richard II*'s "dramatic" meter on the basis of a contemporaneity with the *Sonnets* argued for on the basis of these texts' shared "lyricism" is only apparent: formally, we will see, the dramatic style is inclusive of the lyrical style, making it perfectly possible to include metrically lyrical passages within a play, a possibility in fact used in the characterization of Richard himself.

2. Common properties of all English iambic pentameter

What the two meters have in common, and what has been taken to be the formal basis within generative analyses for their sharing the common name of "iambic pentameter", is the template in (1) together with the correspondence rule regulating rhythmic prominence in (2) (Halle and Keyser 1971; Kiparsky 1975,1977; Liberman and Prince 1977, Piera 1981, Hanson and Kiparsky 1996). The template consists of five rising feet, each composed of a weak metrical position (w) followed by a strong one (s), with these feet grouped ambiguously into rising cola of either two or three feet as shown, partly for reasons to be addressed in section 4, and with the cola grouped into a rising line.

(1) Template for iambic pentameter:

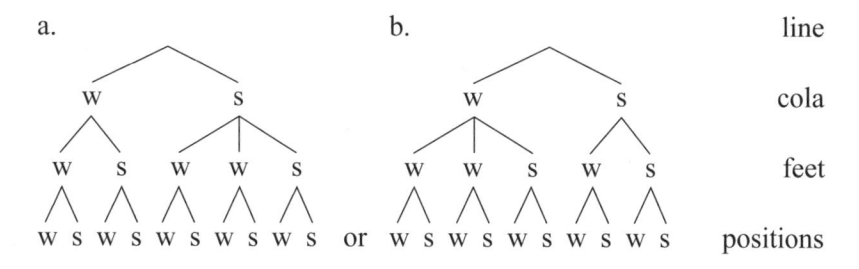

a.   b.   line

```
        w         s                    w           s                       cola
       / \       /|\                  / \         /|\
      w   s     w w s                w   w   s   w   s                     feet
     /\  /\   /\ /\ /\              /\  /\  /\  /\  /\
    w s w s  w s w s w s   or      w s w s w s w s w s                     positions
```

The correspondence rule disallows in a weak position a syllable which according to the phonology of the language is strong relative to another one in the same lexical word – hence in practical terms most stressed syllables

114 *Kristin Hanson*

of polysyllabic lexical words. Exceptions to this are allowed for a syllable immediately following a break, exceptions which will also be characterized more specifically in section 5.

(2) Correspondence rule for prominence for English iambic pentameter:

No weak metrical position contains a syllable which is strong within a lexical word.

As in any meter, a scansion of a line consists of a mapping of the phonological rhythmic structure of the line into the template in a manner consistent with the correspondence rules.

3. Syllable count

In addition to a correspondence rule regulating rhythmic prominence, a meter will also have a rule regulating measure, or the allocation of a specific amount of language to each metrical position. Allocation of a single syllable to each position is the norm in English iambic pentameter, but the rhythmic variety afforded by "trisyllabic substitution", the allocation of two syllables to one position in one of the feet in (1), has also long been recognized as one of its peculiar charms, and one fully exploited by Shakespeare. Building on Tarlinskaja (1976) and Young (1928), Kiparsky (1977) identifies six specific forms this can take, drawing a crucial distinction between what he calls "prosodic rules" illustrated in (3), which define a possible phonological interpretation of the two syllables as actually reduced to one in the rhythmic structure of the language, and "metrical rules", which genuinely allow more syllables to a line than would a one-to-one allocation of syllables to positions. Among the latter are "resolution", allowance of a $\breve{V}C\breve{V}$ sequence in one position, as in *many* in (4), and the disregarding of a proclitic as in *in one* also in (4), as well as extrametricality, allowance of a final extra unstressed syllable ("<>") as in (3c), to which we will return in section 5:

(3) a. And prove thee vertu̯ous, though thou art forsworn. (*Son* 88.4)
         w s   w s w   s   w s w   s
     b. But recko̯ning Time, whose million'd accidents (*Son* 115.5)
         w s   w   s   w   s w   s w s

c. Weeds among weeds, or flowers with flowers gathered   (*Son* 124.4)
   w   s   w   s   w   s   w   s   w   s   <>

(4)   Come to one mark, as many ways meet in one town   (*Hen V* 1.2.208)
        w   s   w   s   w   s   w   s   w   s

Hanson and Kiparsky (1996) reanalyze the two "metrical" rules in (4) as reflexes of a rule defining a fundamentally different form of iambic pentameter than the more conventionally recognized syllable-based one: whereas a meter which has "trisyllabic substitution" only of the type illustrated in (3) may be understood as having a correspondence rule mapping a single syllable into each position as in (5a), a meter which has the types in (4) has a correspondence rule which instead maps a maximum of a single phonological foot, specifically a resolved moraic trochee, into each position:

(5)   Alternative correspondence rules for position for English iambic pentameter:
      a. Each metrical position contains a single syllable.
      b. Each metrical position contains maximally a single phonological foot (resolved moraic trochee).

I will not rehearse the formal argument here. Rather, my point is simply that in that reanalysis, following Kiparsky's (1977) description, the meter with rule (5b) is attributed generally to Shakespeare, and contrasted with the practice of Milton, argued in Hanson (1995, 1996) to strictly observe rule (5a) in *Paradise Lost*. But in fact, the generalization about Shakespeare is too broad. Shakespeare's *Sonnets* have long been recognized as differing from his plays in the comparatively conservative use in them of "trisyllabic feet", and the difference is not one of number, but of kind. Although they show quite an extravagant exploration of what kinds of pairs of syllables might be reduced by rules like those of (3), as well as a handful of words and collocations which have been argued by Weismiller (1989) to have generally been understood as syllabic in the period (such as *heaven* (17.3) or *spirit* (86.5), *abysm* (112.10) or *stol'n* (99.7), *were't* (125.1) or *is't* (39.4)), they have at most a single late and thematically significant example of a genuinely irreducible pair of proclitics (and even that not one acknowledged as such by Weismiller: *to th'* (115.8)), and no productive use of resolution. Hence, the *Sonnets* are best analyzed as in a syllabic meter with the correspondence rule (5a).

116   *Kristin Hanson*

In *Richard II*, however, structures of both types in (4) are abundantly present and fully productive:[1]

(6) a. He was not so resolv'd when last we spake together. (*Rich II* 2.3 29)
      w s w s   w s w s   w s ◇
   b. Ill in myself to see, and in thee, seeing ill.   (*Rich II* 2.1.94)
      w s w s w s   w   s   w   s
   c. While I stand fooling here, his Jack of the clock   (*Rich II* 5.5.60)
      w s w   s w   s   w s   w   s
   d. I task the earth to the like, forsworn Aumerle,   (*Rich II* 4.1.52)
      w s   w   s   w   s   w s w s
   e. And in it are the Lords of York, Berkeley, and Seymour,
      w   s   w   s   w s   w s   w   s   ◇
                                                (*Rich II* 2.3.55)

(7) a. Sluic'd out his innocent soul through streams of blood,
      w   s   w s   w   s   w   s   w   s
                                               (*Rich II* 1.1.103)
   b. One flourishing branch of his most royal root,   (*Rich II* 1.2.18)
      w   s   w   s w s   w   s w   s
   c. For 'twere no charity; yet, to wash your blood   (*Rich II* 3.1.5)
      w   s   w   s   w s   s   w   s
   d. Stoop with oppression of their prodigal weight;   (*Rich II* 3.3.31)
      w   s   w s w   s   w   s   w
   e. Of capital treason we arrest you here.   (*Rich II* 4.1.151)
      w s w   s   w   s w   s   w

Hence, its meter is best analyzed as having correspondence rule (5b).

After considering issues of stress and alignment we will return to some more complex structures involving syllable count. These suffice, however, to illustrate how artfully the two styles may be combined. Technically, I am claiming that the entire play is written in the meter characterized by (5b) (and because its basic correspondence rule is set to a different phonological constituent, that it is in not just a different style but a different meter). Nonetheless, a line with a single syllable in each position is always compatible with that rule, so that a lyrical style may always be represented within it. This is just what happens in many of Richard's most self-absorbed soliloquys, which are followed by abrupt shifts to the more dramatic style when interaction with other characters, especially unwelcome reminders of the usurping Bullingbrook, resumes:[2]

(8) K. Rich
>What must the King do now? Must he submit?
>The King shall do it. Must he be depos'd?
>The King shall be contented. Must he lose
>The name of king? a' God's name let it go.
>I'll give my jewels for a set of beads,
>My gorgeous palace for a hermitage
>My gay apparel for an almsman's gown,
>My figured goblets for a dish of wood,
>My sceptre for a palmer's walking-staff,
>My subjects for a pair of carved saints,
>And my large kingdom for a little grave,
>A little little grave, an obscure grave –
>Or I'll be buried in the king's high way,
>Come way of common trade, where subjects' feet
>May hourly trample on their sovereign's head;
>For on my heart they tread now whilst I live,
>And buried once, why not upon my head?
>...
>   Well, well, I see
>I talk but idlely, and you laugh at me,
>Most mighty prince, my Lord Northumberland,
>What says King Bullingbrook? Will his Majesty
> w   s   w   s   w   s   w   s w s
>Give Richard leave to live till Richard die?   (*Rich II* 3.3.173)

Moreover, the particularly English connotations of the correspondence rule (5b), rooted deep within English metrical tradition and phonology (Saintsbury 1906, Hanson and Kiparsky 1996), seem entirely self-conscious:

(9) *Gaunt*
>Though Richard my live's counsel would not hear,
>My death's sad tale may yet undeaf his ear.

York
>No, it is stopp'd with other flattering sounds,
>As praises, of whose taste the wise are [fond],

> Lascivious metres, to whose venom sound
> The open ear of youth doth always listen;
> Report of fashions in proud Italy,
> Whose manners still our tardy, apish nation
> Limps after in base imitation. (*Rich II* 2.1.15–23)

4. Stress

Kiparsky (1977) argues that the correspondence rule in (2) governing stress in Shakespeare's iambic pentameter has two particularly surprising consequences, one for compound stress and one for phrasal stress. In regulating only syllables which are strong relative to another syllable within the same lexical word, the correspondence rule in (2) may actually require a syllable which is the strongest in a compound or a phrase to be in a weak position in order to allow a less strongly stressed syllable of the regulated type to be in a strong one.

For compounds, this means that those composed of two monosyllabic words may have the stronger first word in either a strong position as in (10a) or a weak position as in (10b), but those including a polysyllabic component word must have the stressed syllable of that word in the strong position as in (11a), never in the weak one as in (11b), even though the latter puts the strongest syllable of the compound as a whole in a strong position:

(10) a. With April's <u>first-born</u> flow'rs, and all things rare (*Son* 21.7)
       w s w   s   w   s   w s w s
   b. As the <u>death-bed</u>, whereon it must expire (*Son* 73.11)
       w s   w   s   w   s w   s w s

(11) a. And his <u>love-kindling</u> fire did quickly steep (*Son* 153.3)
       w s   w   s   w   s w   s   w   s
   b. *And <u>love-kindling</u> fires did so quickly steep (construct)
       w   s   w   s   w   s w s   w   s

This claim has been the focus of considerable controversy, because counterexamples, already noted by Kiparsky (1975, 1977) but dismissed variously as mostly confined to early plays or to specific word types, are in fact persistent (Youmans 1981, Koelb 1979 cited in Youmans 1981, Golston 1998). In *Hamlet* a rough count shows six scansions of the supposedly excluded type, illustrated in (12b); and only four scansions of the predicted type as in (12a). Similarly, in *Cymbeline* a rough count shows ten scansions of the type in (13a), and nine of that in (13b), with both available even to the same word (Youmans 1981):

(12) a. Doth with his lofty and <u>shrill-sounding</u> throat (*Ham* 1.2.152)
         W S W S W S   W   S W   S
   b. That swift as <u>quicksilver</u> it courses through (*Ham* 1.5.66)
        W   S   W S   W S   S W   S

(13) a. Breeds him and makes him of his <u>bedchamber</u> (*Cym* 1.1.42)
        W   S   W   S   W   S W S   W S
   b. In my <u>bedchamber</u>.
                          They are in a trunk   (*Cym* 1.6.196)
      W S W   S W   S W S W S

And although not quite so even-handedly, *Richard II* also shows both types, with about ten examples of the scansion in (14a) and perhaps three as in (14b):

(14) a. Old John of Gaunt, <u>time-honored</u> Lancaster, (*Rich II* 1.1.1)
         W   S W   S   W   S W   S W S
   b. Till thou the <u>lie-giver</u> and that lie do lie (*Rich II* 4.1.68)
        W   S   W S   W   S   W S W S

More significantly, both scansions seem again available to the same word:

(15) a. The grand conspirator, Abbot of <u>Westminster</u>, (*Rich II* 5.4.19)
         W   S   W S   W   S W S   W   S ◇
   b. My Lord of <u>Westminster</u>, be it your charge (*Rich II* 4.1.152)
       W   S   W   S   W   S W S W   S

As Youmans (1983) notes, it is not necessarily problematic to revise the description of the meter to reflect these alternatives, both because of the inherent ambiguity as words of compounds, and because of considerations about subordination we will see below. However, the point I wish to make here is that any such revision will describe the plays only. Kiparsky's original generalization in fact holds, as he noted, absolutely for the *Sonnets*, from which the examples in (10) and (11) come.[3]

120 *Kristin Hanson*

Even more striking differences between the *Sonnets* and the plays emerge with respect to phrasal stress. Here again Kiparsky (1977) claims that for Shakespeare a polysyllabic lexical word must have its strong syllable in a strong position even if that means that in a phrase in which that word is subordinated to a following stronger stress, the latter will have to be in a weak position, as in (16a). Scansions like that in (16b) are predicted to be unmetrical, and claimed to not occur:

(16) a. Or my di<u>vine</u> soul answer it in <u>heaven</u> (*Rich II* 1.1.38)
       w s w s   w s w s   s
    b. *My divine soul shall answer it in <u>heaven</u>.
       w s w   s   w s w s   s

Here too, however, counterexamples have been adduced, all from the plays. Youmans (1983) cites multiple examples with the same word, *divine*, scanned just as in (16b), including that in (17):

(17)   ... If Jupiter
      Should from yond cloud speak di<u>vine</u> things
        w   s   w   s   w s w   s
      And say, "Tis true," I'd not believe them more (*Cor* 4.5.113–15)

Similarly, Golston cites the example from *Hamlet* in (18a), which has just one other example of a phrase of this type, scanned in Kiparsky's predicted way as in (18b):

(18) a. Upon my se<u>cure</u> hour thy uncle stole,   (*Ham* 1.5.61)
       w s w s w   s   w s w   s
    b. With an at<u>tent</u> ear till I may deliver,   (*Ham* 1.2.193)
       w   s w s   w   s w s   w s ◇

And in fact, already *Richard II* suggests the same availability of both scansions, with the line in (19) occurring alongside that in (16a) – perhaps not the strongest example since it could perhaps be scanned differently, but nonetheless worth reconsidering in light of (17) and (18a), and also the fact that (16a) is the only example in the play of a scansion of Kiparsky's predicted type:

(19)   I know it, uncle, and op<u>pose</u> not myself
         w s   w s ◇ w   s   w   s w   s

Against their will. But who comes here?   (*Rich II* 3.3.18–19)
w   s   w   s   w   s   w   s

Thus, in all these plays phrases of the type in question are sparse enough that it is not at all clear that the presence of the few lines here of the predicted type should carry any more weight than the presence of the few counterexamples.

Youmans (1983) suggests that both alternatives might be accommodated by narrowing the description of the syllables regulated by (2) to those which are not themselves rhythmically subordinate, an exception which already has a precedent elsewhere in Shakespeare's practice. In discussing additional restrictions on the scansion of phrases composed of a monosyllabic lexical word grouped phonologically with one or more grammatical words, Kiparsky (1977) observes that the stronger lexical word may be in the weak position only if one of two conditions is met: either the boundaries of the phrase in question match the boundaries of a metrical foot as in (20a), or the pair of syllables is itself subordinated to a following stronger stress in a strong position, as in (20b). Both conditions can be seen to serve to make aspects of the template in (1) which are obscured by the contrary stress pattern nonetheless apparent, (20a) by emphasizing its grouping of positions into feet and (20b) by reasserting the expected prominence distinctions as in (20b), even if neither functions independently as a rule which has to be respected otherwise:

(20) a. Boundary condition:

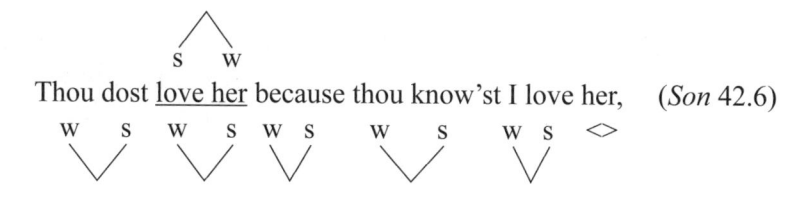

   s   w
Thou dost <u>love her</u> because thou know'st I love her,   (*Son* 42.6)
w s   w s   w s   w   s   w s   ◇

b. Subordination condition:

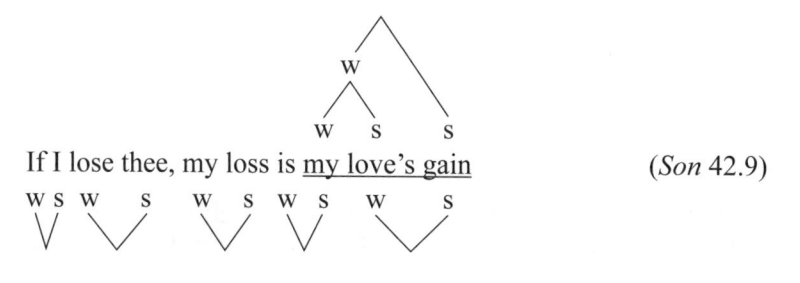

              w
           w   s   s
If I lose thee, my loss is <u>my love's gain</u>   (*Son* 42.9)
w s w   s   w s w s   w   s

Kiparsky already argues that some poets, for example Wyatt, allow exceptions even for lexical words to (2) if (20a) is met, as in (21a). Thus, a revision of the description of Shakespeare's metrical practice to allow lexical exceptions to (2) if (20b) is met is quite natural, as Youmans (1983) suggests, and in fact characterizes quite a regular practice in his successor Donne (Hanson forthcoming):

(21) a. There is <u>written</u> her faier neck rounde abowte:
        w s   w s   w s   w   s w   s
                                                    (Wyatt, *Poems* 7.12)

     b. Shall be<u>hold</u> God, and never tast death's woe
        w   s w   s   w s w s   w   s
                                                    (Donne, "Holy Sonnet" [IV] 8)

However, again such a revision is appropriate only to Shakespeare's plays, not the *Sonnets*. Kiparsky's argument carefully distinguishes the phrases in question like *my divine soul* in (16a) from phrases affected by the Rhythm Rule, which actually changes the stress pattern of a polysyllabic word with final stress if it is subordinated to an immediately following stronger stress in the same phrase, by shifting the first word's final stress to an earlier syllable within the word if there is one which already bears some stress, as in the change in the stress pattern of *thìrtéen* in the phrase *thírtèen mén*. The fact that the initial syllable of *divine* is completely unstressed means that it cannot be affected by the Rhythm Rule. Words like *unseen* in (22), however, can be, and are: such words, Kiparsky claims, are consistently scanned with their strong final syllable in a strong position as in (22a) unless they are in Rhythm Rule configurations as in (22b):

(22) a. The other down, unseen, and full of water: (*Rich II* 4.1.87)
        w s w   s   w s   w   s w s ◇
     b. Are merely shadows to the unseen grief   (*Rich II* 4.1297)
        w   s w s   w   s w s w   s

He further suggests that this consistency shows the rule was obligatory for Shakespeare as it is not for present-day English speakers, which may be too strong: while the pattern in (22) holds true for most of *Richard II*, (23) is a counterexample, suggesting that the rule cannot in fact have been obligatory if (2) is also absolute:

(23)   Than my un<u>pleased</u> eye see your courtesy.   (*Rich II* 3.3.193)
        w   s   w   s   w   s   w   s w s

Still, the evidence that the Rhythm Rule was available in the language, as it still is, is strong, however ambiguous a metrical rule also allowing scansions like (17), (18a) or (19) may make the scansion of lines like those in (24) which obediently follow the pattern in (22) – an ambiguity not unlike that the adoption of the correspondence rule (5b) introduces into the scansion of lines like (3):

(24) a. A little little grave, an obscure grave –   (*Rich II* 3.3.154)
          w s w s w   s   w s   w   s
      b. To pluck him headlong from the usurped throne. (*Rich II* 5.1.65)
          w   s   w   s   w   s   w s   w   s

There is, however, no hint of any evidence like (17), (18a) or (19) suggesting the need to acknowledge any such possibility of ambiguity in the *Sonnets*. The only words which in isolation have stress on their final syllables but appear with that syllable in a weak position when subordinated to an immediately following stronger stress as in (26) to this day also have some stress on their initial syllables, so are available to the Rhythm Rule, and throughout Shakespeare's practice are scanned in a way consistent with its operation, just as Kiparsky's analysis claims:

(25) a. And from the <u>forlorn</u> world his visage hide   (*Son* 33.7)
          w   s   w   s   w   s   w s   s
      b. Nor draw no lines there with thy <u>antique</u> pen   (*Son* 19.10)
          w   s   w   s   w   s   w   s   w   s
      c. Supposed as forfeit to a <u>confin'd</u> doom   (*Son* 107.4)
          w   s   w s w s w s   w   s
      d. For where is she so fair whose <u>unear'd</u> womb   (*Son* 3.5)
          w   s   w s w   s   w   s   w   s

(26)   To some <u>forlorn</u> and naked hermitage,   (*LLL* 5.2)
        w   s   w   s   w   s w   s w s

The only exception is the preposition *among* in (3c), but stress of grammatical words can be shown independently to be treated less restrictively than that of lexical words throughout the English tradition and that of other languages (Halle and Keyser 1971, Kiparsky 1977, Hanson and Kiparsky 1996, Hanson forthcoming), and is in fact not regulated by the correspondence rule as stated in (2).

Curiously, however, the difference between the plays and the *Sonnets* with respect to the interaction of word stress with phrasal stress goes beyond the mere clearer sufficiency of the Rhythm Rule to account for what might otherwise look like the scansions Kiparsky's analysis excludes. For it is not the case that in the *Sonnets* words which lack stress on their initial syllables and so are not subject to it are scanned consistently with Kiparsky's prediction as in (16a) when subordinated to a following stronger phrasal stress; rather, such phrases are avoided entirely, partly, as Youmans (1983) points out, with the help of syntactic inversions like that reversing the normal adjective-noun order in (27) from the *divine terms* which would be found in prose of the period:

(27)   Buy terms divine in selling hours of dross   (*Son* 146.11)
         w   s   w s   w   s w   s   w   s

The reason for this avoidance is not entirely clear, since as (28a,b) and many lines like it show, the *Sonnets* do not require the strongest stress in a domain above the level of the word to be in a strong position any more than the plays do with their lines like (28c) or in fact any of the examples supporting Kiparsky's generalizations above such as (16a) or (18b):[4]

(28) a. To eat the world's <u>due</u>, by the grave and thee   (*Son* 1, 14)
         w s   w   s   w   s w   s   w   s
      b. But like a sad <u>slave</u> stay and think of nought   (*Son.* 57, 11)
         w   s w s   w   s   w   s   w   s
      c. God in thy good <u>cause</u> make thee prosperous!   (*RichII* I iii 78)
         w   s   w   s   w   s   w   s   w   s

In any case, the pattern is shared with Shakespeare's most direct model for an English sonnet cycle, Sidney's *Astrophel and Stella*. Exactly like Shakespeare, Sidney strictly excludes stressed syllables of polysllabic words from weak positions while freely allowing phrasal stress there as in (29a), but includes no lines which manifest the predicted combination of the two in (29b), other than one in (29c) involving a preposition parallel to (3c):

(29) a. But known <u>worth</u> did in mine of time proceed   (*AS* 2.3)
          W S   W S W S W S W S
    b. ?Divine <u>worth</u> did in mine of time proceed   (construct)
          W S   W S W S W S W S
    c. Of touch they are that with<u>out</u> touch doth touch   (*AS* 9.12)
          W S   W S W   S W   S   W S

Whatever the best formal interpretation of these facts, their generic significance is undeniable. Where the missing case appears in the period is in Marlowe's translations from Ovid's narrative poems:

(30) a. He, he <u>afflicts Rome</u> that made me Rome's foe   (*Luc* 1.205)
          W   S W S   W   S W   S W   S
    b. There lives the Phoenix one <u>alone bird</u> ever   (*OE* 2.6.54)
          W   S   W   S   W   S W S   W S<>
    c. Thy hands <u>agree not</u> with the warlike speare   (*OE* 2.3.8)
          W   S W S W   S W   S W   S

And like Shakespeare, in his dramatic verse Marlowe allows freer use of phrases which an absolute interpretation of (2) would disallow. Some such greater freedom must be tolerated by poets if they are to use the full range of words in the language in their natural syntactic configurations. In (16)–(19) and (30) the phrasal stress is borne by a monosyllabic word, but if it is borne by a polysyllabic word as in *divine nature* in (31), under normal word order it is not possible for both to have their strong syllables in strong positions in accordance with (2). Shakespeare's solution as illustrated in (31) lies in the allowance of the lexical stress of *divine* in a weak position if it is subordinated to a phrasal stress in the following strong position as in (20b) which we have already seen suggested by Youmans (1983) to account for (17), (18a) or (19), and shown by him to be preferred to inversion:

(31)   Thou di<u>vine</u> Nature, thou thyself thou blazon'st   (*Cym* 4.2.1700)
              W S W   S W   S W S W   S   <>

Marlowe's solution is different: as shown in (32), he positions the phrasal stress of *precepts* in a weak position, but that allows it to conform to a different condition which still serves to keep the metrical template perceptible, namely, the boundary condition of (20a):[5]

(32)   I do not doubt by your di<u>vine</u> <u>precepts</u>   (*JM* 1.2.334)
         w s w   s   w   s w s   w   s

In sum, with respect to stress, if the counterexamples to Kiparsky's generalizations from the plays are considered together with the conformity to those generalizations in the *Sonnets* in a quest for a general claim about Shakespeare's practice, then they seem merely peskily recalcitrant; but if the two genres are considered separately, the argument they pose for revisions to the metrical rules describing the works in which they appear becomes stronger. Just as with patterns of syllable count, a set of rhythmic structures appears in the plays but not in the *Sonnets*, and quite likely more generally in the period in dramatic verse but not lyric verse. The meter of the plays is again looser, in the technical sense that it allows all the same structures plus additional ones. It is not, however, looser in the sense of being subject to rules only some of the time. Rather, the rules it is subject to form a more complex set than just the one in (2). Here, then, a characteristic of "dramatic" meter seems to be that words are positioned according to multiple rules which can be appealed to resolve conflicts between different metrical desiderata, rather than leaving rephrasing as the only resort as under the absolutism of lyrical meter in which words are positioned according to a single rule, here (2). In fact, the meter of the two poets who allow alternative positions for words in their lyrics – Wyatt and Donne – are often singled out for their particularly "dramatic" styles.

5. Alignment

Of course, even in the *Sonnets* (2) is not really absolute: as mentioned at the outset exceptions to it have always been recognized to be allowed immediately following a break, most commonly a line break, as in (33a), but also sometimes a break within a line as in (33c, e):

(33) a. <u>Na</u>ture's bequest gives nothing, but doth lend   (*Son* 4.3)
          w s   w   s   w   s   w   s   w   s

b. Cousin, throw up your gage, do you begin. (*Rich II* 1.1.186)
   w s   w   s   w   s   w   s w s

c. Yet who knows not, conscience is born of love? (*Son* 151.2)
   w   s   w   s   w   s   w   s   w   s

d. Give me his gage. Lions make leopards tame. (*Rich II* 1.1.174)
   w   s   w   s   w s   w   s   w   s

e. Naming thy name blesses an ill report (*Son* 95.8)
   w   s   w   s   w s w s w s

f. In rage, deaf as the sea, hasty as fire. (*Rich II* 1.1.19)
   w   s   w   s   w s   w s w s

These exeptions belong to a larger set of metrical rules which require reference to breaks of one kind or another. The others include rules for extrametrical syllables, the extra unstressed syllables allowed line-finally as in (34a) or (16a, b) under alternative possible scansions or any of (3c, 20a, b, 22a) above from the *Sonnets* or any of (6a, 6e, 15a) above from *Richard II*, and which are also sometimes allowed immediately preceding a break within a line as in (34c,d) or (19a) above (Kiparsky 1977):

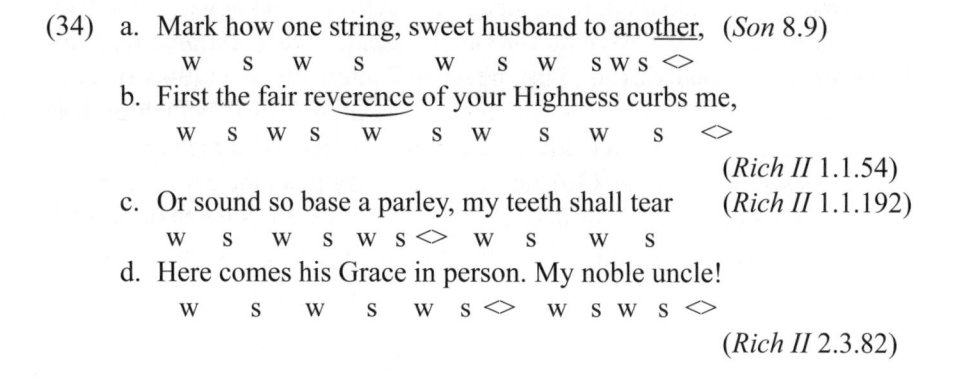

(34) a. Mark how one string, sweet husband to another, (*Son* 8.9)
       w   s   w   s   w   s   w   s w s ◇

b. First the fair reverence of your Highness curbs me,
       w   s   w   s   w   s   w   s   w   s   ◇
                                                               (*Rich II* 1.1.54)

c. Or sound so base a parley, my teeth shall tear (*Rich II* 1.1.192)
       w   s   w   s w s ◇ w   s   w   s

d. Here comes his Grace in person. My noble uncle!
       w   s   w   s   w   s ◇ w   s w s ◇
                                                               (*Rich II* 2.3.82)

They include the rules for the rarer catalexis, unfilled weak positions allowed most commonly line-initially, but again also line-internally immediately following a break:

(35) a. ø Stay, the king hath thrown his warder down. (*Rich II* 1.3.118)
       w   s   w   s   w   s   w   s   w   s

b. *North*
   My liege, old Gaunt commends him to your Ma̱jesty.
   w s w s w s w s w   s ◇
K Rich
   What says he?
North
                  Nay, ø nothing, all is said.
   w   s w   s w s w   s w s
   His tongue is now a stringless instrument.   (*Rich II* 2.1.147–49)
   w   s   w   s w s w s   s

Possibly they even include rules for "premetrical" syllables as suggested by Schlerman (1984), introductory interjections not metrically parsed as in (36):

(36) Well, I will for refuge straight to Bristow castle (*Rich II* 2.2.135)
      ◇ w s w s w   s   w s w   s ◇

Already from these examples it is possible to see clear differences between the *Sonnets* and *Richard II*, many of which are well known (Saintsbury 1906, Tarlinskaja 1987, Wright 1988). The *Sonnets* have extrametrical syllables only line-finally as in (34a), never line-internally as in (34c,d). They have no catalexis, and no lines which suggest "pre-metrical" syllables. It is easy to see how these latter differences might be related directly to performance issues: in a line like (36), an actor can make plain the extraneousness of an interjection to a line, or in one like (35a) fill the missing position with perhaps a gesture[6], or in (34b) make the moving moment of silent emptiness perceptible. As Sir Peter Hall (2000) says, Shakespeare's versification tells the actor everything he needs to know to perform a line.

Still, these extra and missing syllables, like the exceptional stress-placements in (33), must be rule-governed or there would be no meter to tell the actor anything. Kiparsky (1977) argues that all these structures occur only at breaks between major syntactic phrases, a generalization reanalyzed by Hayes (1989) in terms of phonological phrases. And again, although these descriptions do hold across both the *Sonnets* and *Richard II*, they are not quite complete, eliding a slight but interesting difference between the two more subtle than just the absence of line-internal extrametricality, catalexis or pre-metricality already noted. In the *Sonnets,* the exceptional stress placements of (33a,c,e) occur only in the first, third or fourth feet, never in the second or fifth, again with the single exception of grammatical words as in (37), which as we have said are demonstrably metrically freer:

(37) They look <u>in</u>to the beauty of thy mind, (*Son* 69.9)
        W   S   W S W   S W S W   S

These feet are just the ones which also initiate new cola in the template in (1), suggesting that exceptions are again subject to a condition that makes some aspect of the template in (1) especially apparent even as they obscure another, here a coincidence of phrase boundaries with colon boundaries (Hanson 2003) foregrounding the latter. Tarlinskaja (1987) has shown that one characteristic of *Richard II* which distinguishes it from the later plays and in fact aligns it stylistically with the *Sonnets* is the salience of those same line-internal boundaries, especially that in (1a). This can be confirmed from a different perspective here, in that almost all exceptional stress placements and also extrametrical syllables do occur at these boundaries. Yet at the same time there are also sparse exceptions not found in the *Sonnets*, as in (38a), also seen in *Hamlet* in (39). And although no comparison with the *Sonnets* is possible for line-internal extrametrical syllables since there are none, in *Richard II*, they too can be seen as preferentially located at colon boundaries, with a handful of exceptions as in (38b) (or even (38a) under a different possible scansion) thus likewise pointing to the liberation of the meter from what Saintsbury (1906) calls the "periodic" style of confining expression to metrical units like the line or colon, related to the increasing use of alternative line lengths as in (39):

(38) a. It was, <u>villain</u>, ere thy hand did set it down. (*Rich II* 5.3.54)
        W S   W   S W   S   W S W   S
    b. Lord Marshal, command our officers-at-arms (*Rich II* 1.1.204)
       W   S ◇   W   S   W S W S W   S

(39) a. Come sir, to draw toward an end with you.
       Good night, <u>mo</u>ther. (*Ham* 2.3.216–17)
       W   S   W   S

Again, then, a change from absence to presence, however small in number, signals a significant change in metrical style, again in the form of some release from as strong a foregrounding of the template.

6. Conclusion

In three distinct aspects of meter – robustly with respect to syllable count, and more tentatively with respect to stress and alignment – we have seen that *Richard II* includes lines of types which the *Sonnets* do not and which continue to be included in later plays. This is hardly surprising; a lyrical style would be expected to be a more confining form (Hanson and Kiparsky 1997). What is additionally interesting from the point of view of generative metrics, however, is that clarifying the metrical differences between the genres not only supports the kind of attention to interaction of discrete rules that Kiparsky (1977) originally elucidated (Youmans 1983) and that new directions in grammatical theory have endorsed (Golston 1998). It does so in a way that actually strengthens arguments that the notably looser dramatic meter is still a well-defined form, in Saintsbury's (1906, 47) ever perfect phrasing, "– rather loose than merely free –". Or as the Earl of Northumberland says to Bullingbrook, who like Richard "knows the force of language and bends it to his purpose, but ... does not confuse his mental constructs ... with hard unyielding fact ... and ... does not permit mere words ... to take the place of swift, incisive action" (Baker 842):

> *North*
> These high wild wild hills and rough uneven ways
> Draw out our miles and makes them wearisome,
> And yet your fair discourse hath been as sugar,
> Making the hard way sweet and delectable.   (*Rich II* 2.3.4)

Notes

* I would like to thank Elan Dresher, Nila Friedberg and Michael Getty for organising the conference which occasioned this paper, and especially Nila for her extraordinary patience in enabling it to be included in this volume. I would also like to thank Gilbert Youmans for expressing a wish upon reading my work that I had paid more attention to counterexamples, and Donald Friedman for expressing one at the same time that I had paid more attention to genre. Finally I would like to thank Katy Breen for some now long ago research assistance including work on *Hamlet*, *Cymbeline* and other plays which contributed to this paper.
1. For the scansion of *Berkeley* in (6e) see section 4.
2. The scansion given is not the only one possible; the following, for example, is equally compatible with the rules given:

> What says King Bullingbrook? Will his Majesty
> w   s   w   s   w   s   w   s w s

3. This argues, incidentally, for locating a revision to accommodate these scansions within the plays in the metrical rules themselves (perhaps involving evidence of avoided syntactic configurations, as Youmans (1983) suggests), rather than simply in a prosodic ambiguity in the structure of compounds.
4. Of course, inversion is not possible in (28a) and not metrically helpful in (28b), but other rephrasings could reposition the phrasal stress if it were the problem.
5. Compare
   > Alas, my precepts turn myself to smart!   (*OE*)
   > w s   w   s   w   s   w   s

6. I am indebted to Meghan Henry for suggesting this in a class on "Shakespeare's Versification".

References

Baker, Herschel
    1974   Richard II. In *The Riverside Shakespeare*, 3rd ed. Boston: Houghton-Mifflin Co., 800–804.

Evans, G. Blakemore
    1974   Chronology and sources. In *The Riverside Shakespeare*, 3rd ed. Boston: Houghton-Mifflin Co., 47–56.

Golston, Chris
    1998   Constraint-based metrics. *Natural Language and Linguistic Theory*: 16 (4): 719–770.

Hall, Peter
    2000   *Exposed by the Mask: Form and Language in Drama*. London: Oberon Books.

Halle, Morris, and Samuel Jay Keyser
    1971   Illustration and defense of a theory of the iambic pentameter. *College English* 33: 154–176.

Hanson, Kristin
    1995   Prosodic constituents in poetic meter. *WCCFL* 13: 62–77.
    1996   From Dante to Pinsky: a theoretical perspective on the history of the modern English iambic pentameter. *Rivista di Linguistica* 9.1: 53–97.
    2003   Metrical boundaries. Paper presented at the annual meeting of the Poetics and Linguistics Association, Istanbul, June 23–26, 2003.
    forthc.   Nonlexical words in the English iambic pentameter: a study of John Donne. In *The Nature of the Word: Essays in Honor of Paul Kiparsky*, Kristin Hanson and Sharon Inkelas (eds.), Cambridge: MIT Press.

Hanson, Kristin, and Paul Kiparsky
1996   A parametric theory of poetic meter. *Language* 72: 287–335.
1997   The nature of verse and its consequences for the mixed form. In *Prosimetrum: Cross-cultural Perspectives on Narrative in Verse and Prose*, Reichl, Karl and Joseph Harris (eds.), Cambridge: D.S. Brewer, 17–44.

Hayes, Bruce
1989   The prosodic hierarchy in meter. In *Phonetics and Phonology, vol. 1: Rhythm and Meter*, Paul Kiparsky and Gilbert Youmans (eds.), 201–260. San Diego: Academic Press.

Kiparsky, Paul
1975   Stress, syntax and meter. *Language* 51: 576–616.
1977   The rhythmic structure of English verse. *Linguistic Inquiry* 8(2): 189–247.

Koelb, Clayton
1979   The iambic parameter revisited. *Neophilologus* 63: 321–329.

Liberman, Mark, and Alan Prince
1977   On stress and linguistic rhythm. *Linguistic Inquiry* 8(2): 249–336.

Piera, Carlos
1981   Spanish verse and the theory of meter. Ph.D. dissertation, UCLA.

Saintsbury, George
1906   *A History of English Prosody from the Twelfth Century to the Present Day,* 3 vols. London: MacMillan and Co.

Schlerman, Betty Jane
1984   The meters of John Webster. Ph.D. dissertation, University of Massachusetts, Amherst.

Shakespeare, William
1974   *The Riverside Shakespeare*, 3rd edition. G. Blakemore Evans, general editor. Boston: Houghton-Mifflin Co.

Tarlinskaja, Marina
1976   *English Verse: Theory and History*. The Hague: Mouton.
1987   *Shakespeare's Verse: Iambic Pentameter and the Poet's Idiosyncracies*. New York: Peter Lang.

Weismiller, Edward
1989   Triple threats to duple rhythm. In *Phonetics and Phonology, vol. 1: Rhythm and Meter*, Paul Kiparsky and Gilbert Youmans (eds.), 261–290. San Diego: Academic Press.

Wright, George T.
1988   *Shakespeare's Metrical Art.* Berkeley: University of California Press.

Youmans, Gilbert
1983   Generative tests for generative meter. *Language* 59.1: 67–92.

Young, Sir George
   1928   *An English Prosody on Inductive Lines.* Cambridge: Cambridge University Press.

Longfellow's long line

Gilbert Youmans

> There once was a man from Japan
> Who wrote verses that no one could scan.
> When asked, "Why so?"
> He replied, "I don't know,"
> "But I always put as many words into the last line as I can."

Henry Wadsworth Longfellow – two trochees followed by a dactyl. It is fitting, therefore, that the meter of two of Longfellow's best-known narrative poems, *Evangeline* and *The Courtship of Miles Standish*, is dactylic hexameter with frequent trochaic substitutions.

Dactylic hexameter has an impressive pedigree. It is the meter of Homer and Hesiod (see Prince 1989), as well as Vergil's *Aeneid* and Goethe's "Hermann and Dorothea," which Oliver Wendell Holmes called "the German model" for the "measure and the character" of *Evangeline* (Cameron 1978: 140). Despite its pedigree, dactylic hexameter is rare in English verse. As Longfellow said, "The English world is not yet awake to the beauty of that metre," and his choice of "that metre" for *Evangeline* and *Miles Standish* was controversial even in his own day. For example, in 1850, Thomas Powell commented:

> It is somewhat unfortunate for Mr. Longfellow that he has thrown by far the greatest part of his poetical treasure into the most thankless of all forms, the hexameter.... the peculiarity of the measure – to which the English language is so little adapted – renders it very difficult to do justice in it even to the finest poetry. The hexameter is the grave of poetry. It is the crowning monotony of writing. A sort of stale prose. (Cameron 1978: 27)

By contrast, Oliver Wendell Holmes praised *Evangeline's* long line:

> The hexameter has been often criticised, but I do not believe any other measure could have told that lovely story with such effect, as we feel when carried along the tranquil current of these brimming, slow-moving, soul-satisfy-

ing lines. Imagine for one moment a story like this minced into octysyllables. The poet knows better than his critics the length of step which best befits his muse. (Cameron 1978: 140)

The claim by Longfellow's critics that the English language is inherently ill-suited to dactylic hexameter verse bears some examination. So much English poetry has been written in iambic pentameter that this meter is often assumed to be the most "natural" one for English verse. Historically, however, iambic pentameter and other accentual-syllabic meters were continental imports, and they have been restricted mainly to literary verse. By contrast, English oral-traditional verse is typically accentual, with four (or fewer) strong stresses separated by a variable number of unstressed syllables. This sort of variability accommodates the natural characteristics of English more easily than accentual-syllabic meters do. Consequently, English poets writing in binary meters (iambic and trochaic) typically permit ternary substitutions (anapestic and dactylic) with varying degrees of freedom, as lines such as (1) illustrate:

(1) Full mány a glórious mórning have I séen (Shakespeare, Sonnet 33)
     w   s ww   s ww   s   w   s w s

Conversely, poets writing in ternary meters typically permit binary substitutions, as the first line from "The Star-Spangled Banner" illustrates:

(2) Oh, sáy, can you sée, by the dáwn's éarly líght
     w   s   w   w s   w w   s   w w s

Tarlinskaja (1992: 4) discusses the historical tension between accentual-syllabic and purely accentual verse in the English, Russian, and German traditions, and she identifies a transitional form between the two kinds of meter, which she calls the "dolnik" (the accepted Russian term for such verse). In dolnik verse: "The relative syllabic and accentual regularity of structure makes it possible to identify potentially-stressed ('ictic') and potentially-unstressed ('non-ictic') syllabic positions ... . However, ... the number of syllables in non-ictic positions ... is variable. The anacrusis can be 0, 1, or 2 syllables, and the inter-ictic intervals 1 or 2 syllables." This is the typical meter of English ballads and folk songs. [For a careful analysis of ballad meter within the framework of Optimality Theory (Prince and Smolensky 1993), see Hayes and MacEachern 1998.] Tarlinskaja points out that permissible variations in the number of unstressed syllables between stressed ones in such folk verse closely parallels that of natural English speech. Some of Longfellow's best-known poems are written in this meter:

(3)   It wás the schóoner Hésperús,
          That sáiled the wíntry séa;
      And the skípper had táken his líttle daughtèr,
          To béar him cómpaný.
      [Note: Longfellow himself marks the nonstandard emphasis on the final syllable of *daughtèr*.]

(4)   Únder a spréading chéstnùt-trée
          The víllage smíthy stánds;

(5)   Lísten, my chíldren, and yóu shall héar
      Of the mídnìght ríde of Pául Revére,

As these examples illustrate, successive lines of ballad verse normally form linked pairs, which resemble longer lines divided by a caesura:

(6)   Under a spreading chestnut-tree, the village smithy stands;
      [Two short lines reinterpreted as one longer line.]

Conversely, Longfellow's hexameters are typically divided into two half-lines by a mid-line caesura:

(7)   Stróngly búilt were the hóuses, with fràmes of óak and of hémlòck,
       s   w   s   w   w   s   w   w   s   w   s   w   w   s   w
                                                              Evang 1.1.14

   The stressed syllables in these lines, too, are separated by one or two unstressed syllables. Hence, Longfellow's ballad lines and his hexameters present similar metrical challenges. The empirical evidence is that Longfellow met this challenge successfully. Generations of readers have enjoyed his hexameter poems – partly because of "the tranquil current" of his lines. And, whether individual readers take pleasure in them or not, *Evangeline* and *The Courtship of Miles Standish* do demonstrate that the English language can be adapted to hexameter verse.

138 *Gilbert Youmans*

The trochaic tetrameter of *Hiawatha* as described by Hayes (1989) is regular almost to the point of hypermetricality. Longfellow's hexameter poems are freer metrically, like their Greek, Latin, and German models. Prince (1989) describes the classical Greek hexameter line as being composed of five dactyls plus a final spondee, with spondaic substitutions permitted in any of the first five feet, although such substitutions are rare in the third and the fifth feet. The opening lines of *Evangeline* illustrate that Longfellow allowed himself similar variations from strict dactylic meter. In (8), I have underscored binary feet. I have also included interlineal glosses to show the metrical effect of rewriting phrases such as *garments green* in their normal order – *green garments* (the same technique I applied in Youmans 1983, 1989, and 1996). I have marked these rephrasings with an asterisk when they result in a metrically deviant line:

(8)
Thís is the /fórest pri/méval. The /múrmuring /pínes and the /hémlòcks,   333332

Béarded with /móss, and in /gárments /gréen, indi/stínct in the /twílight,   332332
 [*/gréen gárments, /indi/stínct ...]

Stánd like /Drúids of /éld, with /vóices /sád and pro/phétic,   232232

Stánd like /hárpers /hóar, with /béards that /rést on their /bósoms.   222232
 ["*Stand like hóar /hárpers, with/béards ..." has only five feet.]

Lóud from its /rócky /cáverns, the /déep-vòiced /néighboring /ócean   5   323232

Spéaks, and in /áccents dis/cónsolate /ánswers the /wáil of the /fórest.   333332
 ["* ... /in dis/cónsolate /áccents/ ..." has seven feet.]

Thís is the /fórest pri/méval; but /whére are the /héarts that be/néath it   333332

Léaped like the /róe, when he /héars in the /wóodlànd the /vóice of the /húntsman?   333332
 ["* ... /héars the /vóice of the /húntsman /in the /wóodlànd" has seven feet.]

Whére is the /thátch-ròofed /víllage, the /hóme of A/cádian /fármers, –   323332

Mén whose /líves glíded /ón like /rívers that /wáter the /wóodlànds,   10   232332
 [Alternatively, this line could be analyzed as "Men whose lives/ glided/ on like ..."]

Dárkened by /shádows of /éarth, but re/flécting an /ímage of /héaven?   333332

Wáste are those /pléasant /fárms, and the /fármers for/éver de/párted!   323332
 [*Those pléasant /fárms are /wáste, and ...]

Scáttered like /dúst and /léaves, whèn the /míghty /blásts of Oc/tóber   323232

Séize them, and /whírl them a/lóft, and /sprínkle them /fár o'er the /ócean.   332332

Náught but tra/dítion re/máins of the /béautiful /víllage of /Gránd-Pré.   15   333332

Yé who be/líeve in a/ffléction that /hópes, and en/dúres, and is /pátient,   333332

Yé who be/líeve in the /béauty and /stréngth of /wóman's de/vótion,   333232

Líst to the /móurnful tra/dítion, still /súng by the /pínes of the /fórest;   333332

Líst to a /Tále of /Lóve in A/cádie, /hóme of the /háppy.   19   323232

All nineteen of these lines end with binary feet. This turns out to be a categorical constraint in both *Evangeline* and *Miles Standish*, as it was for Longfellow's classical models, although Longfellow's final foot is typically trochaic rather than spondaic. Conversely, the fifth foot is always dactylic in (8). This constraint is nearly categorical, too: there are only eleven exceptions in the two poems combined, such as these two lines from *Evangeline*:

(9)   Whírled them a/lóft through the /áir, at /ónce from a /húndred /hóuse-tòps   1.5.99

Ínto this /wónderful /lánd, at the /báse of the /Ózàrk /Móuntains,   2.4.29

By contrast, in feet 1–4, Longfellow prefers dactylic feet but frequently substitutes trochees (and occasionally spondees). Thus, his first line is regular dactylic until its final trochaic foot; his second line has an additional trochee in foot 3; the third line has additional trochees in feet 1, 3, and 4; and the fourth line has trochees everywhere except for the nearly-obligatory dactyl in foot 5. The incidence of binary feet in the poem as a whole is given in (10):

(10)   Number of Binary feet in *Evangeline* (1397 lines):

Foot 1	Foot 2	Foot 3	Foot 4	Foot 5	Foot 6
319	668	663	657	5	1397
22.8%	47.8%	47.5%	47.0%	0.4%	100%

Binary feet occur at nearly the same rate in feet 2–4, almost fifty percent of the time. They occur at less than half this rate in foot 1. Thus, the lines in *Evangeline* tend to reinforce a dactylic norm early in the line; they allow considerable freedom within the line; and they end with a highly regular cadence.

Horace Scudder, the editor of the Cambridge edition of Longfellow's works, says in his introduction to *Miles Standish* that "the hexameter verse differs in its general effect from that produced by the more stately form used in *Evangeline*, through its greater elasticity. A crispness of touch is gained by the more varying accent and a freer use of trochees" (Longfellow: 164). However, the statistics for *Miles Standish* contradict Scudder's claim:

(11) Number of Binary feet in *The Courtship of Miles Standish* (1017 lines):

Foot 1	Foot 2	Foot 3	Foot 4	Foot 5	Foot 6
228	266	415	422	6	1017
22.4%	26.2%	40.8%	41.5%	0.6%	100%

Thus, binary feet are less frequent in *Miles Standish* than in *Evangeline*. The biggest dropoff is in foot 2: –21.6%. Hence, there is an even greater tendency in *Miles Standish* to delay binary substitutions until later in the line.

Scudder's mistaken claim probably resulted from the fact that trochees are relatively infrequent at the beginning of *Evangeline*, whereas they become progressively more frequent as the poem unfolds. For example, eight (42%) of the first nineteen lines in (8) conform with the dactylic hexameter prototype (333332), whereas only 10.0% of the lines in the poem as a whole conform with this prototype. That is, *Evangeline* establishes its dactylic prototype early, then deviates from it with increasing freedom. By contrast, *Miles Standish* begins with a series of atypical lines, quoted in (12). I have underscored binary feet and major stresses in metrical W positions:

(12)
In the Óld /Cólony /dáys, in /Plýmouth the /length of the /Pílgrims, 332332
Tó and /fró in a /róom of his /símple and /prímitive/ dwélling, 233332
Clád in /dóublet and /hóse, and /bóots of /Córdovan /léather, 232232
Stróde, with a /mártial /áir, Míles /Stándish the /Púritan /Cáptain. 322332

Thus, the lines at the beginning of *Miles Standish* are freer metrically than those at the beginning of *Evangeline*, but *Miles Standish* is more regular overall. For example, 20.8% of its lines conform with the dactylic prototype (333332). This is more than twice the rate of *Evangeline*.

The next step in the analysis of Longfellow's hexameter is to consider the interrelationships among feet. For example, does the presence of a binary foot near the beginning of a line increase or decrease the likelihood of additional binary feet later in the line? To answer questions such as this, I counted the number of lines of each type: lines with one, two, three, four, or five binary feet. There are sixteen possible line types ending with the prototypical ternary-binary sequence (xxxx32). If trochaic substitutions occur independently of each other, then the probability that any one type of line will occur is just the product of the probabilities of occurrence of each foot. For example, in *Evangeline* the frequency of binary feet is 22.8% in foot 1, 47.8% in foot 2, and so on; conversely, the frequency of a ternary foot is 77.2% in foot 1, 52.2% in foot 2, and so on. Hence, the probability of a symmetrical 323232 line is 77.2% x 47.8% x 52.5% x 47% x 99.6% = 9.1%. In fact, 10.7 % (149) of the lines in Evangeline are of this type, which is to say that the presence of a binary foot in foot 2 slightly increases (rather than decreases) the likelihood of another binary foot in foot 4. The statistics for all types of lines are tabulated in (13).

(13) Line Types in Evangeline – 1397 lines:

    (1) One binary foot – 140 (10.0 %)   p = 11.2%
        333332 – 140 (10.0 %)   p = 11.2%
    (2) Two binary feet – 468 (33.5 %)   p = 33.5%
        333232 – 116 (8.3 %)   p = 9.9%
        332332 – 125 (8.9 %)   p = 10.1%
        323332 – 156 (11.2 %)   p = 10.2%
        233332 – 71 (5.1 %)   p = 3.3%
    (3) Three binary feet – 530 (37.9 %)   p = 36.3%
        332232 – 107 (7.7 %)   p = 9.0%
        323232 – 149 (10.7 %)   p = 9.1%
        322332 – 142 (10.2 %)   p = 9.3%
        233232 – 47 (3.4 %)   p = 2.9%
        232332 – 67 (4.8 %)   p = 3.0%
        223332 – 18 (1.3 %)   p = 3.0%
    (4) Four binary feet – 241 (17.3 %)   p = 16.2%
        322232 – 138 (9.9 %)   p = 8.2%
        232232 – 53 (3.8 %)   p = 2.6%
        223232 – 34 (2.4 %)   p = 2.7%
        222332 – 16 (1.1 %)   p = 2.7%
    (5) Five binary feet – 13 (0.9 %)   p = 2.4%
        222232 – 13 (0.9 %)   p = 2.4%
    (6) Other lines (xxxx22) – 5 (0.4 %) – 333322 – 2; 323322; 332322; 322322

Several metrical tendencies emerge from these statistics. Most obvious is Longfellow's preference for early ternary feet. The number of lines with initial ternary feet ranges from a low of 107 to a high of 156, whereas the number of lines with initial binary feet ranges from a low of 13 to a high of 71. Hence, every type of line with an initial ternary foot is more common than every type of line with an initial binary foot. This "early ternary foot" principle is illustrated especially well by the statistics for lines with four binary feet: the longer the first ternary foot is delayed, the less frequent the lines become, from a high of 138 (for 322232 lines) to a low of 16 (for 222332 lines).

Another, though much less significant, tendency is for one binary substitution to increase the likelihood of another one elsewhere in the line. Lines with two binary feet (and therefore one binary substitution) occur 33.5% of the time, exactly equaling the frequency expected for such lines. However, lines with three and four binary feet occur slightly more often than the predicted rate, providing modest evidence for a balance principle; that is, a tendency for one binary foot to be followed by another one nearby in the line. For example, 142 (10.2 %) of the lines in *Evangeline* are structured 322332, with two binary feet in succession. By chance alone, this structure would be expected in only 9.3% of the lines. Similarly, the symmetrical structure 323232 occurs in 149 (10.7 %) of the lines in *Evangeline*, rather than the 9.1% that chance would predict. A "tension metric" based solely on adding up the number of deviations from the dactylic norm might lead us to expect the opposite result – namely, that a binary substitution in one foot would reduce the probability of a binary substitution in another foot. In fact, however, Longfellow shows a modest tendency in the opposite direction: to balance one binary foot with another one nearby.

Table (14) compares the frequencies of line types in Parts I and II of *Evangeline*:

(14) Evangeline:	Part I (664 lines)	Part II (733 lines)
(1) One binary foot	73 (11.0%)	67 (9.1 %)
333332		
(2) Two binary feet	242 (36.4%)	226 (30.1 %)
333232	54 (8.1%)	62 (8.5 %)
332332	79 (11.9%)	46 (6.3 %)
323332	74 (11.1%)	82 (11.2 %)
233332	35 (5.3%)	36 (4.9 %)

(3) Three binary feet	246 (37.0%)	284 (38.7 %)
332232	49 (7.4%)	58 (7.9 %)
323232	74 (11.1%)	75 (10.2 %)
322332	70 (10.5%)	72 (9.8 %)
233232	22 (3.3%)	25 (3.4 %)
232332	26 (3.9%)	41 (5.6 %)
223332	5 (0.75%)	13 (1.8 %)
(4) Four binary feet	99 (14.9%)	142 (19.4 %)
322232	56 (8.4%)	82 (11.2 %)
232232	22 (3.3%)	31 (4.2 %)
223232	13 (2.0%)	21 (2.9 %)
222332	8 (1.2%)	8 (1.1 %)
(5) Five binary feet 222232	3 (0.5%)	10 (1.4 %)
(6) xxxx22	1 (0.2%)	4 (0.55 %)

Table (14) shows a decline in the frequency of prototypical 333332 lines from 11.0% in Part I to 9.1 % in Part II. The largest decline is in symmetrical 332332 lines: from 79 (11.9%) in Part I to 46 (6.3 %) in Part II. Overall, the frequency of binary feet increases from Part I to Part II, reflecting a general loosening of the meter as the poem progresses.

Up to this point, I have been speaking as though the foot is a significant metrical unit for Longfellow. Any such assumption is controversial. Instead of attempting to count binary and ternary feet, why don't I merely count the number of syllables in unstressed (W) positions instead? The answer is: partly out of convenience, partly out of tradition, and partly because there is strong evidence that foot boundaries are significant at least at the ends of Longfellow's hexameter lines. For example, in a systematic 279-line sample from *Evangeline* (every fifth line), 159 out of 279 lines (57%) end with disyllabic trochaic words such as *blóssom* and *fármer*. Another 32 (11.5%) end with disyllabic compounds such as *hémlòcks* and *bláksmìth* (approximating the classical spondee). In all, then, 68% of the lines in *Evangeline* end with disyllabic words. These final disyllables also define the right boundaries of preceding dactyls, which are often trisyllabic words, as in prototypical final cadences such as *néighboring ócean, prímitive dwélling, Córdovan léather, Púritan Cáptain*, and the like. The frequent repetition of such phrases is further evidence of their prototypicality. For example, in *Miles Standish*, Longfellow ends two lines with the phrase *Córdovan léather*, two lines with *Púritan ánthem*, and five lines with *Púritan máiden(s)*. Such metrically convenient phrases recall the epic formulas that are repeated so often in *The Iliad*: *rosy-fingered dawn*, *swift-footed Achilles*, and the like.

However, dactylic words are relatively uncommon in English, so most of Longfellow's dactylic feet are composed of phrases rather than single words. Neverthelss, the fifth foot rarely includes any major phrase boundaries. For example, of the nineteen lines quoted in (8) only one line includes punctuation within the fifth foot:

(15) Yé who be/líeve in a/fféction that /hópes, and en/dúres, and is /pátient,

By contrast, eleven (58%) of the lines in (8) include punctuation within the third foot, the most common location for the mid-line caesura:

(16) Thís is the /fórest prì/méval. The /múrmuring /pínes and the /hémlòcks,

Thus, Longfellow's phrasing tends to reinforce foot boundaries at the beginnings and ends of his lines but to undercut foot boundaries somewhere in the middle. This prevents his hexameters from becoming too monotonously regular.

Prototypical ternary feet include two unstressed syllables: WWS (in anapestic meter) or SWW (in dactylic meter). However, Kiparsky (1977) and Prince (1989) note that trochaic SW sequences can be substituted for WW positions in ternary verse, whereas iambic WS sequences tend to be constrained more strictly in WW positions. Hence, a trochaic word such as *éarly* is acceptable in WW positions in anapestic verse (*by the dáwn's /éarly líght*), whereas an iambic word such as *divíne* would be less acceptable in WW positions (**by the dáwn's /divíne líght*). The same principle applies to Longfellow's hexameters. For example, four-syllable words such as *bènedíction* and *pàtriárchal*, which have secondary stress on the first syllable and primary on the third syllable, can occupy either WWSW or SWSW metrical positions, as illustrated in (17) and (18):

(17) Hómeward se/rénely she /wálked with /Gód's bène/díction u/pón her. 1.1.61
 [*She wálked /hómeward se/rénely ...]

(18) Áll his do/máins and his /hérds, and his /pàtri/árchal de/méanor; 2.3.83–4

Conversely, iambic WS substitutions in WW positions are restricted to minor category words and compounds such as *itself* rather than major category words such as *divine*:

(19) That ùp/róse from the /ríver, and /spréad itsèlf /óver the /lándscàpe. 2.3.31

The lines in (20) illustrate other deviations from the dactylic norm that Longfellow occasionally permitted himself:

(20) Borderlines of metricality

Were the swift /húmming /bírds that /flítted from /blóssom to /blóssom. 2.2.84
[In the first dactyl, the strongest stress is the third syllable. Note that swift is subordinated to the following word.]

Like the gréat /chórds of a /hárp, in /lóud and /sólemn vì/brátions. 2.4.11
[In the first dactyl, the strongest stress is the third syllable. Note that great is subordinated to the following word.]

And at the /héad of the /bóard, the /gréat árm-/chàir of the /fármer. 1.4.114
[The fourth foot is spondaic, with stronger stress on the second syllable.]

All things for/gótten be/síde, they /gáve them/sélves to the /máddening 2.3.131
[The final foot is dactylic unless it is reduced to a trochee by elision.]

Not só /thínketh the /fólk in the /víllage," sàid, /wármly, the /blácksmìth, 1.2.100
[In the first trochee, the second syllable is stronger than the first.]

And when she a/wóke from the /tránce, she be/héld a /múltitude /néar her. 1.5.122
[The first foot has four syllables, requiring elision of she-a(woke).]

Tìll she be/héld him nò /móre, though she /fóllowed fár / into the /fórest. 2.4.66
[The last syllable in the fourth foot is stronger than the first syllable in the fifth foot.]

Into her /thóughts of /him tíme /éntered /nòt, for it /wás nòt. 2.5.28
[In the third foot, the second syllable is stronger than the first syllable.]
Alternatively:
Into her /thóughts of him/ tíme éntered /nòt, for it /wás nòt. 2.5.28
[By this interpretation, the line is pentameter rather than hexameter.]

Such variations are rare, but they demonstrate that Longfellow's hexameters do permit considerable variety. As further evidence of this variety, I will close with two examples of iconic rhythm in *Evangeline*. The line in (21) has no trochaic substitutions and four stressed syllables in W positions. Hence, this line is longer than Longfellow's prototypical dactylic line, and, in fact, it comes close to defining the upper limit for the length and number of stressed syllables that are possible in the lines from *Evangeline*. The metrical expansiveness of the line is appropriate to the meaning it expresses:

(21) Yét ùnder /Bénedìct's/ róof hóspi/tálity /séemed mòre a/búndant: 1.4.18
[Unusually heavy W positions result in an "abundant" line.]

By contrast, line (22) has three trochaic substitutions, and all but one of its W syllables are unstressed. Phonologically, then, the length of this line is near Longfellow's lower limit. In this case, too, the rhythm of the line is appropriate to its meaning:

(22) Darted a /light, swift /boat, that /sped a/way o'er the /water,   2.2.89
[The W positions are unusually "light," resulting in a "swifter" line.]

Such examples illustrate the expressive variety that is possible in Longfellow's hexamaters. Oliver Wendell Holmes praised *Evangeline*'s "slow-moving, soul-satisfying lines," and generations of readers have joined Holmes in taking pleasure in the "tranquil current" of this poem. Some of Longfellow's hexameters "brim" with "more abundant" hospitaility, as in (21). Others move swiftly "o'er the water," as in (22). Such variations demonstrate that Longfellow was a master of his long line, not a slave to it.

References

Cameron, K. W.
    1978   *Longfellow Among His Contemporaries: a Harvest of Estimates, Insights, and Anecdotes from the Victorian Literary World.* Hartford, CT: Transcendental Books.

Hayes, Bruce P.
    1989   The prosodic hierarchy in meter. In *Phonetics and Phonology I: Rhythm and Meter,* Paul Kiparsky and Gilbert Youmans (eds.), 201–60. San Diego, CA.: Academic Press.

Hayes, Bruce P., and Margaret MacEachern
   1998   Quatrain form in English folk verse. *Language* 74: 473–507.

Kiparsky, Paul
   1977   The rhythmic structure of English verse. *Linguistic Inquiry* 8: 189–247.

Kiparsky, Paul, and Gilbert Youmans (eds.)
   1989   *Phonetics and Phonology I: Rhythm and Meter.* San Diego, CA.: Academic Press.

Longfellow, Henry Wadsworth
   1975   *The Poetical Works of Longfellow.* Boston, MA: Houghton Mifflin.

Prince, Alan
   1989   Metrical forms. In: *Phonetics and Phonology I: Rhythm and Meter,* Paul Kiparsky and Gilbert Youmans (eds.), 45–80. San Diego, CA.: Academic Press.

Prince, Alan, and Paul Smolensky
   1993   Optimality Theory: constraint interaction in Generative Grammar. RuCCS Technical Report 2. Piscataway, NJ: Rutgers Center for Cognitive Science, Rutgers University, and Boulder, CO: Department of Computer Science, University of Colorado.

Tarlinskaja, Marina
   1992   Metrical typology: English, German, and Russian dolnik verse. *Comparative Literature* 44: 1–21.

Youmans, Gilbert
   1983   Generative tests for generative meter. *Language* 59: 67–92.
   1989   Milton's meter. In: *Phonetics and Phonology I: Rhythm and Meter,* Paul Kiparsky and Gilbert Youmans (eds.), 341–79. San Diego, CA.: Academic Press.
   1996   Reconsidering Chaucer's prosody. In *English Historical Metrics,* C. B. McCully and J. J. Anderson (eds.), 185–209. Cambridge: Cambridge University Press.

4. Old Norse

The rise of the quatrain in Germanic: musicality and word based rhythm in eddic meters

Kristján Árnason

1. Introduction

It is a well-known fact that Germanic alliterative poetry, from England and Germany in the south to Iceland in the north, shows similarities that cannot be coincidental, indicating a common origin. And the most widely known analysis of the meters, that of Eduard Sievers (1893), is equally applicable to German, English and Icelandic alliterative poetry. What these genres have in common is the use of alliteration as a binding device between colons (short lines), and the nature of the rhythm, with two strong positions to each colon. The strong positions were filled by word stresses in accordance with laws of intonation and sentence stress (cf. Árnason 2002 and references). But the differences found between these versions of what has been assumed to be a common Germanic tradition are also interesting. The main difference between the eddic poems in the North on one hand and the German Heliand and Hildebrandslied and the English Beowulf on the other lies in the stanzaic structure of the eddic poems. This stanzaic division is clearly indicated in the main manuscript of the Poetic Edda, Codex Regius, by punctuation and the use of capital letters at the beginning of each new stanza. The fact that this is absent in the West Germanic corpus tells us that the stanzaic structure must be a Nordic innovation and it also means that understanding the relation between the Germanic sub-genres should start by investigating the development of the Nordic innovation of stanzaic structure.

The present paper will maintain that the basic difference reflected in the stanzaic structure of the eddic poetry *vis à vis* the 'stichic' character of the others lies in the fact that the eddic stanzas are quatrains. The eddic short lines may be combined to form long lines of the West Germanic type, and then a strophe of eight short lines becomes a quatrain with four lines with four beats each.

Metrical investigation has shown that the quatrain is among the most natural of metrical forms. This is so because of the simplicity and naturalness of its 4x4 rhythm (quadruple time, cf. e.g., Attridge 1982, Hayes & McEachern 1998, Hayes 2000). Quatrains are widely known, and their ubiquity can be seen as a consequence of their simplicity.

A further characteristic of the eddic tradition is its elaboration of new metrical variants. Among other things, it distinguishing between the *fornyrðislag* ('the meter of the old sayings') traditionally seen as having eight short lines, and the *ljóðaháttr* ('the meter of the poems, the lyric meter') with six lines of varying length. I propose that both of the eddic forms are quatrains, the *fornyrðislag* a basic one and the *ljóðaháttr* a truncated and catalectic one. The eddic long line, like that of the English Beowulf and the German Heliand and Hildebrandslied thus demands four strong positions. A stanza is formed by repeating this three times to form a quatrain, and it will be maintained below that the rhythm is word based in the sense of Hanson & Kiparsky (1996).

The 4x4 character of the eddic meters makes them more musical than the West Germanic cognates, since the 4x4 rhythm in meter has important characteristics in common with musical structure. And Roman Jakobson's ideas (1987a,b) that verse is more suited for the lyric function in literature and prose better suited for the epic function suggests that the eddic poems, more verse-like in their structure, should be more lyric in their function than, say, *Beowulf* and *Hiltibrandslied*. This is left as a thought for further study, and so is the connection between the musicality of the eddic meters and the rise of skaldic poetry, with its very musical (but foot based) *dróttkvætt* as a basic form, and indeed of the elaboration of artistic prose.

2. Germanic alliterative poetry

As is well known, the fundamental unit in Eduard Sievers' analysis of old Germanic poetry (*Altgermanische Metrik* 1893) was the colon or half-line. The basic structure was that each short line had four positions (*Glieder*), two strong ones, and two weak ones. The distribution of weak and strong positions was free except that a line could not end in two strong positions. This gave five (instead of the six mathematically possible) types of lines. This "Fünftypensystem" is illustrated in (1) with examples of short lines from the Old Icelandic *fornyrðislag* and the Old English *Beowulf*. The rhythm is here pictured with *s* for 'strong' and *w* for 'weak'. In the simplest case each metrical position is filled by one syllable, the strong positions by a stressed syllable and the weak one by an unstressed syllable. But quite commonly more syllables could fill each position, particularly the weak positions. The *A* type with its trochaic character is the most basic one, with the others forming variants according to the distribution of strongs and weaks, labeled by Sievers from *B* to *E*:

(1)   (A)   s w s w
              borgir þessar (Sig.kv. Fáfn. I 1,2)
              'towns these'
              geong in geardum (Beowulf 14a)
              'young in gardens'

    (B)   w s w s
              þeir's hörg ok hof (Völuspá 7,3)
              'those who altars and temples...'
              him on bearme læg (Beowulf 40b)
              'lay in his lap'

    (C)   w s s w
              ok tól gørðu (Völuspá 7,8)
              'and tools made'
              þone God sende (Beowulf 14b)
              'the one who god sent'

    (D)   s s w w
              auð smíðuðu (Völuspá 7,6)
              'wealth produced'
              heah Healfdene (Beowulf 57a)
              'high Halfdan'

    (E)   s w w s
              endlangan sal (Völundarkviða 16,4)
              'the whole hall'
              weorðmyndum þah (Beowulf 8b)
              'prospered in honour'

In Sievers' model, two colons are joined together in pairs to form a larger unit, the long line (German: *Langzeile*). It is customary to print each colon of the *fornyrðislag* separately, as in (2a), but the West Germanic texts are traditionally printed as in (2b), with each long line as a unit. But obviously, a half stanza of *fornyrðislag* can be presented as in 2c:

(2) a Hljóðs bið ek allar
       helgar kindir
       meiri ok minni
       mögu Heimdallar
               (Völuspá 1, 1–4.)

    b Hwæt! wē Gār-Dena in gēardagum
       þēod-cyninga þrym gefrūnon
       hū þā æðelingas ellen fremedon.
               (Beowulf 1–3)

    c Hljóðs bið ek allar / helgar kindir
       meiri ok minni / mögu Heimdallar.

We are thus dealing with closely related metrical forms, as has long been noted and Sievers' line typology was meant to apply to all genres. (Similarly, models like that proposed by Russom (1987, 1998) and Getty (2002) are meant to apply *mutatis mutandis* to all versions of Germanic alliterative poetry.)

In spite of the general acceptance of Sievers' typology, several points of unclarity or disagreement prevail to this day among scholars about the eddic meters. In fact, just about the only thing that everyone agrees about is that each long line has four strong positions. But it seems that many of these problems are solved if we assume that the rhythm of the eddic poems was word based, as is suggested below.

A difference (apart from the stanzaic structure), that has been noted between eddic poetry and the West Germanic cognates is that the eddic poems seem to be more rhythmically regular in having a smaller number of extrametrical syllables. The German *Hildebradslied* and *Heliand* in particular have a more irregular number of syllables than the eddic poems. The *Heliand* has many examples of elaborate "upbeats" or anacruses, as in:

$$\text{s}\text{w}\text{w}\text{s}$$
(3)   (thuo hie erest thesa) werold gescop (Heliand 39b)
       'when he first the world created'

If the parenthesised sequence is analysed as an "upbeat" (somehow extrametrical) the rest of the line can be analysed as an *E*-type in Sievers' classification:

```
      s w    w  s
```
(4) Werold gescop

Similarly, many of the lines of the *Hildebrandslied* have more syllables than needed to fit into the template of four positions (*Glieder*) assumed by Sievers:

```
     s    w    s   w
```
(5) Hiltibrant gimahalta (Hildebrandslied 45a)
     'Hiltibrant spoke'

The seven syllables of this half-line are far more than is directly demanded by Sievers' system, in which case the weak positions are filled by more than one syllable. "Overlong" lines are also common in Beowulf, as can be seen in (6), where the number of syllables goes up to 10:

(6) woroldāre forgeaf (Beowulf 17b) (6 syllables)
     'world honour supplied'

   þær wæs mādma fela (Beowulf 36b) (6 syllables)
   'there was wealth-GEN plenty'

   þæt hit wearð eal-gearo (Beowulf 77b) (6 syllables)
   'that it became fully done'

   sē þe his wordes geweald (Beowulf 79a) (7 syllables)
   'the one who his word's power'

   þa gyt wæs hiera sib ætgædere (Beowulf 1164b) (10 syllables)
   'when still was their peace among'

   Mæg þonne on þæm golde ongitan (Beowulf 1484a) (10 syllables)
   'see that man on the gold'

Geoffrey Russom has argued (1987, 1998) that the difference between the rhythm of the Old Icelandic and the West Germanic poems is at least to some extent due to structural differences between the languages. Icelandic word phonology is different from that of the others in having far fewer unstressed prefixes, for example in past participles like OE *ʒebunden*, OHG *gibuntan*, vs. OI. *bundinn* 'bound'. Furthermore the results of syncope and changes in quantity structure were in some instances more drastic in Nordic than in West Germanic (cf. Riad 1992). Thus disyllabic forms in Old English (*sunu* 'son') and Old High German (*sunu*) correspond to monosyllabic forms in Old Icelandic (*sonr*). This has an effect on the number of syllables per line, so it seems that, *mutatis mutandis*, the same sort of mapping (word based, cf. below) can be assumed to have been at work in both genres. The basic difference between Nordic and West Germanic lies in the stanzaic structure.

3. Quadruple time

Derek Attridge (1982) argues that quadruple time (4x4 rhythm) is a natural form of verse, and the same point is made by Hayes & McEachern (1998) and Hayes (2000). Such a form is illustrated in (7):

(7)   s   s   s   s
      When the bonny blade carouses
      s   s   s   s
      Pockets full, and spirits high,
      s   s   s   s
      What are acres? What are houses?
      s   s   s   s
      Only dirt, or wet, or dry.
          (Samuel Johnson, cf. Attridge 1982: 108)

Quatrain structure is also to be found in the Russian *chastushka* (a form of folk verse):

(8)   s   s   s   s
      Lučše netu togo cvetu
      s   s   s   s
      Kogda jablonja cvetjot.
      s   s   s   s
      Lučše netu toj minuty
      s   s   s   s
      Kogda milen'kij pridjot.

There is no better flower
Than when the apple tree is in bloom.
There is no better minute
Than when the loved one comes
   (Source: Yelena Yershova, cf. also Bailey 1993)

The quatrain form is, then, something to be expected, and such structures can develop spontaneously.

The stanzaic structure of the *fornyrðislag* can easily be represented as a quatrain as in (9):

(9)   s   s   s   s
   Hljóðs bið ek allar / helgar kindir
   silence ask I all / holy creatures
     s   s   s   s
   meiri ok minni / mögu Heimdallar.
   greater and lesser / sons Heimdall-GEN
     s   s   s   s
   Viltu að eg Valföðr / vel fyr telja
   want that I Valföðr / well for tell
     s   s   s   s
   forn spjöll fira / er eg fremst of man
   old lore men-GEN / as I foremost remember
   (Völuspá 1)

'I ask for the attention of all holy creatures, greater and lesser descendants of Heimdall. You want me, Valfather, to recite the old wisdom as I can best remember.'

This is a typical four beat rhythm, and I propose that it is word based in that it counts word stresses. This means that a line is well formed if four word stresses are supplied, which have sufficient strength in the phonological hierarchy, i.e., are not subordinated to other word stresses on the level of phrasal phonology. This means among other things that nouns are more likely to carry an ictus than finite verbs, and the first constituent in a Noun phrase is more likely to carry an ictus than a second constituent. Pronouns and prepositions are weaker and typically do not carry ictuses (cf. Árnason 2002: 227–233).

4. Structural settings

Hanson & Kiparsky (1996, 1997) propose a set of parameters for metrical mapping among which languages and meters can choose their "settings". On the one hand, these are parameters of structure, e.g., defining how many metrical positions are relevant, and whether the structure is trochaic (falling) or iambic (rising). The other set of parameters is that of realization. These define settings for the maximal size of the metrical position: mora, syllable, foot or word. The parameter of prominence site determines where prominence is constrained, i.e., whether it is the weak or the strong position, and finally the prominence type defines the prosodic characteristic in terms of which prominence is defined (weight, stress, strength or pitch accent).

There are language determined connections between the parameters of size and prominence type. For example, if a meter is foot based, i.e., has metrical positions defined as foot slots, foot being a unit relevant to rules of word accent, this means that the prominence relation operative is that of word accent (and not, say phrasal accent). Similarly, a meter which uses the word as a metrical position necessarily refers to prominence relations at the level of phonology on which the prominence relations between words are defined, i.e., phrasal phonology or intonation.

I propose that the eddic meters are word based in that the maximum size of the (satisfied) metrical position corresponds to the linguistic category of phonological word and the prominence type was that of strength.[1]

5. Word count and foot count

The basic structural setting for eddic is, then, that each line has four strong positions, and this is satisfied if the text contains four words that can fill a strong position:

(10)   Ok í |hǫll |Hárs |hána |brenndu (Vsp. 21,5)
       and in hall Óðin-GEN skin burned

A line like:

   *|Mælir |Óðinn við |Mími
    speaks Óðinn to Mímir

(cf. the metrical: mælir *Óðinn við Mímis höfuð*, Vsp. 45)

is unmetrical in the *fornyrðislag* because there aren't enough strong words;

(11) *|Hljóðs bið ek |alla |helga |mǫgu |Sigfǫður
⠀⠀⠀⠀silence ask I all holy sons of Sigfǫðr
⠀⠀⠀⠀⠀s⠀⠀⠀⠀⠀s⠀⠀⠀⠀s⠀⠀⠀⠀s

(11) is unmetrical because there are too many strong words.

The prominence site is S, which means that the essential position to be satisfied is the strong, rather than the weak one (as is the case in English iambic pentameter). What the meter demands is that four strong positions be formed, and if four word stresses are found that can respond to these strong positions, the line is good.

But this means that the number of syllables in the lines of fornyrðislag varies according to the number of syllables in words.

Lines can easily end in two weak syllables, as in (12a) (cf. 9), and the strong positions can stand side by side as in (12b) (cf. 10):

⠀⠀⠀⠀⠀⠀⠀⠀⠀s⠀⠀⠀⠀s⠀⠀⠀s⠀⠀⠀⠀s
(12)⠀a⠀⠀⠀meiri ok minni mögu Heimdallar.
⠀⠀⠀⠀⠀⠀⠀⠀⠀s⠀⠀s⠀⠀⠀⠀s⠀⠀⠀⠀s
⠀⠀⠀⠀b⠀⠀⠀Ok í hǫll Háars / hána brenndu

We saw that Sievers assumed that each colon had four positions (Glieder), two weak ones and two strong ones. The five types are generated by allowing all combinations of strong and weak, except *wwss* with two strongs at the end. But it may in fact be possible to interpret lines like:

⠀⠀⠀⠀⠀⠀⠀⠀⠀⠀⠀s⠀⠀⠀⠀⠀s⠀⠀⠀s⠀⠀⠀⠀s
(13)⠀eða skyldu |goð |öll / |gildi |eiga (Vsp. 23)
⠀⠀⠀⠀or should gods all party have

as *wwss/swsw*, which would mean that Sievers' model in fact breaks down.

In our terms, metrical positions are filled by phonological words, and the strength relations are defined on the level of Intermediate Phrases (ip's) (cf. Árnason 2002, cf. Ladd 1996: 251). But since the prominence site is the strong position, not all weak positions need to be filled, and there is indeed no need to indicate the weak positions in the scansion, as we have seen.

A special constraint which has an effect on the composition of the fornyrðislag is Kuhn's Law (cf. Árnason 2002). According to this law, which has to do with phrasal phonology, so-called sentence particles (*Satzpartikeln*) were grouped together before the first or second stressed word in the clause. The *Satzpartikeln* are weak parts of phonological phrases, typically pronouns, adverbs and finite verbs.Thus *þá gengu*, an adverb and a finite verb, create what Kuhn calls a *Satzauftakt*, a sort of upbeat and do not participate in the mapping of stresses to strong positions.

(14) (þá gengu) |regin |öll á |rök |stóla (Voluspa 23, 1–2)
      s s s s
   then strepped gods all on argument stools

6. The prominence type

Since the rhythm is word based, the prominence type must be some property relevant to the strength of words, i.e., of phrasal phonology. The phrase phonology of Old Icelandic is of course not available for direct observation, but it is clear that lexicogrammatical categories varied in strength, as shown among other things by Kuhn's Law.

On the other hand, the stress of second parts of compounds could fill strong positions, as in:

(15) er Gull|veigu |geirum |studdu (Vsp. 21, 3–4)
    s s s   s
   as Gullveig spears-DAT supported

   s s
   |fram|lundaða
   forward-thinking

   s s
   |upp|himinn
   up-heaven

This shows that compound stress was a phrase level phenomenon in Old Icelandic. Further evidence that parts of compounds were relatively free is shown by the fact that the first part of a compound may alliterate with the second part, as in:

(16)   er í böndum skal
        who in fetters shall

        bíða **r**agna**r**ökkrs
        wait for the end of the world
        (Lokasenna 39, 5–6)

Here the two *r*'s in the compound form *ragna-rökkr* (literally: 'darkness of the gods, *Götterdämmerung*') alliterate, showin that there are two ictuses involved. Similarly *tmesis* in dróttkvætt poetry, shows that compounds can be split up as in (17). Here, the compound place name *Stiklarstaðr* is split up between lines by a part of the Noun Phrase *víðlendr almreyrs lituðr* 'wide-governing soldier/king' (cf. Árnason [1991] 2000: 71–77):

(17)   Vakit frá ek víg at *Stiklar-*
        awaken heard I at *Stiklar-*

        víðlendr, *stöðum* síðan,
        wide-governing *stöðum* later

        Innþrændum lét undir
        the people of inner Trondelag let wounds

        almreyrs lituðr dreyra.
        the bow's straw's colourer bleed.

'I heard that a battle was started at *Stiklarsaðr*. Later the wide-governing soldier (the one who lends colour, i.e., blood, to the arrows – the straws of the bow) made the wounds of the peole if inner Trondelag bleed.'

Looking at the eddic meters as word based seems to solve several problems of long standing in the analysis of the rhythm of the eddic and other

Germanic meters that we cannot go into in any detail here. For example the variation in the number of syllables and the variation in the placement of the stresses can be seen as compositional variants, and Sievers' typology becomes redundant, except as a descriptive account of individual lines. The principles that generate the typology are thus linguistic, and not metrical, as implied by Sievers' typology.

Furthermore, as mentioned in footnote 1, the relation between the eddic style and the skaldic style can be accounted for, it seems. The skalds and court poets used not only the *dróttkvætt* meter, but they also put some of the eddic meters to 'skaldic' use. Thus the so-called *kviðuháttr* 'the meter of the lays', with quadruple rhythm, traditionally represented typographically as an eight line meter, but with more stringency as regards the number of syllables, can simply be seen as *fornyrðislag* using syllabic rhythm, more appropriate for poetry to be presented to kings.

7. Truncation and catalexis: the *ljóðaháttr*

In section 3. it was shown that the *fornyrðislag* can be analysed as a quatrain, each stanza forming four lines with four strong beats (4444). As is well known, variant quatrain forms with alternation between four beat lines and three beat lines, where the second line has only three beats (4343), are common. I will now show that this was also the case in eddic poetry, namely in the *ljóðaháttr*.

The form of the other eddic meter, the *ljóðaháttr*, and its relation to the *fornyrðislag* has long been a matter of discussion (see e.g., Heusler [1889] 1969, [1925] 1956). The *ljóðaháttr* is different from the *fornyrðislag* in a number of respects. The first two colons of the half strophe form an alliterating structure, a long line, similar to a line of *fornyrðislag*. But in addition to this, there is a line (often called 'full line', German: *Vollzeile*). This line is sometimes seen as a sort of extra long colon, but sometimes as having three strong positions. One theory is that the *Vollzeile* somehow developed as a coalescence of two short lines with the effect that the second short line lost its strong position, leaving only three (cf. Hollander 1931, Kristjánsson 1988). In 19th and 20th century editions, it is customary to print the stanza of *ljóðaháttr* in six lines, as in (18).

(18) Inn skal ganga
  in shall walk

Ægis hallir í
Ægir-GEN halls into

á þat sumbl at sjá.
on that drinking to look

Jöll ok áfu
war and strife

færi ek ása sonum
bring I gods-GEN sons-DAT

Ok blend'k þeim svá meini mjöð
and mix I them so malice-DAT mead

'Let us enter the halls of Ægir, and look at the party.
I bring war and strife to the gods; that is how I mix their drink with malice.'
   (Lokasenna 3)

The obvious solution in this context is to see a *Vollzeile* as basically a three beat line, with the last strong beat unrealised, as shown in (19), and then the stanza becomes a 4343 quatrain:

(19) a Inn skal ganga / Ægis hallir í
         á þat sumbl at sjá. Ø
         Jöll ok áfu / færi ek ása sonum
         Ok blend'k þeim svá meini mjöð Ø

     b Þegi þú Gefjun / þess mun ek nú geta
        Be silent you Gefjun / that-GEN will I now mention
        er þik glapti að geði Ø
        when you-ACC distracted at mind

        s   s   s   s
sveinn in hvíti /er þér sigli gaf
ladd the white / when you-DAT necklace gave

    s   s   s   s
ok þú lagðir lær yfir Ø
and you laid thigh over
  (Lokasenna 20)

'Be silent, Gefjun, I'll now tell the story of when the fair lad fascinated you by giving you a necklace, and you went to bed with him.'

Another peculiarity of the *ljóðaháttr* is that it has a special constraint concerning the ending of the three beat line, the *Vollzeile*, which forbids disyllabic words with heavy first syllables. Thus we see that all lines in (19) either end in monosyllables (*í, sjá, mjöð* or *gaf*) or disyllables with light first syllables (i.e., CVCV: *sonum, geta, geði* and *yfir*). On the other hand, this does not apply to the *fornyrðislag* examples (15) and (20).

This constraint, which only applied to *ljóðaháttr* and not the *fornyrðislag* was first noticed by Bugge (1879) and later discussed by Heusler, who calls this ending *stumpf*, i.e., blunt or catalectic (see Heusler 1956: 239–40 and Árnason 2000: 41). This 'blunt' ending can be seen as a strong position or beat without a following weak position. The strong position could be filled either by a monosyllabic word capable of taking sentence stress or a disyllabic one, provided that the first syllable was light. This 'resolution', where two light syllables fill one stressed position, is due to a disyllabic stress making a light syllable rhythmically equal to one stressed syllable (a 'moraic trochee', cf. Hayes 1995, Hanson 1991). The second colon (the end of the first line) also tends to have the same ending.

Thus the half stanza of *ljóðaháttr* starts with a normal 4 beat structure with a (typically) masculine ending, and the *Vollzeile* forms a masculine 3 beat line. It is truncated and catalectic, "doubly catalectic", in that it misses one beat, and the last beat is furthermore masculine. The *fornyrðislag*, on the other hand, typically has a feminine ending, as we have seen:

(20)   Hljóðs bið ek *allar* helgar *kindir* (Vsp. 1)
         Silence I ask all holy creatures

         Veit hún Heimdalar hljóð um *fólgit* (Vsp. 27)
         Knows she Heimdal's sound hidden

It may be noted here that the catalexis practised in the *ljóðaháttr* ranks high on the scale of 'cadentiality' made use of by Hayes and McEachern (1998) and Hayes (2000). The cadentiality, which means something like 'aptitude for functioning as an end or closure to a metrical unit', is thus the measure of the saliency of a form as an end of a text. Typical means for creating cadentiality are truncation or catalexis, but repetition may also serve this purpose. In this light the development of the *ljóðaháttr* with its truncation can be seen as part of the development in Nordic toward more rhythmic stringency, musicality and stylisation.

One of the problems that older scholars have not been able to solve is the number of strong positions in the *Vollzeile*. Arguments have been put forth both ways, that it has two or three strong positions (cf. e.g., Hollander 1931, Kristjánsson 1988: 36). Examples like the ones in (21) are used to support the theory that there were two, rather than three, strong positions. Our analysis provides a solution to this problem, since those lines can easily be accounted for as doubly truncated, i.e., missing two beats in the second line:

(21)
      s   s   s   s
    Fróðr sá þykkisk er fregna kann
    Wise he thinks himself who hear can

      s   s   s   s
    ok segja it sama   Ø   Ø
    and tell the same
      (Hávamál 24)

This sort of truncation, leaving lines with two strong beats in a basically quadripodic meter, is commonly found in the *rímur* poetry. (Another way of looking at this variant might be to assume simply that a colon is left out.)

8. Conclusion

It has been argued here that the eddic meters are quatrain forms developed from older types of rhapsodic structure, such as those seen in West Germanic. We have emphasised the stanzaic character of the eddic poems as compared to the West Germanic texts. The stanzaic nature of the eddic form clearly delineated the beginning and end of the stanza; and the stanzaic units are in fact clearly indicated in the manuscripts. The 4x4 structure in and of itself is a marker of a self-contained structure, and the repetition involved is one of the basic properties of the law of the quatrain (Attridge 1982: 87–8, Hayes & McEachern 1998, Hayes 2000). The quatrain structure of the *fornyrðislag* is manifested in the simple repetition of lines, and the truncation and catalexis of the *ljóðaháttr* lines are even stronger markers of cadentiality.

But we may also ask about the correlation between these formal or metrical characteristics on one side, and the meaning or content of the texts on the other, and look for corroboration of the stanzaic characteristic in the structure of the texts themselves. In certain cases, the contents correspond to the metrical division, like in the poem *Hávamál*, where very often each stanza contains a piece of wisdom or a proverb, and an elaboration on its meaning. In other instances this is not the case, since in spite of their stanzaic structure, many of the eddic poems are epic in content.

However, it is tempting to add here a brief suggestion for an interpretation in literary history. The suggestion is that the increased musicality that came with the development of the stanza in the eddic poems went hand in hand with the development of the artistic prose of the sagas. We can express this in terms of Roman Jakobson's categories (1987a,b) of the function of literary texts: the lyric, the dramatic and the epic functions, corresponding to the grammatical categories of first, second and third person (cf. Hanson & Kiparsky 1997: 20–21). The function of poetry in the texts of the sagas is more often than not to create lyric interludes in the narration (cf. Harris 1997). In this light it is just as likely that the stanzaic structure of the eddic poems may have developed concurrently with the elaboration of the art of skaldic poetry. The great innovation of Nordic literature was then to separate the forms which served a lyric function and those which served an epic function. In other words, this was a step toward a more refined division of labour and stylisation of the literary medium. There may seem to be an interesting contradiction here, namely that 'lyric' forms like *foryrðislag* were used in epic poems like that of *Völundarkviða* 'The lay of Weiland', but this is a small matter compared to the later development, when whole sagas were recomposed as poems in the very elaborate and 'musical' style of the *rímur* (see Craigie 1938, 1952).

Notes

1. Since any language has both a level of word phonology and a level of phrasal phonology, it is possible that different metrical forms can refer to these different levels. This seems to have been the case in Old Icelandic. The eddic meters were word based and the skaldic meters (like the *dróttkvætt*, see Árnason 2000), on the other hand, were foot based with word accent as the prominence type. (And this was also the character of the later *rímur* meters.)

References

Árnason, Kristján
    2000   *The Rhythm of* dróttkvætt *and Other Old Icelandic Meters*. Reykjavik: The University of Iceland, Institute of Linguistics. Original edition Institute of Linguistics [1991].
    2002   Kuhn's laws in Old Icelandic prose and poetry. *Journal of Germanic Linguistics* 14: 201–241.

Attridge, Derek
    1982   *The Rhythms of English Poetry*. London: Longman.

Bailey, James
    1993   *Three Russian Lyric Folk Song Meters*. Bloomington: Slavica Publishers, Inc.

Bugge, Sophus
    1879   Nogle bidrag til det norröne sprogs og den norröne digtnings historie, hentede fra verslæren. *Beretning om forhandlingerne på det første nordiske filologmøde* [1876], København: Gyldendalske boghandels forlag, 140–149.

Craigie, William A.
    1938   *Early Icelandic rímur: MS no. 604 4to of the Arna-Magnæan Collection in the University Library of Copenhagen. Corpus codicum Islandicorum medii aevi;* 11. Copenhagen: Levin & Munksgaard.
    1952   *Sýnisbók íslenzkra rímna: Frá upphafi rímnakveðskapar til loka nítjándu aldar*. Valið hefir Sir William A. Craigie. London, Reykjavik.

Getty, Michael
    2002   *The Metre of Beowulf: Constraint-Based Approach*. Berlin: Mouton.

Hanson, Kristin
    1991   Resolution in modern meters. Ph.D.Dissertation, Stanford University.

Hanson, Kristin, and Paul Kiparsky
    1996   A parametric theory of poetic meter. *Language* 72: 287–335.
    1997   The nature of verse and its consequences for the mixed form. In *Prosimetrum: Crosscultural Perspectives on Narrative in Verse and*

Prose, Joseph Harris & Karl Reichl (eds.), 17–44. Cambridge, Mass: D.S. Brewer.

Harris, Joseph
1997   The prosimetrum of Icelandic saga and some relatives. In *Prosimetrum: Crosscultural Perspectives on Narrative in Verse and Prose*, Joseph Harris & Karl Reichl (eds.), 131–163. Cambridge, Mass: D.S. Brewer.

Hayes, Bruce
1995   *Metrical Stress Theory. Principles and Case Studies.* Chicago: The University of Chicago Press.
2000   Faithfulness and componentiality in metrics. Manuscript, UCLA.

Hayes, Bruce, and Margaret McEachern
1998   Quatrain form in English folk verse. *Language* 74: 473–507.

Heusler, Andreas
1969   Der Ljóðaháttr. Eine metrische Untersuchung. In *Kleine Schriften II*. Berlin: Walter de Gruyter & Co., 1969, 690–750. Originally published in *Acta Germanica* I,2: 89–174 [1889]
1956   *Deutsche Versgeschichte. I. (Zweite unveränderte Auflage)*. Berlin: Walter de Gruyter. Original edition [1925].

Hollander, Lee M.
1931   Hat die Vollzeile des Liodaháttr zwei oder drei Hebungen? *The journal of English and Germanic Philology* XXX: 475–493.

Jakobson, Roman
1987a.   Linguistics and poetics. In *Language in Literature,* Krystyna Pomorska and Stephen Rudy (eds), 62–94. Cambridge, Massachusetts: Harvard University Press.
1987b.   Marginal notes on the prose of the poet Pasternak. In *Language in Literature,* Krystyna Pomorska and Stephen Rudy (eds), 301–317. Cambridge, Massachusetts: Harvard University Press.

Kristjánsson, Jónas
1988   *Eddas and Sagas: Iceland's Medieval Literature.* Reykjavík. Hið íslenska bókmenntafélag.

Ladd, D. Robert
2000   *Intonational Phonology.* Cambridge: Cambridge University Press.

Riad, Tomas
1992   *Structures in Germanic Prosody. A Diachronic Study with Special Reference to the Nordic Languages.* Stockholm: Department of Scandinavian languages, Stockholm University.

Russom, Geoffrey
1987   *Old English Meter and Linguistic Theory.* Cambridge: Cambridge University Press.

1998. *Beowulf and Old Germanic Metre*. Cambridge: Cambridge University Press.
Sievers, Eduard
   1893   *Altgermanische Metrik*. Halle: Max Niemeyer.

5. Mora counting meters

The function of pauses in metrical studies: acoustic evidence from Japanese verse*

Deborah Cole and Mizuki Miyashita

> "That rhythm, that rhythm.
> it makes them one."
> - Ofelia Zepeda

> "...silence does not simply exist but
> is actively created by participants."
> - Nancy Bonvillian

1. Introduction

In this paper, we use acoustic evidence to establish that a line containing 8 moras is the metrical template for traditional Japanese poetry: lines that have been previously analyzed as having 5 or 7 moras are underlyingly octomoraic. We do this by demonstrating that pauses function as additional moras in the meter to regulate line length. We also argue that phonetic data should be used in metrical studies (by consulting native speakers' productions of metered texts) because they provide information about metrical structure not available in traditional text-based approaches, which view reader intuitions as unreliable. We make a needed contribution to metrical studies by analyzing meter in Japanese, a *prominence insensitive* language, meaning a language without stress accent. Therefore, Japanese meter lacks an alternating pattern of strong and weak positions because stressed or unstressed syllables do not exist in the phonology of Japanese.

Our paper is organized as follows. In section 2, we give brief backgrounds of metrics, traditional Japanese poetry, and a previous phonetic study of haiku by Lehiste (1997). Section 3 contains our data, which are phonetic measurements of readings of tanka, a form of Japanese poetry longer than haiku[1] by two lines. Our analysis appears in section 4, and in section 5 we embed our results in a general discussion of methodology and theory in the study of meter.

2. Metrical studies

Metrical studies have commonly analyzed languages that are prominence sensitive, meaning languages with stress. For example, iambic pentameter, which aligns word stress to metrical positions, has received much attention in metrical studies (Halle and Keyser 1971, Kiparsky and Youmans 1989, Hanson and Kiparsky 1996, Hayes 1984). These studies focus on written texts as sources of data that provide evidence of the poet's competence. Our study is experimental and uses native speaker readings of texts as evidence of the metrical structure of tanka, a verse type written in Japanese, a language without phonological stress.

2.1. Japanese poetry – haiku and other verse types

A traditional Japanese poem is commonly described as consisting of combinations of 5 and 7-mora lines (Kozasa 1997). For example, a haiku verse consists of three lines having counts of 5, 7, and 5 moras. Native Japanese speakers are taught to count 'letters' or 'symbols' when they compose haiku in elementary school. This is because a single *kana* symbol in the Japanese writing system generally corresponds to a mora, but not to a syllable (Shibatani 1990).

A mora (μ) is an abstract phonological unit. Light syllables have one mora and heavy syllables have two moras (Hayes 1989). In Japanese, a mora dominates both the onset and its adjacent vowel in a syllable (Katada 1990). Diphthongs and long vowels are bimoraic, and coda consonants are monomoraic. Examples of Japanese syllable types and number of moras per syllable are shown in (1) below. (C indicates a consonant, V indicates a vowel, and μ indicates a mora.)

(1) Syllable Types
    a. light syllable (monomoraic):
        V_μ *i*   'stomach (organ)'
        CV_μ *ki*   'tree'
    b. heavy syllable (bimoraic):
        $V_{\mu\mu}$ *oo*   'king'
        $CV_{\mu\mu}$ *kuu* 'empty'
        $V_\mu V_\mu$ *ai*   'love'
        $CV_\mu V_\mu$ *kai*   'shell'
        $CV_\mu C_\mu$ *san* 'three'

As mentioned, haiku consists of 17 moras that are distributed in three lines of 5 moras, 7 moras and 5 moras. An example of mora distribution in haiku is shown below.

(2)　Haiku example (Issa 1997)

　　　ya se ga e ru　　'skinny frog'
　　　μ μ μ μ μ

　　　ma ke ru na Is sa 'do not lose, I (Issa)'
　　　μ μ μ μ μμ μ

　　　ko re ni a ri　　'am here'
　　　μ μ μ μ μ

There are other Japanese verse types besides haiku. In (3)a – (3)f are some Japanese verse types listed by Kozasa (1997). All are combinations of 5 moraic lines and 7 moraic lines. For our study, we look at tanka. The reasons for choosing tanka over haiku are discussed in section 3.1.

(3)　Names of Verse Types　　Mora Count Alternations
　　　a. bussokusekika　　　　5-7-5-7-7-7
　　　b. chooka　　　　　　　　5-7-5-7- ... -5-7-7
　　　c. haiku　　　　　　　　　5-7-5
　　　d. kata-uta　　　　　　　　5-7-7
　　　e. sedooka　　　　　　　　5-7-7-5-7-7
　　　f. tanka　　　　　　　　　5-7-5-7-7

2.2. Octomoraic template

Austerlitz (1987) claims that pauses are an inherent part of the underlying metrical structure of haiku. Although lines in Japanese verse have traditionally been described as consisting of 5 or 7 moraic constituents, several researchers have concluded that lines actually consist of slots which correspond to 8-mora timing. Kozasa (1997) uses the term bimoraic tetrameter meaning a line consisting of four binary moraic feet. Bekku (1977) claims that a speaker reads a line in a four beat rhythm: 2 *haku* (moras) in one beat. Kogure and Miyashita (1999) analyze haiku lines as having 8 moraic slots that consist of two cola, which are defined as prosodic units containing two feet (Hammond 1987).

The common description of lines of Japanese verse as combinations of 5 or 7 moras merely describes the number of *uttered* moras. Lines are read with an inclusion of breaks, or silent moras, corresponding to a specific number of paused segments. In what follows, we demonstrate that 3 empty moras follow 5-mora utterances and 1 empty mora follows 7-mora utterances, making all lines structurally octomoraic.[2] We thus provide empirical evidence for the existence of silent constituents claimed to exist by scholars of Japanese literature.

2.3. Lehiste's phonetic study of haiku

Lehiste's interest in her 1997 study was to address claims about an isochronous unit of speech timing in Estonian. To show that Estonian is neither mora timed nor syllable timed, she compared readings of haiku in Japanese to readings of haiku written in Estonian, which unlike Japanese haiku counts syllables instead of moras.

Here, we specifically address her claims about the Japanese readings. Her results showed that 5-mora lines were strikingly equal in length and 7-mora lines were strikingly equal in length. Lehiste also examined the lengths of the pauses that occurred in the readings at the ends of lines. She observed that the average pause duration at the end of 5μ lines (419 msec) was longer than the average uttered mora (182 msec) and that average pause duration at the end of 7μ lines (119 msec) was shorter than the average uttered mora[3]. Lehiste noted that Austerlitz (1987) assigns a metrical function to pauses, and she hypothesized two functions that pauses could serve in the meter.

Function 1: Pauses constitute 1 additional mora

Function 2: Pauses provide flexibility in the overall timing of the onset of lines.

Lehiste discounts both hypotheses. Function 1 is denied because the pause after 5-mora lines was too long to be one mora, and after 7-mora lines the pause was too short to be one mora. Function 2 is denied because she observed no regularity between longest lines being followed by shortest pauses and shortest lines being followed by longest pauses. Her denial of these functions leaves at least two questions unanswered: 1. Why were the average pauses after 5-mora lines longer than those after 7-mora lines? and 2. How do we account for literary descriptions of haiku as having 8 moras per line?

Our study provides answers to these questions. We follow Lehiste's lead in metrical studies by using native speaker readings of Japanese meter to understand the kinds of prosodic alternations that occur in Japanese poetry. We conclude that pauses are an inherent part of the structure of Japanese meter.

3. Description of our study

We explain the function of pauses in Japanese verse and their varying lengths by proving the existence of an octomoraic template. Line duration in Japanese verse is regulated by alternately realizing lines as 5 uttered moras + 3 paused moras or as 7 uttered moras + 1 paused mora. While we would expect the average duration of 5 uttered moras to differ from the average duration of 7 uttered moras, assuming an underlying 8 mora template we would expect the average duration of *total lines* (uttered moras + paused moras) to be relatively equal. Crucially, we would expect a correlation between the measured durations of pauses and utterances and the number of moras hypothesized to exist in the underlying metrical structure.

3.1. Tanka for data

As mentioned above, we chose tanka verse types for our study. A tanka consists of 5 lines: The first three lines are the same as haiku, and the last two lines are 7-mora lines. An example tanka is shown in (4) which gives the uttered mora counts for each line. Our choice of tanka over haiku was motivated by our interest in the line-final pauses. Since pauses are inserted at the end of lines, pauses at the ends of the first four lines should be clearly measurable in recitation because they are immediately followed by the utterance of another line. Haiku provides only two measurable pause positions between the first and second, and second and third lines. So although the last lines of a tanka also end with a pause, we did not include them in our data because with no immediately following utterance it would be impossible to measure the duration of the silence.

(4) Tanka 5-line verse form. (Takuboku 1968)

> line 1. yawaraka ni   'softly'
> μ μ μ μ μ (5)
> line 2. tsumoreru yuki ni   'into the accumulated snow'
> μ μ μ μ μ μ μ (7)
> line 3. hoteru ho o   'blushing cheek'
> μ μ μ μ μ (5)
> line 4. uzumuru gotoki   'as if being buried'
> μ μ μ μ μ μ μ (7)
> line 5. koishite mitashi   'wish to fall in love'
> μ μ μ μ μ μ μ (7)

In (5), we provide a revised example of a tanka analyzed using the octomoraic template proposed by Kozasa (1997) and Bekku (1977). The first and the third lines have three moraic pauses at the end (* = pause), and the second and the fourth have monomoraic pauses. The last line also has a one-mora pause.

(5) Line1   ya   wa   ra   ka   ni   *   *   *
             μ   μ   μ   μ   μ   μ   μ   μ
     Line2   tsu mo   re   ru   yu   ki   ni   *
             μ   μ   μ   μ   μ   μ   μ   μ
     Line3   ho   te   ru   ho   o   *   *   *
             μ   μ   μ   μ   μ   μ   μ   μ
     Line4   u   zu   mu   ru   go   to   ki   *
             μ   μ   μ   μ   μ   μ   μ   μ
     Line5   ko   i   shi te   mi   ta   shi *
             μ   μ   μ   μ   μ   μ   μ   μ

The terminology we use for the remainder of our paper is introduced in (6). We call the uttered or pronounced moraic segments *utterance positions* (marked with μ above). The pauses at the end of lines are *pause positions* (marked with * above). Hereafter, *line* refers to both utterance positions and pause positions. A line and its structure based on these terms is illustrated in (6d).

The tanka we used in our experiment were taken from *Ware o aisuru uta* 'Love song to myself' by Takaboku Ishikawa (1886–1912) which contains

151 tanka. Subjects were given the printed forms of poems that were written in both *kanji* and *kana* symbols. *Kana* symbols are moraic, generally one symbol corresponds to one mora, but *kanji* symbols can correspond to one or two moras. Printed tanka are continuous and do not indicate line breaks, as in (7b).

(6) Terminology
    a. Utterance positions (Upos)
    b. Pause positions (Ppos)
    c. Line = Upos + Ppos or {[Utterance Positions]+[Pause Positions]}
    d.

Utterance Positions	Pause Positions

(7)   a. yawaraka ni
       tsumoreru yuki ni
       hoteru ho o
       uzumuru gotoki
       koishite mitashi

    b. やはらかに積もれる雪に熱てる頬を埋むるごとき恋してみたし

The printed tanka in (7b) has only three printed lines. The vertical lines are read from top to bottom and right to left. The first printed line comprises the first two metrical lines of tanka, the second printed line corresponds to the next two metrical lines of tanka, and the last printed line is the fifth metrical line. This particular division of lines is not the only one used in the book. We assume that the variation in printing was used to achieve a visually pleasing form on the page.

The fact that poems are not printed in a way that indicates the division of the lines in the tanka verse form allowed us to test for line break intuitions not indicated in the text. Further, the fact that the printed poems included *kanji* symbols allowed us to test hypotheses about moraic counts also not directly represented in the text.

3.2. Method

We conducted an experiment with five native speakers of Japanese, all of whom were graduate students at the University of Arizona. A subject's task was to read tanka aloud into a microphone that automatically records into CSL (Computerized Speech Lab Model 4300B Software Version 5X). Their instructions were to "read them as you usually would." The purpose of the test was explained following the completion of the recording. We collected recordings of subjects reading five different poems and measured the durations of utterances and following pauses for the first four lines.

4. Results

In this section we present our measurements of the durations of utterances and pauses for the first 4 lines of each tanka, which were lines containing 5μ, 7μ, 5μ and 7μ utterance positions respectively. We measured a total of 97 lines.

4.1. Mean durations of utterance positions (Upos)

Figure (8) shows the portion of the line (shaded) discussed.

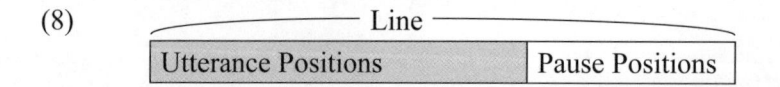

(8) ⸻ Line ⸻
| Utterance Positions | Pause Positions |

Although readers were not given instructions about how to read lines, and although readers did not hear each other read, the durations of 5-mora utterances across speakers were strikingly equal as were the durations of 7-mora utterances. Further, when we calculated the mean duration of moras for both 5 and 7-mora utterances, they were strikingly equal to each other. Average utterance durations appear in Table 1. M indicates the mean duration of the utterance and $M(\mu)$ indicates the mean duration of the averaged moras in the utterances. SD indicates standard deviation for M and $SD(\mu)$ indicates standard deviation for $M(\mu)$. All values shown here are given in milliseconds (msec).

Table 1.

	5-mora utterance	7-mora utterance
M	801	1060
SD	81.1	134
M(μ)	160	152
SD(μ)	16.2	19.2

These data suggest that the timing of uttered moras is strictly regulated in the recitation of tanka. The fact that the standard deviations for the mean durations of utterance lengths (81 msec and 134 msec) are smaller than the length of an average mora (160 msec for 5 uttered moras and 152 msec for 7 uttered moras) tells us that the variation among speakers in the overall timing of an utterance does not standardly vary as much as the length of a mora. In other words, a reader should not utter a line containing 5μ Upos in such a way that it could be mistaken as having 6μ Upos or a line containing 7μ Upos as having 8μ Upos.

4.2 Mean duration of pause positions (Ppos)

Figure (9) shows the portion of the line (shaded) discussed in this section, and the data appear in Table 2. Again, all values are given in milliseconds (msec).

(9) Line: Utterance Positions | **Pause Positions**

Table 2.

	pause after 5 μ utterance	pause after 7 μ utterance
M	424	134
SD	138	78.7
M(μ)	142	134
SD(μ)	45.9	78.7

When we measured line-final pauses, we found, as Lehiste did, that the average duration of pauses after 5μ Upos (424 msec) was much longer than the average duration of pauses after 7μ Upos (134 msec). However, the duration

182 *Deborah Cole and Mizuki Miyashita*

of pauses after 5 μ utterances were strikingly equal across speakers (standard deviation = 138 msec), and the duration of pauses after 7 μ utterances were even more equal (standard deviation = 78.7 msec). Assuming an octomoraic template, the mean mora length for pauses after 5 μ utterances was calculated by dividing the mean pause duration (424 msec) by 3. The mean mora length after a 7 μ utterance is the same as the mean duration because we assume there is only a single mora pause.

4.3. Mean duration of lines

Figure (10) shows the portion of the line discussed in this section.

(10) Line
| Utterance Positions | Pause Positions |

The results of combining the durations of the Upos with the Ppos to measure the duration of whole lines are given in Table 3.

Table 3

	5 μ utterance + pause	7 μ utterance + pause
M	1216	1195
SD	166	162
M(μ)	152	149
SD(μ)	20.7	20.3

Here we present the results of calculating the mean duration and standard deviation for the total lines having either 5μ Upos and 7μ Upos. Mean mora lengths were calculated in all cases by dividing the mean duration of line lengths by 8, under the assumption that tanka have an octomoraic template. When the pauses are included in the measurement of line duration, 5 mora lines and 7 mora lines are strikingly equal (1216 and 1195 msecs respectively). Mean mora length for these lines is also strikingly equal (152 and 149 msecs).

The data in Table 3 show the surprising result that 5-mora lines are slightly longer on average than 7-mora lines, a situation that would not have a satisfactory explanation if lines were analyzed as only having the 5 or 7 uttered moras. Our analysis of 5 mora lines being followed by a 3 mora pause offers a preliminary explanation for why this might be the case, i.e., both 7 mora lines and 5 mora lines really have 8 moras worth of structure that need to be represented in the reading.

4.4. Showing the relationship between underlying moras and measured durations

The scatter plot in (11) shows 194 measurements: 97 measurements of utterance durations of both 5 and 7 moras and 97 measurements of the pause durations occurring after each of these utterances. Assuming an octomoraic template, we wanted to see if the measurements of the pauses would correlate with an analysis of pauses after 7 uttered moras being 1 mora long and pauses after 5 uttered moras being 3 moras long. The x-axis shows the written mora counts for lines (5 and 7) and assumed mora counts for the pauses (3 and 1) for the lines of tanka in our data set. The y-axis shows the duration measurements of these four categories in milliseconds.

(11) Plotting mora counts against measured durations

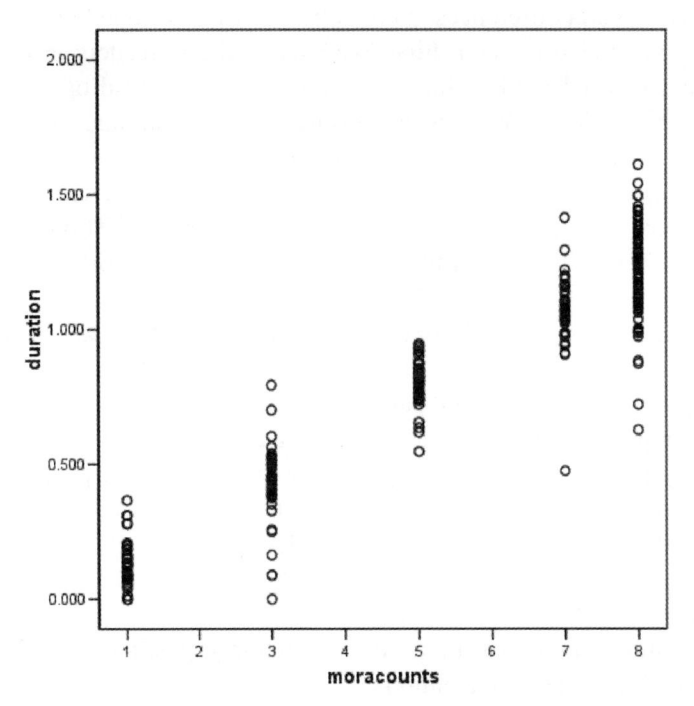

The scatter plot shows a positive correlation between the number of moras claimed by Japanese scholars and theorists to be in the meter and the measurements of the pause durations (1 and 3 mora counts) and utterance durations (5 and 7 mora counts). The clustering of the measurements as well as the linear increase in duration measurements over equal intervals are evidence that pauses after 5 uttered moras are structurally 3 moraic units, and pauses after 7 uttered moras are structurally only one moraic unit.

4.5. Discussion

Our study of tanka readings by native speakers of Japanese found a correlation between the hypothesized number of underlying moras and the duration of the spoken or paused unit. We also showed that when lines are analyzed as including paused moras, they show a tendency towards equal durations, regardless of whether the number of utterance positions written in the text is 5 or 7 moras. Our data support the existence of an octomoraic template, which includes functional pauses in Japanese meter and provide concrete evidence for the claims mentioned in 2.2.

There were several differences in our approach from the one Lehiste used in her study of Japanese meter. First, we used multiple readers instead of one. Second, we used the five-line verse form, tanka, instead of the three-line haiku form, which enabled us to measure two non-final lines of 5 and 7 moraic utterances per poem while avoiding an effect of lengthening at the end of the poem. Crucially, because we posited an octomoraic template for Japanese meter, we were able to answer the unanswered questions left by Lehiste's (1997) rejection of her two hypothesized functions for pauses (see 2.3).

Recall that Lehiste rejected Function 1, which stated that pauses constitute one additional mora, because the pauses after 5-mora lines were longer than the average uttered mora and pauses after the 7-mora lines were shorter than the average uttered mora. An analysis of the line as having 8 moras explains why pauses after 5 uttered moras were longer than pauses after 7 uttered moras, and our data corroborates Lehiste's observation. We have therefore modified her statement of Function 1.

Function 1 (revised):
Pauses constitute 1 additional mora after 7 utterance positions, but 3 additional moras after 5 utterance positions.

We also accept a line-regulating function for pauses. Lehiste proposed and rejected the hypothesis that pauses serve to provide flexibility for the overall timing of the onset of lines. Our data supports the following revision of Function 2.

Function 2 (revised):
Pauses function to keep line durations equal, regardless of the number of utterance positions.

Pauses, then, function in Japanese meter to fill in the silent moras not written in the text and make lines have an overall duration of 8 moras.

5. More support for the octomoraic template

In this section we provide further support for the existence of the octomoraic template and discuss the relevance of pauses to metrical theories in general.

5.1. The possibility of an additional mora in traditional poems

In some tanka poems, variations of the 5-mora 7-mora patterns can occur. For example, in lines whose template calls for 7 Upos, the poet can write 8 moras to be uttered, and speakers can easily parse this by omitting a pause. However, more than 8 written moras are unparseable as a line of tanka. Lines whose template calls for 5 Upos can have up to 6 uttered moras, but no more. Presumably this is because more than one additional mora would make a 5 Upos line indistinguishable from a 7 Upos line. We included several samples of 6 mora lines in our initial tests and as we expected, the utterance duration was longer than the average utterance duration for 5-mora lines and the pause duration was shorter (these 6-mora lines were *not* included in the data sets presented above). Further, overall line duration appeared to remain equal, as preliminary investigations showed that line length was well within one standard deviation of the 5-mora lines we measured. This phenomenon needs further investigation, but it appears to support the existence of a fixed octomoraic template within which variations on numbers of Upos can occur.

5.2. The shifting of pause positions in 7-mora lines

Another type of support for the octomoraic template is addressed in this section. Our results support the existence of a pause after a 7-mora line corresponding to a single mora. However, in section 2.3, we noted that Lehiste denied Function 1 because average pauses after 7-mora lines were too short to be one mora. We propose that pauses after 7-mora utterances can be shorter than the average uttered mora because of the possibility for the pause position to shift in a line.

All of the 7-mora lines in the tanka read in our study contained a pause that occurred at the end of the line. One type of variation in 7-mora lines is that a pause can occur in non-final positions. A sample line where this shifting occurs is shown below. A paused mora is indicated by *, which may be realized at the beginning of a line as in (12) or in the middle as in (13).

(12) pause at the beginning
    line: * en no u e na ru   'above the balcony'
    template: (μ)$\mu\mu$ μ $\mu\mu$ μ μ

(13) pause in the middle (variation)
    line: en no * u e na ru   'above the balcony'
    template: $\mu\mu$ μ (μ) μ μ μ μ

In this line, the pause must occur either at the beginning or in the middle of the line. The line's syntactic constituency is the reason for this phenomenon.

(14) en-no   uenaru
     balcony-genitive locative

This line contains two constituents: a 3-mora element and a 4-mora element. Kogure and Miyashita (1999) claim that in haiku a colon boundary coincides with a word boundary, as shown in (15).

(15) $\{[(*\mu)(\mu\mu)]_{Wd}\}_{Colon} \{[(\mu\mu)(\mu\mu)]_{Wd}\}_{Colon}$

This colon boundary separates the line evenly, and the pause can occur only at the edge of the colon in which the 3-mora phrase occurs, either before the 3-mora constituent or directly after it.

When a line consists of 3-mora constituent *followed* by a 4-mora constituent as in (15), no pause is measured between second and third lines. In our experiment, we only selected 7-mora lines that consisted of 4-mora constituents followed by 3-mora constituents. If our data had included haiku with 7-mora lines that allow a pause at the beginning of the line, then readers would not count a pause at the end of lines. We would then expect that the mean mora length of the pause after 7-mora utterances would be less than monomoraic. These constituency facts offer further support for the existence of an octomoraic template and may explain why Lehiste found pauses at the end of 7-mora lines to be shorter than the average mora.

5.3. Defining meter in a prominence insensitive language

Metrical studies are based on the idea that the prosodic structures already present in language are exploited in meter (Hanson and Kiparsky 1996, Lehiste 1992). In traditional Japanese meter, the relevant prosodic structure is the mora. If meter is the mapping of language to the metrical template, which results in alternations between prosodic structures (as in stressed vs. unstressed syllables in English meter), what is alternating in tanka? This study shows that a paused mora is the unit that alternates with the uttered mora in the prominence insensitive meter of Japanese.

5.4. An analogy to timing in music

In various cultures, poems are referred to as songs. In fact, the word *tanka* means short song (tan 'short' + ka 'song').[4] In songs, rhythm provides alternations between sound and silence. Oehrle (1989) discusses the relevance of rhythm to English meter and speech timing. He states that different underlying time signatures result from the inclusion of rests (as opposed to simply marking every beat with sound). For example, four-beat time can be realized as three quarter notes and one quarter rest. We schematize this in (16) using the following notation: (• for quarter note, * for a quarter rest, and | for measure division).

(16) Four beat time realized as 3 quarter notes and 1 rest.
|•••*|•••*|

If you tap or count this rhythm, you get 1, 2, 3, rest 1, 2, 3, rest. However, if you ignore this rest, you get 3 beat time resulting in waltz. The beat is then 1, 2, 3 1, 2, 3, as illustrated in (17) below.

(17) Ignoring the rest results in 3 beat time
|•••|•••|

In tanka, the alternations between uttered and paused moras constitute the meter. Ignoring the pause in tanka destroys the underlying meter, i.e., the octomoraic template. Our study shows that speakers are sensitive to these alternations and adjust their timing by increments in the range of 121–156 msec to create lines (similar to the | divisions above) that are surprisingly equal in length.

5.5. Future research

This study shows that pausing can be used as a basic metrical unit in a language that does not mark prominence with stress. From this we propose two contrasting hypotheses to be tested in future research.

(18) Hypothesis A: Pauses function structurally in meter cross-linguistically.
Hypothesis B: Pauses function structurally in meter only in languages without stress systems.

If Hypothesis A is correct, the pauses that occur in the performance of meters written in languages with stress, like the empty beats at the ends of lines of English quatrains[5] for example, could be shown to serve a structural function as well. If Hypothesis B is correct, the pauses in English quatrains would not serve a structural function but would be simply a byproduct of performance. Methodologies for investigating meter that view performance data as irrelevant start with the assumption that Hypothesis B is correct.

The results of this study, however, lead us to be most interested in investigating Hypothesis A. To be tested, Hypothesis A relies on methodologies that consult native speaker intuitions in metrical performance. Although Lehiste's study that we used as a starting point for this paper was technically about speech timing and not metrical structure, she has argued elsewhere (1992) for phonetic approaches to the study of meter:

> Phonetic measurements of utterances are the only aspect of language directly subject to observation; and experimental phonetics provides a point at which metrical theories can be tested with respect to at least one kind of objective reality. (Lehiste 1992: 98)

We have shown here that native speaker intuitions about the structure of poetic meter can be reliably consulted by analyzing performances. We have also shown that determining whether or not pauses function as part of the metrical system requires listening to readers' performances of texts, since pauses are not indicated within the written versions of the texts. We believe that phonetic approaches as laid out by Lehiste and continued here will broaden our understanding of the structures in language that function in meter as well as of speaker competence in manipulating these structures. Although it can be argued that some older traditions, like Old English verse, cannot be subjected to native speaker readings, we have shown that in the case of at least one living verse form, a performance based analysis gives the facts of traditional Japanese meter a more satisfactory explanation than a purely text-based one.

In future research, we will investigate further the tendency towards isochronous line lengths. This investigation may provide some insight into the controversy of why people perceive Japanese to be mora timed, but in spontaneous speech speakers produce moras that are timed in only a relatively regular way (Warner and Arai 2001). It may be that by crystallizing its suprasgmental system in the structure of its traditional poetry (Lehiste 1997), a language makes "salient" (Hayes and MacEachern 1998) precisely the structures that are needed in establishing that language as a "psychological reality" (Ochs 1990) in learners.

6. Conclusion

We conclude that the template for Japanese meter has 8 moraic slots. A line has either 5 or 7 utterance positions. Lines containing 5 utterance positions are followed by 3 pause positions, and lines containing 7 utterance positions are followed by 1 pause position. Variation in meter is achieved by varying the number of utterance positions in a line and shifting the utterance positions within a line. Silent moras function as part of the template to make all lines have a duration of 8 moras.

Further, our study supports Lehiste's claim (1992) that phonetic information is necessary for testing metrical theories. In this, we see traditional linguistic methodology, i.e., consulting native speaker intuitions, as foundational to metrical studies instead of seeing metrics as purely text-based. Further, whereas metrical studies following Halle and Keyser (1971) claim that metrics is an account of the poet's competence, our study suggests that metrics is also an account of reader competence, and that this competence is relatively equivalent across readers, at least in the case of reading tanka. Finally, we see the shift to phonetic data over purely text-based data as a recognition of poetry's oral history (Foley 1988), which expands the field of metrics to include analysis of non-written songs in cultures whose literatures still have strong ties with oral tradition (such as Fitzgerald's (1998) treatment of meter in Tohono O'odham). This shift opens the door for innovative methodologies in the study of meter and pushes metrical theory to account for a broader range of data.

Notes

* We would like to thank Therese de Vet, Colleen Fitzgerald, Mike Hammond, Jason Haugen, Rachel Hayes, Jane Hill, Kumi Kogure, Ilse Lehiste, Stephen Liebowitz, Andrea Massar, Marina Tarlinskaja, Timothy Vance, Natasha Warner, Jessica Weinberg, Ofelia Zepeda, and an anonymous reviewer for helpful discussion and suggestions. All mistakes and errors are ours.
1. The haiku verse form originated by dropping the last two lines from the tanka verse form.
2. See Homma (1991) and Asano (2002) for recent studies of tanka.
3. Standard deviation for 5μ lines = 126 msec, and for 7μ lines = 172 msec
4. Similarly, in Nahuatl, the word for poetry is *inxo:chitl incuicatl* meaning 'DET flower DET song'. "This is a so-called 'difrasismo' or ceremonial couplet where the two go together to make a metaphor that means a third thing." (Jane Hill, personal communication.)
5. The kind of pauses we refer to are like those that occur in nursery rhymes as in: Hickory Dickory Dock (pause), The mouse ran up the clock (pause).
See also Hayes and MacEachern (1998).

References

Asano, Makiko
    2002   Studies in Japanese prosody. PhD. dissertation, Harvard University.

Austerlitz, R.
    1987   The Japanese five- and seven-syllable line. *Bochumer Jahrbuch Ostasienforschung* 10: 77–81.

Bekku, Sadanori
    1977   *Nihongo no Rizumu*. Tokyo: Kodansha.

Bonvillian, Nancy
    1997   *Language, Culture, and Communication: The Meaning of Messages*. Upper Saddle River, New Jersey: Prentice-Hall, Inc.

Fitzgerald, Colleen M.
    1998   The meter of Tohono O'odham songs. *International Journal of American Linguistics* 64 (1): 1–36.

Foley, John Miles
    1988   *The Theory of Oral Composition: History and Methodology*. Indianapolis: Indiana University Press.

Halle, M., and S. Keyser
    1971   *English Stress: Its Form, Its Growth, and Its Role in Verse*. New York: Harper & Row.

Hammond, Michael
    1987   Hungarian cola. *Phonology* 4: 267–269.

Hanson, K., and P. Kiparsky
    1996   A parametric theory of poetic meter. *Language* 72: 287–335.

Hayes, Bruce
    1984   The phonology of rhythm in English verse. *Linguistic Inquiry* 15: 33–74.
    1989   Compensatory lengthening in moraic phonology. *Linguistic Inquiry* 20: 253–306.

Hayes, Bruce, and Margaret MacEachern
    1998   Quatrain form in English folk verse. *Language* 74: 473–507.

Homma, Yayoi
    1991   The rhythm of *tanka*, short Japanese poems: Read in prose style and contest style. In *Proceedings of the XIIth International Congress of Phonetic Sciences* 2, 314–317, Aix-en-Provence, France.

Issa [Kobayashi, Issa]
    1997   *The Spring of My Life and Selected Haiku*. Translated by Sam Hamill. Boston: Shambhala Publications, Inc.

Katada, F.
    1990   On the representation of moras: Evidence from a language game. *Linguistic Inquiry* 21: 641–646.

Kiparsky, Paul, and Gilbert Youmans (eds.)
1989   *Phonetics and Phonology: Rhythm and Meter*, San Diego: Academic Press, Inc.

Kogure, Kumi, and Mizuki Miyashita
1999   Audible silence: Silent moras in Japanese verse. In *Proceedings of Western Conference On Linguistics* 98, 258–272, California State University, Fresno.

Kozasa, Tomoko
1997   Rhythm or meter: Moraic tetrameter in Japanese poetry. Ms., California State University, Fresno.

Lehiste, I.
1992   The phonetics of metrics. *Empirical Studies of the Arts* 10 (2): 95–120.
1997   The phonetic realization of the haiku form in Estonian poetry, compared to Japanese. In *Speech Production and Language in Honor of Osamu Fujimura*, S. Kiritani, H. Hirose and H. Fujisaki (eds.), 241–249. Berlin: Mouton de Gruyter.

Ochs, Elinor
1990   Indexicality and socialization. In *Cultural Psychology*, James Stigler, Richard A Shweder, and Gilbert Herdt (eds.), 287–308. Cambridge: Cambridge University Press.

Oehrle, Dick
1989   Temporal structures in verse design. In *Phonetics and Phonology: Rhythm and Meter*. Paul Kiparsky and Gilbert Youmans (eds.), 87–120. San Diego: Academic Press, Inc.

Shibatani, Masayoshi
1990   *The Languages of Japan*. Cambridge: Cambridge University Press.

Takuboku [Ishikawa, Takuboku]
1968   *Nihon no shishu 2: Ishikawa Takuboku shishu*. Tokyo: Kadokawa Shoten.

Warner, Natasha, and Takayuki Arai
2001   The role of the mora in the timing of spontaneous Japanese speech. *The Journal of the Acoustical Society of America* 109 (3): 1144–1156.

Zepeda, Ofelia
1995   *Ocean Power: Poems from the Desert*. Tucson, Arizona: University of Arizona Press.

Iambic meter in Somali*

Colleen M. Fitzgerald

1. Introduction

Much research in Generative Meter focuses on the manifestations of metrical structure in stress languages such as English (Kiparsky 1975, 1977; Hayes 1989), Finnish (Kiparsky 1968, Hanson and Kiparsky 1996), Spanish (Piera 1980), Middle English (Golston 1998), and Tohono O'odham (Fitzgerald 1995, 1998). The metrical structure of these languages can generally be determined from the stress patterns of words, which then interact with the stress patterns in poetic meter. An interesting counterpoint to stress languages comes from pitch accent languages like Japanese, where accent is unrelated to metrical structure. Instead, support for metrical structure comes from elsewhere in the phonology of Japanese. In this way, the meter of verse is one way to provide evidence for the bimoraic foot as the relevant foot type for Japanese (Poser 1990, Kogure and Miyashita 1999, Tanihara 2001), even without rhythmic stress.

This paper examines poetic meter in another pitch language, Somali. The data is drawn from a verse form in Somali that counts moras, known as the *masafo*. While the *masafo* has traditionally been analyzed as regulating half-line length in terms of moras, I argue that this is not the appropriate characterization. Rather, Somali verse is considerably more varied in the types of half-lines that actually occur, and there is no decisive evidence favoring a 9 mora half-line. Instead, I claim that Somali verse provides evidence supporting metrical structure, and that the type of extensive variation is exactly what is predicted if the half-line is characterized in terms of quantitative iambic feet.

The basic structure of the paper is as follows. First, I present background on prosodic phonology, specific to Somali and more general theoretic assumptions. Second, I turn to the basics of the *masafo*, the mora-counting verse form analyzed in this paper. Third, I compare two parsings of the meter, one with iambs, the other with moraic trochees, and show that the iambic parse is superior.

2. Prosodic phonology

Somali prosodic phonology is oriented around the syllable and the mora, although there is little, if any discussion of whether feet are relevant for the language. While this section does not argue for feet, it does establish the basic prosody of Somali as quantity sensitive. Quantity sensitivity is a hallmark of two types of metrical feet, the iamb and the moraic trochee (Hayes 1995).

Somali allows short and long for both vowels and consonants, but only vowels are moraic. Short vowels contribute one mora, while long vowels and diphthongs contribute two moras.[1] The prosody is based on a pitch system, more similar to Japanese pitch accent than English stress (for example, pitch accent is not rhythmic). The paradigms below illustrate how accent assignment depends on mora count, and is assigned on the basis of grammatical information. Nouns that are masculine (or singular) have a penultimate mora accented, while those that are feminine (or plural) accent the final mora (Hyman 1981, Orwin 1996). The generalization depends on the assumption that coda consonants are not moraic.

(1)   Penultimate accent   Final accent
    a.   ínan   'boy'   inán   'girl'
    b.   nácas   'stupid man'   nacás   'stupid woman'
    c.   bálli   'water reservoir'   ballí   'water reservoirs'
    d.   daméer   'young donkey, masc'   dameér   'young donkey, fem.'
    e.   éi   'dog'   eí   'dogs'

Words with a short vowel surface with a high accent, as in (1a–c). Words with long vowels and diphthongs, (1d–e), surface with either a falling accent (high accent on the first mora) or rising accent (high accent on the second mora).

These specific aspects of Somali prosody are put into a larger context now, by outlining some general assumptions about metrical structure (following the asymmetric typology of Hayes 1987, 1995) with particular regard to foot shape and the construction of feet. The asymmetric foot typology consists of three feet, the iamb, the moraic trochee, and the syllabic trochee. The first two are quantitative, while the syllabic trochee consists of two syllables and syllable weight is unimportant. An iambic foot may take three possible shapes, where parentheses indicate the boundaries of the foot: (LH), (H), and (LL). Feet are always maximized when possible, so that (LH) is better than L(H). Only two possible shapes are allowed for the moraic trochee: (H) and (LL). It is also important to note that two types of constituents are disallowed; *(HL) and *(L) are not well-formed feet in the Hayesian typology.

This foot typology is generally used to assign stress patterns to words cross-linguistically. Thus, iambic feet typically have a stress on the final element of the foot (LH́, LĹ or H́). Trochaic feet typically stress the initial element of the foot, whether quantity sensitive (ĹL or H́) or not (σ́σ). For our purposes, stress is irrelevant to the metrical shape of Somali verse. Instead, what matters is the quantitative shape of the foot. The opposite state of affairs is obtained in English iambic pentameter, where quantity has typically been given no status in the iambic foot, except for resolution. The approach here thus differs from traditional accounts of English meter in its treatment of the iamb, but is similar to traditional accounts of the classical meters of Latin and Greek.[2]

3. The *masafo* verse

The *masafo* verse is one of a number of alliterative verse forms used in Somali. A caesura divides each line into two half-lines; these half-lines are the basic unit for this verse form.[3] In addition to the line division marked by the caesura, alliteration also signals the internal line division into half-lines (named "A" and "B"). The alliteration of half-lines has been argued to show that half-lines are constituents, and that they form the constituent "line" together (Fabb 1999). The lines directly below are alliterated in d, as indicated by underlining. Alliterative elements are most often content words rather than function words.

(2)   The beginning of *The Sayid's Reply*[4]:

Ogaadeen ha ii **d**irin, **d**acwad baan ka leeyahay
War, **d**uul haad Amchaaraha, adiga Kaa ma **d**ayayee
Deyntaan ku leeyahay, **d**un ha iiga qaadin e
Wuchuu aniga iga **d**ilo, **d**iyo hayga siinin e

The four lines display consistent alliteration (most often of the half-line initial element), but inconsistent length in terms of the line and the half-line. The rest of this section attempts to establish the regularities of this verse and the best way to characterize the verse.

196   *Colleen M. Fitzgerald*

The approach here involves an analysis of the scansion of 442 *masafo* lines (884 half-lines) by the Sayid, Maxamad Cabdulle Xasan (texts from Jaamac Cumar Ciise 1974). Short vowels were scanned as light, while long vowels and diphthongs were scanned as heavy.

While the *masafo* is commonly described as having half-lines with nine moras, the actual length varies considerably. The chart in (3) gives the mora count for all 884 half-lines of the corpus. There is a distinct preference for either 9 or 10 moras, as 75% of the half-lines consist of either 9 or 10 moras. Overall half-line length ranges from 6 to 15 moras.

(3)   Overall mora count in half-lines

# of Moras	Total Half-lines	% of total
6	2	.2%
7	5	.6%
8	46	5.2%
9	380	43%
10	283	32%
11	105	11.9%
12	39	4.4%
13	16	1.8%
14	7	.8%
15	1	.1%

These numbers can be broken down based on whether we look at the first half-line (A) or the second half-line (B) portion of the line, which give somewhat different results, as in (4). These numbers are interesting because the two types of half-lines do not behave identically. Here the distribution is somewhat skewed – half-lines A tend to be somewhat longer, and half-lines B tend to be somewhat shorter. What this suggests is that there is a dependency between the two half-lines, such that the two half-lines appear to compensate each other in mora count. There is also a stronger preference for 9 mora lines among half-lines B than half-lines A.

The chart in (5) provides a summary for the number of moras for the entire line. If 9 mora half-lines were the norm, then the norm for full lines would be predicted as 18 moras. However, such lines constitute just under one-quarter of all lines. In fact, it is more likely that lines will have 19 or

20 moras per line. These three line lengths (18, 19, and 20 moras) make up 78.1% of all lines. There is definitely a clustering around a particular size, but the distribution is spread among various lengths.

(4) Mora count by half-line type (A versus B)

Half-line A	% of A	# of Moras	Half-line B	% of B
0	0%	6	2	.5%
0	0%	7	5	1.1%
7	1.6%	8	39	8.8%
164	37.1%	9	216	48.9%
154	34.8%	10	129	29.2%
59	13.3%	11	46	10.4%
34	7.7%	12	5	1.1%
16	3.6%	13	0	0%
7	1.6%	14	0	0%
1	.3%	15	0	0%

(5) Mora Count Total by Line

Full Line Total – MORA		
Moras	Total # of Lines	% of Full Lines
17	7	1.6%
18	102	23.1%
19	124	28.1%
20	119	26.9%
21	68	15.4%
22	16	3.6%
23	6	1.3%

The numbers in (5) suggest that half-lines should be viewed in the context of the line (a similar argument is made on the basis of alliteration in Fabb 1999). There seems to be a *compensatory relationship* between the length of the two half-lines. The previous charts have all shown general length trends for half-lines, lines, and the two half-line types. In (6), the particular combinations are shown by frequency of occurrence, showing which half-line As combine most frequently with which half-line Bs.

(6) Half-lines A and B combinations by mora count

Half-line A	Half-line B	Total # Moras	Lines Total	% of total	
9	9	18	93	21%	
10	9	19	75	17%	60.6% of total
10	10	20	54	12.2%	
9	10	19	46	10.4%	
11	9	20	28	6.3%	
11	10	21	22	5%	
10	11	21	20	4.5%	
9	11	20	18	4.1%	30.3% of total
12	8	20	17	3.8%	
12	9	21	11	2.5%	
13	8	21	11	2.5%	
11	11	22	7	1.6%	
10	8	18	4	0.9%	
9	8	17	4	0.9%	
8	10	18	3	0.7%	
13	9	22	3	0.7%	
9	12	21	3	0.7%	
8	9	17	3	0.7%	
14	9	23	3	0.7%	
12	10	22	3	0.7%	
11	7	18	2	0.5%	9.1% of total
12	7	19	2	0.5%	
14	8	22	2	0.5%	
10	12	22	1	0.2%	
12	11	23	1	0.2%	
13	6	19	1	0.2%	
13	10	23	1	0.2%	
14	6	20	1	0.2%	
14	7	21	1	0.2%	
8	12	20	1	0.2%	
15	8	23	1	0.2%	

The chart in (6) gives the half-line A length, the half-line B length, the total mora count, the total number of lines, and the percent of the overall total. The right hand side column totals the percentages for each horizontal block: the top block is combinations that are at least 10% of the overall total, the middle block consists of combinations over 1% (but not more than 10%) of the overall total, and the bottom block is the remaining combinations, all under 1% of the total count. This chart suggests the dependency between half-line types that tries to maintain a steady number of overall moras. For example, there are five different attested ways to construct a 20 mora line out of differently sized half-lines. For example, when the first half-line is 10, half-line B would have 10 moras. When half-line A has 11 moras, the second half-line would have 9 moras. A half-line A of 12 moras would be followed by a half-line B of 8 moras. These five different half-line combinations make up more than a quarter of the overall total. If half-lines have a consistent moraic length (for example, 9 moras), how can we explain this odd clustering of combinations?

This section has detailed the facts on mora count, as this has been the prototypical way to describe the *masafo* meter. There are many meters that have a fair amount of divergence from the ideal metrical shape. However, if we treat the *masafo* as a 9 mora half-line, there is too much divergence. The prototypical shape for the half-line occurs less than half the time (43% of the half-lines consist of 9 moras). The traditional conception of the half-line as a 9 mora unit is weakened by proliferation of half-lines of different sizes. Furthermore, the suggestion that there is a compensatory relationship between half-lines also argues against a consistent 9 mora half-line as the proper abstract unit. In other words, the facts in this section suggest that the there is too much divergence for 9 moras to be the appropriate abstract shape of this verse type.

4. An iambic analysis of the *masafo*

This range in possible *masafo* half-lines has lead to the postulation of different templates by different researchers (for example, Banti and Giannattasio 1996; Fabb 1997, Orwin 2001). I claim that an examination of the surface properties of this meter show that the *masafo* is an iambic meter. In fact, I claim that variation itself provides at least one argument in favor of the iambic analysis.

Different predictions for length are made by the two quantitative feet, the moraic trochee and the iamb. Moraic trochees always consist of two moras, either one heavy or two light syllables. The line length in (7) shows that the overall mora count depends on the number of feet.

(7) Moraic trochee predictions for a half-line:
a. 4 feet per half-line (8 moras total): (μμ)(μμ)(μμ)(μμ)
b. 5 feet per half-line (10 moras total): (μμ)(μμ)(μμ)(μμ)(μμ)

The predictions made by iambic footing allows for more variation because iambs can consist of either 2 or 3 moras per foot. An iamb can be a light-light sequence, a light-heavy sequence, or a single heavy syllable. Assuming that there are four feet, and two possible sizes, this gives us five possible line lengths.

(8) Iambic predictions for 4 feet per half-line:
a. 8 moras: (μμ)(μμ)(μμ)(μμ)
b. 9 moras: (μμμ)(μμ)(μμ)(μμ)
c. 10 moras: (μμμ)(μμμ)(μμ)(μμ)
d. 11 moras: (μμμ)(μμμ)(μμμ)(μμ)
e. 12 moras: (μμμ)(μμμ)(μμμ)(μμμ)

The comparison between (7) and (8) suggests two observations, both of which favor an iambic analysis of the *masafo*. First, if we view metrical feet as determining the number of positions per line, iambs offer a better way to have a consistent number of metrical positions. All the example lines in (8) consist of four iambic feet; this delivers five different line lengths. In contrast, the bimoraic size of the moraic trochee means that the variation must in part come from a variable number of feet. This would require a verse type without a fixed number of metrical positions (such meters do exist, as in Tohono O'odham meter in Fitzgerald (1995, 1998)). Second, a fixed number of metrical feet (four feet per half-line) predicts that half-lines will vary from 8 to 12 moras. An analysis with four iambic feet predicts the half-line length of 84% of the half-lines.

The next factor to look at is how light and heavy syllables are ordered line-internally. The half-lines schematized in (7) and (8) are abstract and less concerned with order than with how many moras in each foot. The next chart, in (9), looks at half-line types in terms of how light and heavy syllables occur sequentially. This shows that the prosodic organization of *masafo* lines is given a better parse under an iambic analysis than a moraic trochee analysis.

The chart in (9) consists of half-line types with at least 10 tokens. This represents 586 half-lines, or 66% of the total. Each half-line type is determined by ignoring word boundaries, and instead, focusing on the sequencing of heavies and lights within a half-line. Overall, there are 173 total half-line types and 93 of these types consist of only a single half-line token.

The first column of the chart gives the shape of each half-line type (with at least 10 tokens), followed by the actual number of token half-lines. The "iambic" column (and the two columns following it) shows how iambic feet parse the line, how many feet per line, and how many syllables cannot be footed. The final three columns repeat the same information, but using moraic trochees as the foot.[5]

(9) Competing metrical parses of half-line types

Half-Line	#	Iambic	Feet	σ	Moraic Trochee	Feet	σ
LLHLHH	62	(LL)(H)(LH)(H)	4	0	(LL)(H)L(H)(H)	4	1
LLHLHLL	59	(LL)(H)(LH)(LL)	4	0	(LL)(H)L(H)(LL)	4	1
LLLLLHH	43	(LL)(LL)(LH)(H)	4	0	(LL)(LL)L(H)(H)	4	1
LHLLLHH	38	(LH)(LL)(LH)(H)	4	0	L(H)(LL)L(H)(H)	4	2
LLLLLHLL	36	(LL)(LL)(LH)(LL)	4	0	(LL)(LL)L(H)(LL)	4	1
LLHLLLH	28	(LL)(H)(LL)(LH)	4	0	(LL)(H)(LL)L(H)	4	1
LHHLHH	28	(LH)(H)(LH)(H)	4	0	L(H)(H)L(H)(H)	4	2
LHHLHLL	23	(LH)(H)(LH)(LL)	4	0	L(H)(H)L(H)(LL)	4	2
HLLLHH	23	(H)(LL)(LH)(H)	4	0	(H)(LL)L(H)(H)	4	1
LLHLHLH	22	(LL)(H)(LH)(LH)	4	0	(LL)(H)L(H)L(H)	4	2
HHLHH	22	(H)(H)(LH)(H)	4	0	(H)(H)L(H)(H)	4	1
LLHLLLLL	21	(LL)(H)(LL)(LL)L	4	1	(LL)(H)(LL)(LL)L	4	1
LHHLHLH	21	(LH)(H)(LH)(LH)	4	0	L(H)(H)L(H)L(H)	4	3
HLLLHLL	21	(H)(LL)(LH)(LL)	4	0	(H)(LL)L(H)(LL)	4	1
LLLHHL	20	(LL)(LH)(H)L	3	1	(LL)L(H)(H)L	3	2
LLLHLHH	19	(LL)(LH)(LH)(H)	4	0	(LL)L(H)L(H)(H)	4	2
LHLLLHLL	15	(LH)(LL)(LH)(LL)	4	0	L(H)(LL)L(H)(LL)	4	2
HHLHLL	15	(H)(H)(LH)(LL)	4	0	(H)(H)L(H)(LL)	4	1
LLLHLHLH	13	(LL)(LH)(LH)(LH)	4	0	(LL)L(H)L(H)L(H)	4	3
LLLLLHLH	12	(LL)(LL)(LH)(LH)	4	0	(LL)(LL)L(H)L(H)	4	2
LHHLLLH	12	(LH)(H)(LL)(LH)	4	0	L(H)(H)(LL)L(H)	4	2
HLHLHH	12	(H)(LH)(LH)(H)	4	0	(H)L(H)L(H)(H)	4	2
LLHLLLLH	11	(LL)(H)(LL)(LL)(H)	5	0	(LL)(H)(LL)(LL)(H)	5	0
LLLHLHLL	10	(LL)(LH)(LH)(LL)	4	0	(LL)L(H)L(H)(LL)	4	2

Iambic footing gives fairly consistent results. Only two half-line types do not parse evenly into feet, and these two types only have a single unfooted syllable. Second, almost all half-line types consist of 4 feet (1 type is 3 feet, 1 type is 5 feet). So iambic footing allows most syllables to be parsed into four feet, with a small amount of variation. In nearly every type, the third foot of the half-line begins with a light syllable (the half-line medial light syllable has been characterized as a key property of Somali *masafo*).

In contrast, trochaic footing gives somewhat less satisfactory results. All but two half-line types can be footed with 4 feet, so there is consistency in metrical structure. However, only one half-line type evenly parses all syllables into feet. In other words, a moraic trochee parse of half-lines nearly always results in syllables that do not belong to any foot. Many of the half-line types have more than one unfooted syllable, with two half-line types that have three unfooted syllables under the moraic trochee parse. Many of the half-lines have an unfooted medial syllable occurring between the middle two feet, but this is not true for every half-line. The appearance of the medial light syllable appears far less consistent under the moraic trochee parse.

Iambic feet provide a consistent, even parse for a wide variety of *masafo* half-line types, as shown by the comparison in the chart in (9). The variety in the different types is provided with a nice explanation under an iambic analysis. The way to think of this meter is as having an ideal shape, but the ideal shape is obscured somewhat on the surface by satisfying competing priorities (for example, parse all syllables, binarity, alliterate, the presence of the medial light syllable, etc.).

5. Conclusion

This paper has endeavored to show two things. First, that the *masafo* half-line allows considerable surface variation, suggesting that the appropriate invariant shape of this meter is something other than a 9 mora half-line. Second, it shows that the iambic foot can account for the actual length of half-lines. Iambic feet account for three dimensions of the Somali *masafo*. First, the verse is clearly quantitative; so is the iamb. Second, there are certain patterns that occur frequently; these are the patterns where the half-line has four iambic feet. Given that there are three types of iambic feet possible, this covers the range of most frequent types from 8 moras to 12 moras. The types of variation are exactly what we would predict given four iambic feet. Finally, there is considerable variation in the half-line shape, rather than having a fairly set, dominant pattern with substantially smaller number of variant half-line types. Why is it that no matter what we consider, there is never more than 49% of the half-lines with 9 moras? Why is it that, for example, 10 mora half-lines often occur as the second most frequent pattern? If the half-line is viewed as having 4 metrical positions, where each position is an iambic foot, each position could have one of three possible realizations (H, LL, or LH). If the meter had no other constraints on it except the drive towards four iambic feet, then we would still expect extensive variation in half-line types.

By no means have I provided a complete account of this meter; I have tried to show the arguments in favor of an iambic characterization of this meter. There are certainly some empirical issues that have not been addressed here. However, the iambic analysis does provide convincing account of the frequency and variation in half-line types.

There are two alternative conceptions of the *masafo*. In the analysis offered by Banti and Giannattasio (1996), variation is built into the verse design. This is shown in (10), where curly braces and simultaneous breves (light) and macrons (heavy) indicate optional choices.

(10)   *Masafo* line according to Banti and Giannattasio (1996)

$$\left\{ \begin{array}{c} \cup \_ \\ \cup\cup \\ \cup \cup \cup \end{array} \right\} \cup\cup \cup \cup\cup \left\{ \begin{array}{c} \_ \cup \\ \cup\cup \end{array} \right\}, \left\{ \begin{array}{c} \cup \cup \\ \cup\cup \\ \cup \cup \cup \end{array} \right\} \cup\cup \cup \cup\cup \cup\cup$$

A conceptual problem to this approach is that under generative metrics, all surface lines should share some abstract shape or template. This problem is avoided in another characterization of *masafo* that appears in Fabb (1997). For him, half-lines consist of five metrical positions, 2 strong positions on either side of a single weak position. This appears in (11).

(11)   *Masafo* line according to Fabb (1997)

```
        Half-line              Half-line
          /|\                    /|\
         / | \                  / | \
        S S W S S              S S W S S
```

Metrical positions are filled with H or LL (if S) or with L (if W). This is reminiscent of the moraic trochee parse from above. Variation is handled by a number of substitution rules that relate to whether positions can take three moras, for example. The equivalence of H or LL definitely suggests a quantitative foot, although that favors a moraic trochee. But the substitution of three moras into certain positions favors an iambic analysis; only the LH uneven iamb has three moras per foot. The analysis offered by Fabb (1997) thus hints at quantitative feet, but this paper actually pushes that further. I explicitly argue that this is iambic meter and that the types of variation that are attested in this system are exactly those types predicted by a half-line consisting of four iambic feet. Importantly, the iambic feet used in this analysis are those that represent the three possible quantitative iambs (LH, H, and LL) argued to occur in natural language by Hayes (1995), rather than the stress-based iamb, (σσ́), traditionally used in discussions of English and other verse traditions.

The iambic analysis here is rather abstract and depends upon examining the particular half-lines that occur and the frequency of their occurrence. This follows a current trend in generative metrics that makes use of frequency and statistical occurrences (Hayes and MacEachern 1998, Golston 1998, and Golston and Riad 2000). The bulk of such work makes use of the stress patterns (and often, the metrical structure) found in the language as a whole. In the case of Somali, there is no rhythmic stress system. The meter does not regulate accentual patterns in any way. Instead, the meter is quantitative. Word prosody of Somali does not provide decisive evidence for metrical structure. The question can be raised whether such metrical structure is found anywhere in Somali. Here I have argued that we do have such evidence; even without word prosody, the verse patterns show that the *masafo* genre is best characterized in terms of iambic feet.

Notes

* Portions of this paper were presented at the University of Toronto conference on Recent Developments in Generative Metrics (Fitzgerald 1999), and more recently at the School of Oriental and African Studies in London. For helpful discussion and comments, thanks to Nigel Fabb, Magda Dumitru, Sayaka Abe, and Nila Friedberg. I also owe a special thanks to Martin Orwin for many interesting discussions, as well as for his generous help with Somali verse, and his comments on a previous draft. The literature (in English) on Somali meter includes Andrzejewski and Lewis (1964), Banti and Giannattasio (1996), Fabb (1999), Johnson (1979, 1984, 1996), Orwin (1994, 1996, 2000, 2001), and Orwin and Riiraash (1997). Any errors here should be attributed to me.

1. Here diphthongs are treated as always bimoraic, contra Johnson (1979) and later arguments from Orwin (1996).
2. In fact, the Hayesian foot typology is inspired by this classical tradition.
3. Commas are conventionally used to indicate caesura, which divide each line into two half-lines; caesura always correspond to a word-boundary and often are accompanied by pauses (Banti and Giannattasio 1996.)
4. The Somali title is "Dacwad baan ka leeyahay", and the translation comes from Andrzejewski and Lewis (1964: 75). The lines translate as: "Concerning your plea 'Do not incite the Ogaadeen against us' I also have a complaint. The people of the Ethiopian region look for nothing from you, So do not press my claim against them. Do not claim on my behalf the blood money which they owe me."
5. Note that there is no foot type of either (HL) or (L), and that footing is treated as a directional left-to-right parse, maximizing foot structure.

References

Andrzejewski, B. W., and I. M. Lewis
    1964   *Somali Poetry: An Introduction.* Oxford: Clarendon Press.

Banti, G., and F. Giannattasio
    1996   Music and metre in Somali poetry. In *Voice and Power: The Culture of Language in North-East Africa,* R.J. Hayward and I.M. Lewis (eds.), 83–128. London: SOAS.

Fabb, Nigel
    1997   *Linguistics and Literature.* Cambridge: Basil Blackwell.
    1999   Verse constituency and the locality of alliteration. *Lingua* 108, 223–245.

Fitzgerald, Colleen M.
    1995   'Poetic meter >> morphology' in Tohono O'odham. Paper presented at the Annual Meeting of the Linguistic Society of America.
    1998   The meter of Tohono O'odham songs. *International Journal of American Linguistics* 64:1, 1–36.
    1999   Mora-counting meter in Somali. Paper presented at Formal Approaches to Poetry: Recent Developments in Generative Metrics. University of Toronto, Canada.

Golston, Chris
    1998   Constraint-based metrics. *Natural Language and Linguistic Theory* 16: 719–770.

Golston, Chris, and Tomas Riad
    2000   The phonology of Classical Greek meter. *Linguistics* 38:1, 99–167.

Hanson, Kristin, and Paul Kiparsky
    1996   A parametric theory of poetic meter. *Language* 72:2, 287–335.

Hayes, Bruce
- 1987 A revised parametric metrical theory. Proceedings of the Northeastern Linguistic Society 17.
- 1989 The prosodic hierarchy in meter. in *Rhythm and Meter,* P. Kiparsky and G. Youmans (eds.), 201-260. San Diego: Academic Press.
- 1995 *Metrical Stress Theory.* Chicago: The University of Chicago Press.

Hayes, Bruce, and Margaret MacEachern
- 1998 Quatrain form in English folk verse. *Language* 74:3, 473–507.

Hyman, Larry
- 1981 Tonal accent in Somali. *Studies in African Linguistics* 12: 169–203.

Jaamac Cumar Ciise, Sheekh (ed.)
- 1974 *Diiwaanka gabayadii Sayid Maxamad Cabdulle Xasan.* Mogadishu: Akademiyaha Dhaqanka, Wasaaradda Hiddaha iyo Tacliinta Sare.

Johnson, J.W.
- 1979 Somali prosodic systems. *Horn of Africa,* 2/3, 46–54.
- 1984 Recent researches into the scansion of Somali oral poetry. In *Proceedings of the Second International Congress of Somali Studies,* T. Labahn (ed.), 313–331. Hamburg: Buske.
- 1996. Musico-moro-syllabic relationships in the scansion of Somali oral poetry. In *Voice and Power: the Culture of Language in North-East Africa,* R.J. Hayward & I.M. Lewis (eds.), 73–82. London: SOAS.

Kiparsky, Paul
- 1968 Metrics and morphophonemics in the Kalevala, in *Studies Presented to Professor Roman Jakobson by His Students,* C. Gribble (ed.). Cambridge, Mass.: Slavica.
- 1975 Stress, syntax and meter. *Language* 51: 576–616.
- 1977 The rhythmic structure of English verse. *Linguistic Inquiry* 8, 189–441.

Kogure, Kumi, and Mizuki Miyashita
- 1999 Audible silence: Silent moras in Japanese verse. Proceedings of Western Conference in Linguistics.

Orwin, Martin
- 1994 Aspects of Somali phonology. School of Oriental and African Studies, University of London PhD Dissertation.
- 1996 A moraic model of the prosodic phonology of Somali. In *Voice and Power: the Culture of Language in North-East Africa,* R.J. Hayward & I.M. Lewis (eds.), 51–71. London: SOAS.
- 2000 A literary stylistic analysis of a poem by the Somali poet Axmed Ismaciil Diiriye 'Qaasim'. *Bulletin of the School of Oriental and African Studies* 63/2: 194–214.
- 2001 On consonants in Somali metrics. Afrikanistische Arbeitspapiere.

Orwin, Martin, and Maxamed Cabdullaahi Riiraash
    1997   An approach to relationships between Somali metre types. *African Languages and Cultures* 10/1: 83–100.

Piera, Carlos
    1980   Spanish verse and the theory of meter. PhD Dissertation, UCLA.

Poser, William J.
    1990   Evidence for foot structure in Japanese. *Language* 66:1, 78–104.

Tanihara, Kimio
    2001   Line crossover as rhythm adjustment in Japanese verse. Master's thesis, University at Buffalo.

6. Modelling statistical preferences

Constraints, complexity, and the grammar of poetry[*]

Nila Friedberg

1. Introduction

Readers of poetry make aesthetic judgements about verse. It is quite common to hear intuitive statements about poets' rhythms, such as 'this poet sounds complex'. Yet, it is far from clear what these statements really mean. Does 'complex' mean 'non-monotonous', 'hard to produce', or, maybe, something else? Are our aesthetic intuitions supported by any concrete facts? How exactly, if at all, should complexity be captured from the linguistic point of view?

The question of what it means for the rhythm to be complex in itself is not new. It was raised by the Russian symbolist poet Andrei Bely in his essay "Lyrics and Experiment" as early as 1910. Bely, himself a mathematician, attempted to account for his own aesthetic judgements by means of concrete numbers and graphs (see Hall, this volume). Bely defined complexity in terms of the deviations from the iambic template. Poets who deviate from the template often, and in a variety of different ways, have complex rhythm. Poets who deviate from the template infrequently, or deviate in the same way, have simple rhythm.

Sixty years later, the theory of generative metrics (Halle and Keyser 1971, Kiparsky 1975, 1977, Hayes 1989, among others) adopted a very similar approach to complexity. The theories of Halle and Keyser (1971), Kiparsky (1975), and Hayes (1989) differ with respect to whether word, foot, or phrasal boundaries are considered relevant for measuring complexity. Yet one fact remains the same: complexity is still understood as a deviation from the metrical template.

In this paper, I argue that there is more to complexity than deviation from the template. If complexity is understood as an *aesthetic* principle, many alternative formal definitions of this concept emerge, for example "How hard is it to construct a certain rhythm, or to invent a certain metrical rule?" I model the statistical preferences of the 18th and 19th century Russian poets using a constraint-based model (Friedberg 1997, 2000) alternative to Hayes and MacEachern (1998). Focusing on Taranovsky's (1953) statistics about stress omission in the eighteenth and nineteenth century Russian iambic tetrameter, I model hierarchies of preferences of major Russian poets with the help of **Preference constraints**, arranged into a scale of relative strength. Looking across poets and times, two types of preference-patterns emerge. Simple patterns are generated by four constraints. Complex patterns, such as Pushkin's, are generated by five constraints. In addition, simple patterns are derived by ordering the constraints in several distinct ways. Complex patterns can be derived in just one way.

Hence, I argue that simple grammars are computationally easy (and easy to construct), whereas complex grammars are computationally hard (and difficult to construct).

From a theoretical point of view, this paper argues for a theory that combines aspects of the Generative (Halle and Keyser 1971, Kiparsky 1975, 1977, among others) and Quantitative (Bely 1910, Tomashevsky 1921, 1929, Taranovsky 1953, Gasparov 1974, Bailey 1975, Tarlinskaja 1976) approaches to verse. I view preferences as categorical rather than numerical, and demonstrate that it is the combination of the two approaches that allows us to advance our understanding of what metrical complexity is.

2. Stress omission in the Russian iambic tetrameter

A line of iambic meter can be defined as a sequence of weak (W) and strong (S) metrical positions, where every odd metrical position is weak, and every even position is strong. In English and Russian poetry, weak positions ideally correspond to unstressed syllables whereas strong positions correspond to stressed syllables. An ideal match with the iambic template is exemplified by the following line from Donne (capitalized W and S refer to metrical positions, capitalized syllables are stressed):

(1) Thy FIRM-ness MAKES my CIR-cle JUST
     W   S   W   S   W   S W S
                            "Valediction: Forbidding Mourning"

However, poets rarely follow the ideal template. One of the most common deviations in Russian poetry is inserting unstressed syllables into strong positions, as indicated by *za-* in (2)[1]:

(2) Kog- DA ne v SHUT- ku za- ne- MOG
     W   S W   S   W S W   S
     When [he] became seriously ill   (Pushkin, *Eugene Onegin*)

The majority of Russian words are polysyllables, which typically lack rhythmic secondary stress. Thus, if Russian poets intend to utilize as many words of different prosodic shapes as possible, they cannot compose a line of iambic verse without filling strong positions by unstressed syllables (see Scherr 1980, Tarlinskaja 1987).

In terms of stress omission, the lines of iambic tetrameter can be classified into a number of logical possibilities, or 'rhythmical forms' (Taranovsky 1953). In this paper, a strong position bearing stress is indicated by a small s, whereas a strong position filled by an unstressed syllable is indicated by a small w:

(3) I.   no omissions of stress: ssss
    II.   omission on the first foot   wsss
    III. omission on the second foot   swss
    IV.   omission on the third foot   ssws
    V.   omission on the first and third foot   wsws
    VI.   omission on the second and third foot   swws
    VII. omission on the first and second foot   *wwss (non-occurring)
    VIII. omission on the first three feet   *wwws (non-occurring)
    IX.   different types of omission on the last foot, i.e.,
          sssw, ssww, swsw, etc   (non-occurring)

According to Taranovsky (1953), no Russian poets omit stress on the last foot, as in (3.I). In addition, most of them, except Pavlova (Bely 1910) avoid a line type *wwss*. The rest of the patterns of omission (*i.e.*, I–VI) are well formed. Which of these patterns are the most preferred and the least preferred among poets?

Following the work of Bely (1910) and Tomashevsky (1921, 1929), Taranovsky (1953) provides exact statistics about the frequency of each rhythmical form in the works of various poets. What makes the data especially valuable is that Taranovsky shows the preferences of poets on a year-by-year basis and on a poem-by-poem basis as well as over a long period of time. For example, (4) shows Pushkin's metrical preferences in different samples of verse:

(4) Pushkin's metrical preferences

rhythmical form	1823–30 'Eugene Onegin'	1822–23 'The Bakhchisaraj' Fountain	1814–20
ssws	47.5	49.9	53.7
ssss	26.6	28.9	27.3
swss	9.7	10.5	9.2
wsws	9	6.7	5.2
wsss	6.6	3.8	4.3
swws	0.5	0.2	0.3

Note that even though the difference between the frequency of occurrence of *swss* (9.7%) and *wsws* (9%) in 'Eugene Onegin' may seem insignificant, the same preference pattern emerges in both small and large samples of Pushkin's verse, such as in 1822–23 and 1814–1820 samples. Thus, we may conclude that it was important for Pushkin to preserve the hierarchy in (5):

(5)   ssws >> ssss >> swss >> wsws >> wsss >> swws

What this fact suggests is that while poets may not be aware of numbers per se (e.g., Pushkin may not have known he was using the form *swss* 9.7% of the time), their relative preferences for different types are a real part of their poetical grammars. The exact numbers change from sample to sample; what remains constant is the hierarchy of preferences.

The hierarchy in (5) is not specific to Pushkin. It was used by many other poets at different stages of their careers. If we restate Taranovsky's data in terms of relative frequency, the majority of Russian poets will consistently fall into one of the six preference patterns in (6). The numbers of rhythmical forms are the same as the ones used by Taranovsky.

In proposing these patterns I adopted the following approach: if the same poet uses the same hierarchy in more than one verse sample, his hierarchy is treated as a pattern. Conversely, if a poet employs a certain hierarchy in only one sample, I treated it as accidental, and did not consider it a pattern. My goal is to suggest a mechanism that would generate the hierarchies in (6).

(6) Preference patterns among Russian poets

pattern type	pattern 1	pattern 2	pattern 3	pattern 4	pattern 5	pattern 6
most preferred ⇓ least preferred	ssws 4 ssss 1 swss 3 wsws 6 wsss 2 swws 5	ssws 4 ssss 1 wsws 6 wsss 2 swss 3 swws 5	ssws 4 ssss 1 swss 3 wsss 2 wsws 6 swws 5	ssws 4 ssss 1 swss 3 wsss 2 swws 5 wsws 6	ssss 1 ssws 4 swss 3 wsss 2 swws 5 wsws 6	ssws 4 ssss 1 wsss 2 wsws 6 swss 3 swws 5

3. Constraint-based approaches to meter

Constraint-based approaches to poetic meter (Golston & Riad 1995, Fitzgerald 1998, Golston 1998, Hayes & MacEachern 1998, Getty 1998, Getty 2002, among others) were originally inspired by Optimality theory (OT – Prince & Smolensky 1993) in generative phonology. OT suggests that Universal Grammar consists of a set of violable constraints, which are arranged into a hierarchy on a language-specific basis. The input candidate competes with a number of other logically possible forms. The grammatical form is the one that wins the competition, i.e., satisfies the given hierarchy of constraints better than other candidates. Although OT can generate more than one winner in the competition by simply not ranking certain constraints with respect to each other, it makes no predictions about the frequency of winning candidates.

There are a number of ways one could model the frequencies of attested metrical types within OT framework (Kiparsky 1993, Nagy & Reynolds 1994, Anttila 1997, Zubritskaya 1997, Hayes and MacEachern 1998). Although the approaches vary in terms of how frequencies are modeled, all of them aim to model the *exact* numbers. However, we have seen that in case of Russian verse, the exact numbers vary from sample to sample, yet what remains constant is a sense of relations – i.e., what a poet prefers more or less. Thus, I propose an alternative way of modelling metrical tendencies by introducing the notion of **constraint strength** (Friedberg 1997, Friedberg 2000).[2] More specifically, I suggest that:

I. Hierachies of poets' preferences can be generated with the help of **Preference constraints,** or P-constraints, which are different in nature from OT constraints.
II. P-constraints vary in terms of strength.

III. A form violating a strong P-constraint is rare; a form violating a weak P-constraint is frequent.
IV. P-constraints are ordered into a scale (from strongest to weakest).
V. The strength of a particular constraint may vary across poets.

How will this model accommodate the constraints responsible for absolute restrictions on the one hand, and P-constraints on the other? One solution is to follow Hayes & MacEachern (1998), who suggest that constraints may be simply divided into violable and inviolable ("undominated") families; the latter are ranked above the former. An alternative solution adopted in this paper is to introduce a constraint *NULL PARSE[3] which acts as a border between metrical tendencies and absolute restrictions. According to this approach, the difference between tendencies and rules derives from the position of constraints in a tableau. That is, any constraint ranked above *NULL PARSE is an absolute restriction, which no metrical line can violate, whereas any constraint ranked below *NULL PARSE is a metrical tendency. The advantage of the Null Parse approach is that it claims that no line type is inherently unmetrical: the same constraint can be an absolute restriction (ranked above *NULL PARSE) in one poem, but merely a tendency (ranked below *NULL PARSE) in another.

4. Constraints

To account for the preference patterns in (6), one may propose two groups of constraints. The inviolable constraints (or at least inviolable for many poets) which are ordered above *NULL PARSE, account for absolute restrictions in meter; whereas preference constraints, ordered below *NULL PARSE, account for metrical tendencies.

Crucial to the analysis is the assumption that a line of iambic tetrameter has a hierarchical organization: metrical positions are grouped into feet, while feet are grouped into hemistichs (or half-lines). I will indicate hemistich boundary with a dash (e.g., *ws-ws*).

The relevant constraints are formulated in (8) and (9).

(8) **Absolute restrictions** – inviolable for most poets in the corpus.

> ENDING The last strong position in a line must be stressed (cf. Hayes and MacEachern 1998).

HEAD   A hemistich must have one stress, which is its head
(Dresher and van der Hulst 1998).
This constraint rules out *ww-ss*, and *ww-ws*.

These absolute restrictions rule out all the impossible lines, and cut down the number of rhythmic types from sixteen to six types. For example, the constraint ENDING rules out all lines which end in a *w*, whereas the constraint HEAD rules out *ww-ss*, *ww-ww*, *ww-ws*, *ss-ww*, and *sw-ww*.

Following the theory of Dresher & van der Hulst (1998), I assume that a stressed foot is a head of a hemistich in the same way a stressed syllable is a head of a foot.

In (9) I summarize the constraints responsible for deriving metrical preferences:

(9)   **P-Constraints** – responsible for generating preference hierarchies.[4]

BIN1   The first hemistich must be binary,
i.e., have 2 stresses

BIN2   The second hemistich must be binary,
i.e., have 2 stresses

BIN1&2   At least one of the hemistichs must be binary
(predicts that *ws-ws* and *sw-ws* are less frequent
than other forms). This constraint is an instance of a
Local Conjunction (Smolensky 1995)
between Bin1 and Bin2.[5]

ALIGNL(LINE)   Mark the left edge of a line with stress
(predicts that *ws-ws* and *ws-ss* are less frequent
than other forms).

ALIGNR(HEM)   Mark the right edge of a hemistich with stress
– in order to make the hemistich prominent
(predicts that *sw-ws* and *sw-ss* are less frequent
than other forms).[6]

SYMMETRY   Two hemistichs should have the same number of
stresses (predicts that *ws-ws and ss-ss* are most
common).

*LAPSE   Avoid *ww* sequences (after Golston & Riad 1995,
Hanson and Kiparsky 1996, Hayes & MacEachern
1998). Predicts that *swws* is less frequent than other
forms).

218 Nila Friedberg

FIT A line must contain stress omissions in order to fully utilize the vocabulary of Russian (Hanson & Kiparsky 1996). The constraint predicts that *ssss* is less frequent than other forms.

FAITH A strong position must be stressed (predicts that all forms are less frequent than *ss-ss*).

5. Deriving frequency hierarchies

Let us derive the hierarchies of preferences of different poets using the preference constraints formulated above. A number of comments about the tableaus are in order here. The line types in the tableaus are arranged in decreasing frequency: the topmost candidate in the leftmost column being the most frequent (ssws) and the bottom candidate being the least frequent (swws). Each candidate line is evaluated against a constraint. The order in which the candidates violate the constraints represents the order of their relative preference: the least preferred candidate looses first, the most preferred one loses last. Violations that contribute to deriving a preference hierarchy are marked by ☒, whereas other violations are marked by a star (*). The boundaries of hemistichs are marked with a dash (e.g., *ss-ss*).

(10) Pattern 4: Lomonosov (1745–1746)

		strongest	⇒		weakest
	constraint strength scale	BIN1&2	ALIGNL(LINE)	ALIGNR(HEM)	FIT
most frequent	ss-ws 4				
	ss-ss 1				☒
⇓	sw-ss 3			☒	
	ws-ss 2		☒		
least frequent	sw-ws 5	☒		*	
	ws-ws 6	☒	☒		

Consider pattern 4: the two least preferred rhythmical forms have something in common: both *wsws* and *swws* have only one stress per hemistich. They are predicted to be the least frequent by the highest ordered BIN1&2, which requires at least one of the hemistichs to have two stresses. Among these two candidates, we now have to choose the least frequent. *wsws* can be selected by ordering ALIGNL(LINE) (which requires the left edge of a line to bear stress) right after BIN1&2. Note that ALIGNL(LINE) performs two functions: on the one hand, it selects the least frequent among candidates 5 and 6, on the other hand, it rules out the next candidate in the hierarchy, i.e., *wsss*. We are now left with candidates *ssws*, *ssss* and *swss*. What differentiates the less frequent *swss* from the more frequent *ssss* and *ssws* is the fact that *swss* does not have stress on the right edge of the hemistich, that is, it violates ALIGNR(HEM). Once *swss* is selected, we have to choose the most frequent candidate among *ssss* and *swss*. *ssss* violates FIT and *ssws* emerges as the most frequent rhythmical form.

An interesting fact is that in 1741 Lomonosov did not use *swws* and *wsws*. Thus, in 1741 BIN1&2 was an absolute restriction, ordered above *NULL PARSE, whereas in 1742 it became a preference constraint, ordered below *NULL PARSE. In (11) I show Lomonosov's pattern in 1741 employing the Null Parse mechanism. Ill-formed lines are shown in parentheses; as in OT, a fatal violation is indicated by an exclamation mark. First, the absolute restrictions rule out all the ill-formed line types. After a form is ruled out by an absolute restriction, further computation becomes irrelevant, and the row is shaded. Once we are left with the well-formed line types *ssss, ssws, swss, wsss*, the computation of preferences proceeds.

(11) Lomonosov 1741

absolute restrictions ⟶   Other P-constraints

	END	HEAD	BIN1&2	*NULL PARSE	
ss-ss					
ss-ws					
sw-ss					
ws-ss					
∅-parse				*!	
(sw-ws)			*!		
(ws-ws)			*!		*
(ww-ss)		*!			*
(ss-sw)	*!				

220   *Nila Friedberg*

Let us now generate the preference patterns of well-formed lines (below the absolute restrictions are not shown).

(13)   Pattern 5

	Bin1&2	AlignL(Line)	AlignR(Hem)	Fit
ss-ss				
ss-ws				*
sw-ss			☒	
ws-ss		☒		
sw-ws	☒		*	
ws-ws	☒	☒		

(14)   Pattern 6

	AlignR(Hem)	Bin1&2	AlignL(Line)	Fit
ss-ss				
ss-ws				☒
sw-ss			☒	
ws-ss		☒	*	
sw-ws	☒			
ws-ws	☒	☒		

Note that in pattern 6, Bin can be ordered either right before or anywhere after AlignL(Line), still yielding the same pattern. *Lapse could have been inserted anywhere in the tableau without changing the results.

Note also that patterns 5 and 6 actively use only four constraints, i.e., they do not utilize Symmetry and *Lapse, which are not included into the tableau. However, some patterns cannot be generated without Symmetry and *Lapse. For example, pattern 3 cannot be generated without *Lapse (10); Patterns 1 and 2 cannot be generated without actively using both Symmetry and *Lapse (16) and (17).

Looking across the patterns generated so far, one may generalize that they differ in terms of computational complexity. Patterns 1 and 2 actively manipulate five constraints, whereas patterns 6 and 5 employ only four. Patterns 1 and 2 actively use Symmetry and *Lapse, whereas patterns 5 and 6 do not.

Patterns also differ in terms of the number of ways they can be generated. Different constraint orderings were tested using a computer program written in Prolog by B. Elan Dresher. The results are outlined in section 6.

(15) Pattern 3

	*Lapse	Bin1&2	AlignL(Line)	AlignR(Hem)	Fit
ss-ws 4					
ss-ss 1					☒
sw-ss 3				☒	
ws-ss 2			☒		
ws-ws 6		☒	*		
sw-ws 5	☒	*		*	

(16) Pattern 2

	*Lapse	AlignR(Hem)	AlignL(Line)	Fit	Sym
ss-ws 4					☒
ss-ss 1				☒	
ws-ws 6			☒		
ws-ss 2			☒		☒
sw-ss 3		☒			*
sw-ws 5	☒	☒			*

(17) Pattern 1 (Pushkin's 'Eugene Onegin')

	*Lapse	AlignL(Line)	Hem Sal	Fit	Sym
ss-ws 4					*
ss-ss 1				☒	
sw-ss 3			☒		**
ws-ws 6		☒			
ws-ss 2		☒			☒
sw-ws 5	☒		*		*

6. Prolog results

The program generated 55 patterns out of which 6 are attested. Most of the remaining patterns have *ssws* or *ssss* as the most preferred line, similarly to the attested ones.[7] These patterns may be accidental gaps, that is, they might be possible eighteenth or nineteenth century preference patterns.[8]

The program also tested how many solutions there exist for each pattern; we have seen that some hierarchies can be derived in more than one way since constraint orderings can vary, or different sets of constraints can be employed. In (18) I provide the list of patterns with the number of possible solutions for each as well as the number of active constraints employed:

(18)   Patterns

Pattern type	The number of ways a hierarchy can be generated	The number of constraints actively employed
Pattern 1	1	5
Pattern 2	7	5
Pattern 3	10	5
Pattern 4	10	4
Pattern 5	35	4
Pattern 6	42	4

Pushkin's metrical preferences in 'Eugene Onegin' can only be generated in one way. Recall that Pushkin employs five rather than four constraints in 'Eugene Onegin', and the constraints SYMMETRY and *LAPSE are absolutely crucial. On the other hand, in patterns generated in 42 ways, only 4 constraints are active, and SYMMETRY and *LAPSE are not crucial. Based on this correlation, I propose that metrical patterns can be classified into complex and simple. These patterns are identified on the basis of more than one characteristics:

(19)   *Most complex patterns* (i.e., pattern 1)
    (a) Actively employ five constraints
    (b) Actively employ SYMMETRY
    (c) Actively employ *LAPSE
    (d) Can be generated in 1 way

Simplest patterns (i.e., patterns 5 and 6)
(a) Actively employ four constraints
(b) Do not actively employ either SYMMETRY or *LAPSE
(c) Can be generated in many ways.

It should be noted that 'simple' and 'complex' are merely a continuum; poets do not know that their grammar can be generated in 10 ways. The classification simply suggests that some grammars are computationally easier than others. Between the two extremes of this continuum (i.e., complex and simple) there exists a transitional area, such as patterns 2, 3, and 4, which fulfill some of the conditions for complex patterns, but not all of these conditions.

We can further classify the P-constraints into two types: **core constraints**, actively used by all poets, and **periphery constraints**, used only by some poets. Looking across the patterns we notice that the constraints referring to edges of constituents, namely ALIGNL(LINE) and ALIGNR(HEM) are actively used by all poets, irrespective of which weighting solution is chosen. On the other hand, the SYMMETRY constraint is only actively utilized in complex grammars. A possible explanation for this fact is that from a cognitive point of view, edge constraints are not as complex as the notion of SYMMETRY: edge constraints merely require one to mark beginnings and ends, whereas the notion of SYMMETRY involves a comparison between two half-lines.

7. Examining individual poets

Consider how the metrical grammar of Lomonosov changed over the course of his career. Lomonosov represents an especially interesting example of metrical development because he was the first to use the iambic meter in Russian (Zhirmunsky 1971) (see (20)).

At the beginning of his career Lomonosov employed a simple pattern. Note that in 1739 and 1741 not only was he using a simple grammar but he was also using more absolute restrictions: the forms *swws* and *wsws* do not occur, indicating that BIN was an absolute constraint. Gradually, however, Lomonosov started to employ rhythmical forms *swws* and *wsws*, and his patterns became transitional (1748–49), and then complex (1750). Thus the increase in the number of rhythmical forms roughly correlates with the increase in the complexity of a pattern.

(20) Lomonosov[9]

1739	1741	1742	1745–1746	1748–1749	1750	1752–1757, 1761
simple 35 ways pattern 5	simple 35 ways pattern 5	simple 35 ways pattern 5	simple 10 ways pattern 4	transitional 10 ways pattern 3	complex 1 way pattern 1	transitional 10 ways pattern 3
ssss	ssss	ssss	ssws	ssws	ssws	ssws
ssws	swss	ssws	ssss	ssss	ssss	ssss
swss	ssws	swss	swss	swss	swss	swss
wsss	wsss	wsss	wsss	wsss	wsws	wsss
		swws	swws	wsws	wsss	wsws
		wsws	wsws	swws	swws	swws

Out of the twenty samples of Pushkin's verse, ten samples, including 'Eugene Onegin', use a complex pattern (Friedberg 2000, Friedberg 2002). The remaining ten samples represent a transitional pattern; that is to say, simple patterns are not used at all.

8. Conclusion

This paper argued that our intuitive statements about what sounds complex and what sounds simple are often based on very concrete parameters such as the number and the type of constraints employed and the number of ways a poet's hierarchy of preferences can be generated.

I have also demonstrated that complexity may be expressed not only through directly observable data, such as the shape of a line or a stanza, but also through more abstract phenomena, such as statistical preferences. Unlike lines or stanzas, preference hierarchies do not constitute physical objects that the reader can directly see or hear. Rather, these hierarchies result from calculations performed over a large body of verse. Nevertheless, the patterning of preference hierarchies provides us with intuitively appealing judgments about poets and thus constitutes an important measure of complexity.

Finally, we have seen that there are different ways of interpreting the term 'complex'. In traditional GM, 'complex' refers to the degree the poet deviates from the ideal template; 'complex' could also mean 'how many rhythmical forms a poet employs'. In the theory proposed here, 'complex' refers to the patterning of rhythmical forms in the preference hierarchy. Instead of attempting to find one 'true' definition of complexity, I suggest that all the three meanings have to be taken into account in a formal analysis of style, since a feeling of 'metrical complexity' is probably caused by a combination of different factors. Moreover, a poem may sound complex for a variety of reasons unrelated to meter, including the choice of metaphors or the poet's ideas. Last but not least, a poet may choose a simple pattern in order to sound different from other poets who aim to sound complex.

Appendix

a. Complex Patterns
   Pattern 1 – given by 1 ordering (4>1>3>6>2>5):
Lomonosov 1750 (i.e., poems written in 1750); *Bogdanovich* 1790–92; *Zhukovskij* 1803–1813, 1814–1832, 1814–16, 1818–19, 1821, 1823–1832; *Viazemskij* 1811–1815, 1816–1819, 1823–25, 1826–27; *Pushkin* 1814–15, 1816, 1817–18, 1819–20, 'The Bakhchisaraj fountain', 1822–23, 'Eugene Onegin' (written 1823–30), 1814–1820, 'The Gypsies' (written in 1824, no swws used), 'Count Nulin' (written in 1824–5, no swws used); *Del'vig* 1817–1819; *Kozlov* 1821; *Vasilii Pushkin* 1828; *Shevirev* 1825; *Lermontov* 1839–40

b. Transitional Patterns
   Pattern 2 – given by 7 orderings (4>1>6>2>3>5):
Jazykov 1825–28, 1829–31; Baratynskij, poems 1828; Polezhaev 1825–26, 1827–31, 1834–38; Pushkin lyrics 1823–24, lyrics 1827, lyrics 1828–29, 'Poltava' 1828 (no swws), lyrics 1830–1833, 'Mednyj Vsadnik' 1833;Viazemskij 1831; Lermontov, poems 1833–34, poems 1836.
   Pattern 3 – given by 10 orderings (4>1>3>2>6>5):
Lomonosov 1752–1757, 1761; Sumarokov 1767–72, Kostrov 1778, Kotel'nitski 1795; Zhukovskij 1797–1800; Pushkin 'Ruslan and Liudmila' 1817–1820, Venevitinov, Ryleev 'Dumy' 1821–23; Kuxelbeker 1818–20, 1821–24, 1832–35; Xomiakov 1826–27; Lermontov 1828, lyrics 1830; Pushkin, 'Kavkazskij plennik'1820–21, 'Bratja razbojniki' 1821–22 (no swws)

c) Simple patterns
   Pattern 4 – given by 10 orderings (4>1>3>2>5>6):
Lomonosov 1745–46; The same hierarhcy of preferences emerges from Bely's (1910) calculations, suggesting that the pattern is statistically significant.
   Pattern 5 – given by 35 orderings (1>4>3>2>5>6):
Lomonosov 1739, 1741 (no wsws or swws), 1742

Pattern 6 – given by 42 orderings (4>1>2>6>3>5):
Pletnev 1822–25, Baratynskij lyrics 1819–20, Baratynskij lyics 1821–1828, narrative poems 1826, Kozlov 1827, Shevirev 1827, Lermontov 'Izmail bei'1832, B.Orsha 1835, Mtsyri 1840

Accidental Patterns given by single samples:
Lomonosov 1747 (4>1>3>5>6>2); Lomonosov 1762–1764, Del'vig 1814 (4>3>1>6>2>5); Kniazhnin (till 1791), Petrov 1766, Krylov 1793 (1>4>3>2>6>5); Xomiakov 1828–39; Lermontov long poems 1829 (4>1>2>3>6>5); Kapnist 1792 (1>4>3>6>2>5); Pushkin 1821–1822, Lermontov 'Daemon', Nekrasov (4>1>6>3>2>5); Polezhaev (4>1>6>5>2>3); Lomonosov 1759 (4>1>3>6>5>2); Nikolaev (1>4>3>6>5>2).

PROLOG RESULTS

The numbers correspond to Taranovsky's numbers assigned to each rhythmical form:
(4) ssws (2) wsss (6) wsws (1) ssss (3) swss (5) swws

Hierarchy of preferences	Attested patterns	Given by N constraint rankings	Pattern number
1 6 4 2 3 5		112	
1 4 2 3 6 5		77	
1 4 2 6 3 5		77	
1 4 3 5 6 2		66	
1 4 3 5 2 6		66	
1 4 3 2 6 5		53	
6 1 4 2 3 5		49	
1 6 4 3 2 5		44	
4 1 2 6 3 5	✔	42	Pattern 6
1 6 4 3 5 2		40	
4 1 3 5 2 6		36	
1 4 3 2 5 6	✔	35	Pattern 5
4 2 6 1 3 5		35	
6 4 2 3 5 1		30	
4 2 6 3 5 1		30	
4 2 3 1 6 5		28	
4 3 5 1 2 6		25	
4 3 5 2 6 1		25	
4 2 3 6 5 1		24	
4 3 1 5 2 6		23	
1 4 6 2 3 5		21	
4 2 1 3 6 5		21	
4 2 1 6 3 5		21	
4 3 2 6 5 1		17	
4 3 2 1 6 5		16	

435162		15	
435621		15	
431256		15	
642135		14	
431265		14	
412365		14	
614325		13	
432561		12	
432165		12	
143625		11	
643251		10	
413256	✔	10	Pattern 4
413265	✔	10	Pattern 3
432615		9	
614352		8	
643521		8	
416235	✔	7	Pattern 2
462135		7	
413562		6	
462351		6	
642315		5	
426315		5	
423615		4	
643215		3	
431562		3	
431625		3	
436251		3	
436215		3	
413625	✔	1	Pattern 1
462315		1	

Notes

* I would like to thank Elan Dresher, Kristin Hanson, Paul Kiparsky, and Keren Rice for stimulating ideas and encouragement. Thanks also to James Bailey, David Beck, Nigel Fabb, Bruce Hayes, Daniel Hall, William Idsardi, Ron Smyth, Barry Scherr, members of the University of Toronto Phonology Project, the audiences at Montreal-Ottawa-Toronto phonology workshop, LSA 1999, and Penn Linguistic Colloquium 1999. This research was supported in part by a SSHRC research grant to Elan Dresher and Keren Rice.

1. For more on the difference between English and Russian versification see Tarlinskaja (1987).

2. The idea that the order of constraint violations can bear on the relative frequencies of forms is also expressed in Getty (2002).
3. Thanks to Elan Dresher for this suggestion. For the discussion of null parse see McCarthy & Prince (1993), Hammond (this volume).
4. The question is how do we motivate the given constraints? One motivation has to do with the patterning of rhythmical forms on preference hierarchies: forms that violate a certain constraint tend to occur as neighbours on frequency hierarchies. For example, there is a statistical correlation exhibited by *sw-ss* and *sw-ws* which turns out to be significant at the 0.05 level by Pearson's correlation test. This correlation argues in favour of ALIGNR(HEM) constraint. Similarly, the statistical correlation of *ws-ws* and *ws-ss* (significant at 0.05) argues in favour of the ALIGNL(LINE) constraint, since lines which do not mark their left edge with stress pattern as a natural class.

   Second, many of the constraints are not specific to Russian poetry, and occur cross-linguistically either in verse or in natural language, e.g., constraints on Binarity and Alignment (Prince and Smolensky 1993), Headedness (Dresher and van der Hulst 1998), NoLapse (Hanson and Kiparsky 1996), Symmetry (Ghini 1993), and saliency of edges (Hayes and MacEachern 1998).
5. Thanks to Paul Kiparsky for pointing out to me that the original formulation of BIN in Friedberg (1997) was an instance of local conjunction (Smolensky 1995). Thus the constraint on Binarity will be used as a Local Conjunction of constraints BIN1 and BIN2: BIN1&2 will be violated only if both of the hemistichs are not binary (i.e., *ws-ws* or *sw-ws*). The reason local conjunction is suggested has to do with the patterning of *ws-ws* or *sw-ws* in Lomonosov. At the early stages of his career, Lomonosov did not use either of the two lines, suggesting that they pattern as a natural class.
6. The previous names of ALIGNL(LINE), ALIGNR(HEM), and FIT were respectively MARKL(LINE), MARKR(HEM), and CONTRAST (Friedberg 1997, discussed in Hall, this volume).
7. The program was constrained in the following way. FAITH is ordered below ALIGNL(LINE), ALIGNR(HEM) and BIN1&2 by Kiparsky's (1982) Elsewhere Condition which states that specific rules should apply before general ones. FAITH is a general principle which requires the stressing of every strong position in a line. On the other hand, the other three constraints refer to the stressing of specific constituents, such as the foot or hemistich.
8. The program also generated preference hierarchies where *wsws* is the most preferred line. There are no hierarchies of this type in Taranovsky's (1953) database, However, the XIX century metrical reform, originated by Zhukovsky, involved the promotion of *wsws* (Taranovsky 1953). Thus, the constraint system should be able to generate *wsws* as most preferred: the reason this form never became the most preferred has to do with the frequency of word shapes that fill the *wsws* pattern (Taranovsky 1971, see also Hall, this volume).

9. I have omitted accidental patterns from the table.

References

Anttila, Arto
    1997   Deriving variation from grammar: a study of Finnish genitives. In *Variation, Change, and Phonological Theory*. F. Hinskens et al. (eds.), 35–68. Amsterdam: John Benjamins.

Bailey, J.
    1973.   The evolution and structure of the Russian iambic pentameter from 1880 to 1922. *International Journal of Slavic Linguistics and Poetics* 16: 119–46.
    1975.   *Toward a Statistical Analysis of English Verse*. Lisse/Netherlands: Peter de Ridder Press.

Bely, A.
    1910   *Simvolizm; kniga statei*. Moskva: Knigoizdatel'stvo: Musaget.

Dresher, B. E., and H. van der Hulst
    1998   Head-dependent asymmetries in prosodic phonology: Visibility and complexity. *Phonology* 15/3: 317–52.

Fitzgerald, C.
    1998   The meter of Tohono O'odham songs. *International Journal of American Linguistics* 64: 1–36.

Friedberg, N.
    1997   Rules, tendencies, and the theory of meter, as exemplified by Russian verse. M.A. thesis, University of Toronto.
    2000   Poetic meter and constraint-based theories. In *Proceedings of the 1999 Annual meeting of the Israeli Association for Theoretical Linguistics*, A. Wyner (ed.), 27–50. Haifa: University of Haifa.
    2002   Metrical complexity in Russian iambic verse: A study of form and meaning. Ph.D. dissertation, University of Toronto.

Gasparov, M.L.
    1974   Sovremennyj russkij stix: metrika i ritmika. Moscow: Nauka.

Getty, M.
    1998.   A constraint-based approach to the meter of Beowulf. Doctoral dissertation, Stanford University.
    2002   *The Meter of Beowulf: a Constraint-based Approach*. Berlin: Mouton de Gruyter.

Ghini, M.
    1993   Phi-formation in Italian: A new proposal. In *Toronto Working Papers in Linguistics* 12(2), C. Dyck (ed.), 41–78.

Golston, C.
1998 Constraint-based metrics. *Natural Language and Linguistic Theory* 16: 719–770.
Golston, C., and T. Riad
1995 Direct metrics. Paper presented at LSA, San Diego.
Halle, M., and S.J. Keyser
1971 *English Stress, Its Form, Its Growth, and Its Role in Verse*. New York: Harper and Row.
Hanson, K.
1993 Resolution in modern meters. Doctoral dissertation, Stanford University.
Hanson, K., and P. Kiparsky
1996 A parametric theory of poetic meter. *Language* 72: 287–335.
Hayes, B.
1983 A grid-based theory of English meter. *Linguistic Inquiry* 14: 357–393.
1988 Metrics and phonological theory. In *Linguistics: The Cambridge Survey*, F.J. Newmeyer (ed.), 220–249. Cambridge: Cambridge University Press.
1989 The prosodic hierarchy in meter. In *Phonetics and Phonology, vol. 1: Rhythm and Meter*, P. Kiparsky & G. Youmans (eds.), 201–260. San Diego: Academic Press.
Hayes, B., and M. MacEachern
1998 Quatrain form in English folk verse. *Language* 74: 473–507.
Kiparsky, P.
1973 Elsewhere in phonology. In *A Festschrift for Morris Halle*, S. Anderson and P. Kiparsky (eds.), 93–106. New York: Holt, Rinehart and Winston.
1975 Stress, syntax and meter. *Language* 51: 576–617.
1977 The rhythmic structure of English verse. *Linguistic Inquiry* 8: 189–249.
1982 Lexical phonology and morphology. In *Linguistics in the Morning Calm*, I.S. Yang (ed.), 3–91. Seoul: Hanshin.
1993 Variable rules. Handout distributed at the Rutgers Optimality Workshop (ROW1).
McCarthy, John, and Alan Prince
1993 Prosodic morphology I: Constraint interaction and satisfaction. Technical Report #3, Rutgers University Center for Cognitive Science.
Prince, A., and Paul Smolensky
1993 Optimality Theory: constraint interaction in Generative Grammar. Manuscript, Rutgers University and University of Colorado at Boulder.

Reynolds, B., and N. Nagy
- 1994   Phonological variation in Faetar: An optimality account. *Chicago Linguistic Society 30-II: Papers from the Parasession on Variation and Linguistic Theory* 277–292. Chicago.

Scherr, B. P.
- 1980   Russian and English versification: similarities, differences, analysis. *Style* 19: 353–375.
- 1986   *Russian Poetry; Meter, Rhythm, and Rhyme*. Berkeley: University of California Press.

Smolensky, Paul
- 1995   On the internal structure of the constraint component Con of UG. ROA-86-0000, http://roa.rutgers.edu.

Taranovsky, Kiril F.
- 1953   *Russki dvodelni ritmovi*. Beograd: Srpska Akademija Nauka.
- 1971   O ritmicheskoi structure russkix dvuslozhnyx razmerov. In *Poetika i stilistika russkoi literatury. Pamiati akademika V.V. Vinogradova*, 420–428. Leningrad: Nauka.

Tarlinskaja, M.
- 1976   *English Verse: Theory and History*. The Hague: Paris.
- 1987   Meter and language: binary and ternary meters in English and Russian. *Style* 21 (4): 626–649.

Tomashevsky, B.
- 1921   *Russkoje stixoslozhenije*. München: Wilhelm Fink Verlag.
- 1929   *O stixe*. München: Wilhelm Fink Verlag.

Zhirmunsky, Viktor Maksimovich
- 1966   *Introduction to metrics*. Mouton: The Hague.
- 1971   *Vvedenie v metriku* [Introduction to Metrics]. München: Wilhelm Fink Verlag.

Zubritskaya, K.
- 1997   Mechanism of sound change in Optimality Theory. *Language Variation and Change* 9: 121–148.

Modelling the linguistics–poetics interface*

Daniel Currie Hall

1. Introduction: On the relation between verse and linguistics

In the scientific study of poetry, it is widely held that attested patterns of verse are the product of an interaction between the formal properties of language and those of meter. For example, Taranovsky ([1971] 1980: 25) writes of investigating "the manner in which the living tendencies present in the language are transformed into the laws of verse." The goal of this paper is to model that interaction more explicitly than it has been in previous theories of verse, taking as a case study the variable patterns of stress omission observed in Russian iambic tetrameter. The model presented here is analogous to the phonetic source-filter model of phonation and articulation, in which speech sounds are the result of applying a filter to the sound wave produced by the vibration of the vocal folds. Here, the source is the natural prosody of the Russian language, and the filter is a metrical grammar consisting of ranked constraints, similar to those used by Friedberg (1997, 2001).

Jakobson ([1960] 1981: 18) argues for the relevance of the study of verse to general linguistics, writing that "[p]oetics deals with problems of verbal structure, just as the analysis of painting is concerned with pictorial structure. Since linguistics is the global science of verbal structure, poetics may be regarded as an integral part of linguistics." It is thus reasonable to expect that theories of linguistics should shed light on problems of poetics, and vice versa. The model of poetic variation presented here is based in part on Optimality Theory (Prince and Smolensky 1993; hereafter OT), a quite general model of constraint interaction that has been applied primarily to phonology, but also to syntax (e.g., Pesetsky 1997) and semantics (e.g., Hendriks and de Hoop 2001). In showing how a grammar of categorically ranked constraints can play a role in accounting for statistical patterns in Russian verse, this paper potentially offers a way of using OT to deal with non-categorical phenomena in other areas of linguistics.

2. What a theory of verse must account for

Metrical verse is defined by its use of regular alternations between strong (long or stressed) positions and weak (short or unstressed) ones. Verse forms can generally be characterized by templates such as the one in (1).

(1)　　Template for a line of iambic tetrameter:　WS　WS　WS　WS

Sometimes the template is followed exactly. In (2), for example, each strong position is filled by a stressed syllable, and each weak position by an unstressed one.

(2)　　Ĭámbĭcs márch frŏm shórt tŏ lóng –
　　　　　　　　　　　　(S. T. Coleridge, "Metrical Feet," l. 5)

Frequently, though, the correspondence is inexact, and there are mismatches between what Zhirmunsky (1966: 23) defines as **meter** – "the ideal law governing the alternation of strong and weak sounds in the verse" – and **rhythm**, "the actual alternations of strong and weak sounds, resulting from the interaction between the natural characteristics of the linguistic material and the metrical law." An example of such a mismatch may be seen in the second line of (3), in which the word *folded* represents a temporary rhythmical reversal of the iambic pattern.

(3)　　Bŭt thóu wĭlt névĕr móre ăppéar
　　　　<u>Fóldĕd</u> wĭthín mў hémĭsphéar,
　　　　　　　　　　　　(Henry King, "The Exequy," ll. 31–2)

The task of the metricist, then, is not merely to identify the template, but also to explain why some deviations (such as (3)) are allowed, while others (such as (4)) are not.

(4)　　*Bŭt thóu wĭlt névĕr <u>ăppéar</u> móre[1]　　(construct)

In English iambic verse, reversals like the one in (3) are common. In Russian, however, the most prevalent form of deviation is stress omission, i.e., the association of an unstressed syllable with a metrically strong position.

The importance of stress omission in Russian verse was established by the work of Andrei Bely. Bely (1910) proposed a graphical method of gauging the complexity of verse, in which each metrically strong position is represented as a table cell, and stress omissions are marked with dots. Rhythmical complexity is revealed by connecting the dots, as in (5).

(5)   a. Rhythmically simple verse: b. More complex verse:

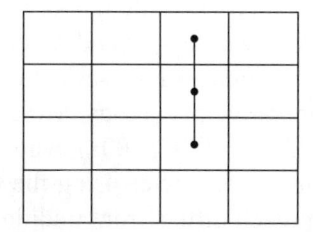

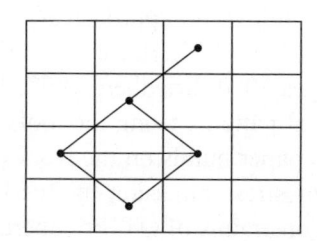

Bely's work revealed a number of generalizations about the rhythm of Russian tetrameter. In the verse tradition under consideration here, stress omission is not permitted (a) on the final foot of a line, (b) on three consecutive feet, or (c) on the first two feet of the line.

Taranovsky (1980) describes the attested patterns of stress omission in terms of **regressive accentual dissimilation.** The final strong position of the line is the 'strongest' (in Taranovsky's terminology) – that is, the one most likely to be filled by a stressed syllable. Strong positions alternate in relative likelihood of being stressed: the penultimate strong position is stressed less often than the final one; the antepenultimate syllable is stressed more often than the penultimate one; and so on. The effect of accentual dissimilation diminishes towards the beginning of the line: in tetrameter, the difference between the last two strong positions is much greater than the difference between the first two. Taranovsky's data on the 'strength' of each strong position are summarized in (6).

(6)   Average likelihood of stressed σ:

$$(_w S) \; (_w S) \; (_w S) \; \left(_w S\right)$$

    86%   89%   45%   100%

A complete theory of metrics, then, should not only be able to describe a template and explain what deviations from that template are possible; it should also provide some account of why some permissible deviations are more frequent than others.

3. Accounting for preferences in generative metrics

This paper follows the approach of generative metrics (Halle and Keyser 1971; Kiparsky 1975, 1977; Hanson and Kiparsky 1996; Hayes and MacEachern 1996; Hayes 2000; Friedberg 1997, 2001 *inter alia*), which seeks to account for metrical patterns using the tools of generative phonology. More specifically, this paper builds on the work of Friedberg (1997, 2001), who derives patterns of stress omission in Russian iambic tetrameter using the ranked, violable constraints of OT. Friedberg's approach differs from traditional OT in that her tableaux do not select single optimal output forms, but rather determine the relative well-formedness of several permissible line types.

In Friedberg's system, a line is metrical if and only if it does not violate any constraint ranked higher than *NULLPARSE, the constraint that penalizes the null candidate. Two such constraints are shown in (7). (These constraints are drawn from Friedberg 2001: 20 and Friedberg 1997: 39; HEAD in particular is based on Dresher and van der Hulst's (1995) work on head–dependent asymmetries.)

(7)   Constraints ranked above *NULLPARSE:
   a. ENDING - The last strong position in a line must be stressed.
   b. HEAD - A hemistich must have a head, which must be stressed.

These constraints rule out lines with stress omission on the last foot (XXXW) and lines in which there are two stress omissions in the same hemistich (WWXX, XXWW).[2]

Any constraint ranked below *NULLPARSE is violable. Some of the violable constraints proposed by Friedberg (1997: 39–45; 2001: 22) are shown in (8).

(8)   Constraints ranked below *NULLPARSE:
   a. *LAPSE - Stress omissions should not occur on adjacent feet.
   b. MARKL(LN) - The leftmost strong position of the line should be stressed.

c. MARKR(HS) - The rightmost strong position of a hemistich should be stressed.
d. CONTRAST - A line should contain at least one stress omission.
e. SYMMETRY - The two hemistichs should have the same number of stresses.
f. BINARYCOLON - At least one hemistich must contain two stresses.
g. STRESSS - All strong positions should be stressed.

Ranked in the order in which they are listed in (8), these constraints predict the relative frequency of occurrence of the six different line types that occur in Pushkin's *Eugene Onegin*, as illustrated in the tableau in (9). The line type SSWS, which is judged most harmonic by the constraint ranking, is the most frequent, while SWWS, the least harmonic of the six permissible line types, occurs least often. In a standard OT calculation, the presence of a more harmonic alternative suffices to rule a candidate out; in Friedberg's theory, the less harmonic candidate is dispreferred, but it is not deemed unmetrical unless it is so ill-formed as to be worse than the null candidate.

(9) Tableau for line types in Pushkin's *Eugene Onegin* (based on Friedberg 1997: 46)

	*LAPSE	MARKL	MARKR	CONT	SYMM	BINCOL	STRS
1. SSWS					*		*
2. SSSS				*			
3. SWSS			*		*		*
4. WSWS		*				*	**
5. WSSS		*			*		*
6. SWWS	*		*			*	**

Various rankings of the constraints in (8) correctly generate the patterns of stress omission found in the work of a number of poets.

This approach does, however, have certain theoretical and empirical limitations. For example, the constraint hierarchy in (8) and (9) does not make explicit the notion that the line type SSSS, in which all strong positions are filled by stressed syllables, represents perfect conformity to an abstract metrical ideal. There is one constraint (STRESSS) that prefers SSSS over all other line types, but another constraint (CONTRAST) specifically penalizes SSSS. This conceptual objection can be at least partially answered by formulating STRESSS as a faithfulness constraint (as in Friedberg 2001), giving the metrical template privileged status as the input form. Even so, STRESSS is not always active; in the *Eugene Onegin* grammar in (9), for instance, it is ranked so low as to have no influence on the hierarchy of line types produced.

The model also has some difficulty in fully capturing the principle of FIT. As originally formulated by Hanson and Kiparsky (1996: 294), FIT pertains to the choice of meter: "Languages select meters in which their entire vocabularies are usable in the greatest variety of ways." For example, iambic pentameter is a good meter for English verse, because most English words are easily accommodated by the iambic template (given a certain degree of licence for deviation). However, the same principle also applies to rhythm, as the natural prosodic tendencies of a language determine which kinds of deviation from the metrical template will be most useful. Russian, because it has many polysyllabic words with no secondary stress, must permit stress omissions, or else it would be forced to exclude much of its vocabulary from syllabo-tonic verse altogether. As Friedberg (1997: 47) notes, "Even Lomonosov, who aspired to write iambic poetry with no omissions of stress, still has more cases of SSWS than SSSS."

The constraints in (8) and (9) clearly derive line types with stress omission, but they do not present stress omission as a consequence of properties of the Russian language. Instead, the grammar combines meter and rhythm into a single set of constraints. While STRESSS unambiguously mandates adherence to the metrical template, and CONTRAST unambiguously mandates deviation, the meaning of the other constraints (which penalize particular forms of deviation) and their ranking is less obvious. If the grammar prefers WSWS to SWWS, is this because WSWS is a less severe departure from the template from a metrical point of view, or because SWWS is a less useful line type from the point of view of Russian vocabulary and syntax? The grammar in (9) succeeds in generating the patterns that result from tension between meter and language, but does not model the tension itself.

Finally, the model is empirically limited in that while it can predict whether one line type will be preferred to another, it cannot predict how strong or weak the preference will be. For example, the grammar in (9) predicts that SSSS will be preferred to SWSS, and SWSS to WSWS; as the data in (10) reveal, both predictions are correct, but the difference in frequency between SSSS and SWSS (26.6% *vs.* 9.7%) is much greater than the difference between SWSS and WSWS (9.7% *vs.* 9.0%).

(10) Actual frequencies of line types in *Eugene Onegin* (Friedberg 1997, citing Tomashevsky 1929):

1. SSWS 47.5%
2. SSSS 26.6%
3. SWSS 9.7%
4. WSWS 9.0%
5. WSSS 6.6%
6. SWWS 0.5%

4. An alternative account: The source-filter model

This paper proposes an alternative theory that makes more fine-grained predictions about output frequencies by explicitly modelling the interaction between language and meter.

(11) a. A phonetic source and filter:

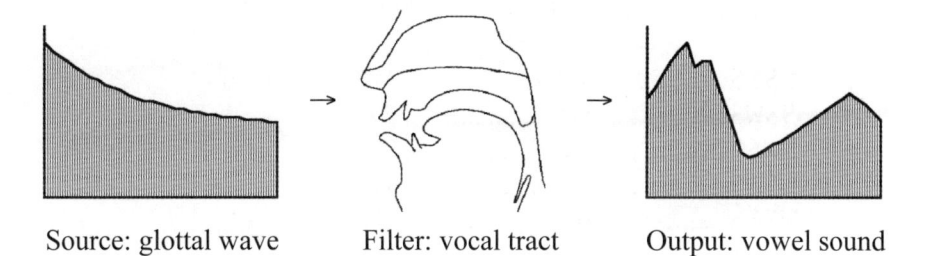

Source: glottal wave   Filter: vocal tract   Output: vowel sound

b. A metrical source and filter:

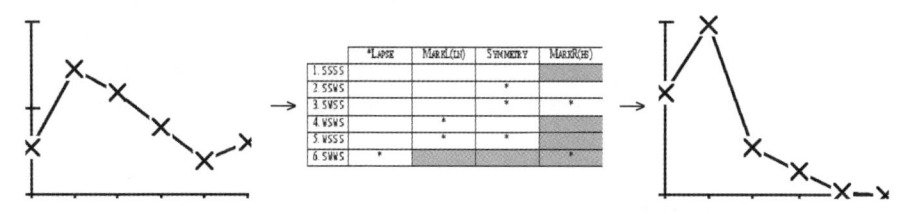

Source: natural prosody   Filter: metrical grammar   Output: verse rhythm

The proposed theory is metaphorically based on the phonetic source-filter model of phonation and articulation, illustrated in (11a), in which the shape of the vocal tract filters the sound wave produced by the vocal folds, reinforcing some frequencies and dampening others to produce distinctive patterns of formants. In the metrical source-filter model (11b), the rhythmic patterns of a natural language serve as a source of variability that is filtered through a metrical grammar. The output is poetic rhythm, which results from the reinforcing and dampening of natural patterns by the metrical template.

Taranovsky (1980) provides two sets of data that might serve as the natural-language source for Russian iambic tetrameter; these are listed in (12). The column labelled 'theoretical' shows Taranovsky's predictions about how likely each line type is to occur naturally in (non-poetic) Russian; the column labelled 'fortuitous' indicates the results of his study of chance iambic sequences in an actual sample of Russian prose. The figures in (12) show the frequency of each line type as a proportion of all sequences of well-formed iambic tetrameter in prose; they have been adjusted to add up to 100% because Taranovsky's original calculations include the unmetrical WWSS.

(12) Prose frequencies from Taranovsky (1980):

Line Type	Theoretical	Fortuitous
SSSS	11.3%	10.9%
SSWS	29.5%	29.3%
SWSS	26.6%	20.2%
WSWS	14.2%	17.6%
WSSS	6.3%	9.3%
SWWS	11.4%	12.7%

The filter through which this source passes is a metrical grammar consisting of ranked, violable constraints similar to those used by Friedberg. For the data under consideration here – the range of eighteenth- to early twentieth-century poetry surveyed by Taranovsky – the constraints in (13) appear to be sufficient.

(13) Constraints in the metrical filter:

  a. *Lapse - Stress omissions should not occur on adjacent feet.
  b. MarkL(ln) - The leftmost strong position of the line should be stressed.

c. SYMMETRY - The two hemistichs should have the same number of stresses.
d. MARKR(HS) - The rightmost strong position of a hemistich should be stressed.

The constraints in (13), all originally proposed by Friedberg, are repeated from (8). Ranked in the order in which they appear in (13), they form the grammar in (14), which generates an ordering of the six line types in which perfect adherence to the template (SSSS) is the most harmonic option.

(14) Deriving SSSS > SSWS > SWSS > WSWS > WSSS > SWWS:

	*LAPSE	MARKL(LN)	SYMMETRY	MARKR(HS)
1. SSSS				
2. SSWS			*	
3. SWSS			*	*
4. WSWS		*		
5. WSSS		*	*	
6. SWWS	*			*

The raw frequencies are filtered through the metrical grammar as follows: Three candidate line forms are selected at random based on the frequencies in (12), and the grammar in (14) selects the optimal candidate from the set. The predicted frequency of each line type is equal to the likelihood of its being generated by this procedure.[3]

The procedure is mathematically similar to rolling a six-sided die three times and selecting the lowest number rolled. In this case, however, the die is weighted by the prosody of Russian prose, and it is the grammar in (14) that determines which of the rolled numbers is chosen. Some examples of how the procedure works are shown in (15).

(15) Selecting the optimal candidate from a random set:

a. Roll: 2: SSWS 2: SSWS 5: WSSS Selection: 2: SSWS
b. Roll: 3: SWSS 4: WSWS 1: SSSS Selection: 1: SSSS
c. Roll: 5: WSSS 4: WSWS 6: SWWS Selection: 4: WSWS
d. Roll: 6: SWWS 6: SWWS 6: SWWS Selection: 6: SWWS

In (15a), SSWS – the second-best candidate according to the metrical grammar and the most frequent one in the input frequencies – comes up twice; since the other randomly chosen candidate, WSSS, is less optimal, SSWS is chosen as the output. In (15b), the presence in the candidate set of SSSS, the most harmonic line type, guarantees that it will be selected by the grammar. None of the best three line types is present in the candidate set in (15c), and so the grammar chooses WSWS, the best one available. (15d) shows the only circumstance in which the procedure will select the least harmonic line type: SWWS must turn up all three times in order to be chosen.

Calculating each line type's chance of being selected by this procedure yields a set of predicted frequencies in which the prose pattern of (12) is, in effect, filtered through the metrical preferences of the grammar in (14). The most harmonic line types are reinforced; the least harmonic ones are damp- ened. The table in (16) compares the predicted frequencies with the range of frequencies attested for each line type in the verse surveyed by Taranovsky.

(16) Raw, filtered, and attested frequencies:

Type	Fortuitous Raw	Fortuitous Filtered	Theoretical Raw	Theoretical Filtered	Attested
1. SSSS	10.9	**29.3**	11.3	**30.4**	25 – 32
2. SSWS	29.3	**49.4**	29.5	**49.2**	41 – 54
3. SWSS	20.2	**15.2**	26.6	**11.6**	3 – 19
4. WSWS	17.6	**5.1**	14.2	**8.3**	3 – 11
5. WSSS	9.3	**0.9**	6.3	**0.4**	3 – 8
6. SWWS	12.7	**0.2**	11.4	**0.2**	0 – 2

For every line type except WSSS, the predictions of the source-filter model fall within the range of attested frequencies. As shown in (16), and graphically in the chart in (17), filtering either set of raw frequencies through the metrical grammar generates an overall pattern much closer in shape to that of actual Russian iambic tetrameter of the eighteenth to early twentieth centuries.

In (17), dotted lines trace the pattern described by Taranovsky's data for theoretical and fortuitous sequences of iambic pentameter in Russian prose; solid lines indicate the results of filtering each of these sets of frequencies through the metrical grammar; and the shaded boxes show the ranges of frequencies attested for each line type in verse. The line types are listed in the order in which they are ranked by the metrical constraint grammar, from most harmonic to least. The two most harmonic line types, SSSS and SSWS, are reinforced by the grammar; the other four are dampened. The second-least harmonic line type, WSSS, is predicted by the model to be somewhat less common than it is in actual verse; for the other line types, the poets and the model appear to be in agreement.

(17) The effects of the metrical filter:

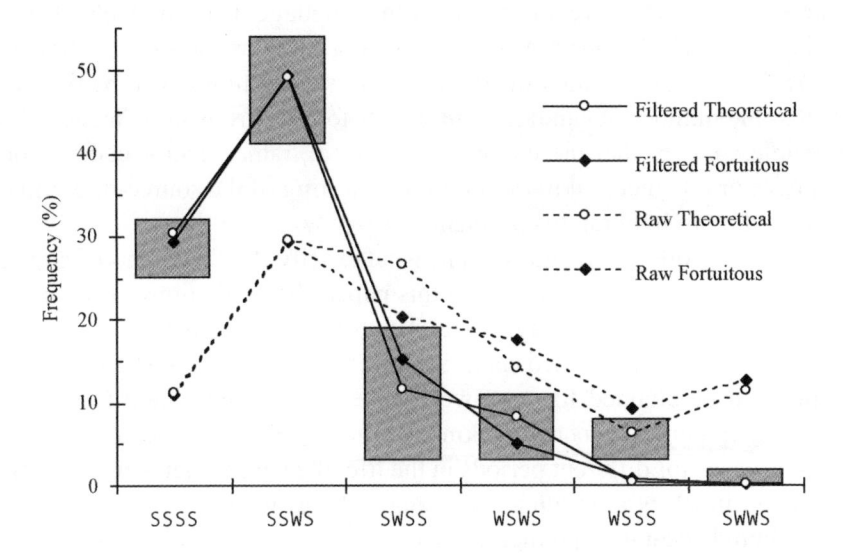

5. Evaluation

The results in (16) and (17) provide some indication of the empirical viability of the source-filter model, at least in its application to the particular question of Russian iambic tetrameter. A number of theoretical questions, however, remain unanswered.

Of these questions, there is one that pertains specifically to the model itself: Why does the randomly chosen candidate set contain exactly three candidates? Empirically, the number three seems to provide just the right balance between the source and the filter. If the number of candidates is decreased, the filtered frequencies become more like the raw frequencies, and presumably, more like prose. (If there were only one candidate, it would necessarily be the best one available, and so the likelihood of the model selecting a given line type would be equivalent to the likelihood of that line type occurring 'naturally.') If the number of candidates is increased, then the most harmonic line type predominates inordinately, since its chance of being included in the candidate set approaches 100% as the number of candidates grows. Too small a set produces the rhythm of prose; too large a set produces the monotony of perfectly regular iambic meter.

Clearly, some intermediate number of candidates must be chosen if the model is to portray at all realistically the poetic compromise between the rules of meter and the requirements of the language. Unfortunately, there is no immediately obvious reason for selecting three as the magic number *a priori*. Ideally, one or both of the following should turn out to be the case: (a) that the number of candidates in the set follows from some independent principle, and (b) that the number is universal, rather than specific to one language or one metrical tradition. Further testing of the source-filter model may shed more light on this problem.

Another, more general question is, what exactly should the model attempt to predict? In the case presented in this paper, the predictions of the model fared well when set beside aggregate data from various poets writing over a period of approximately two centuries. It remains to be seen whether similar results can be attained for narrower ranges of data. Friedberg (1997) provides grammars that generate rankings of line types for individual poets, and in some cases for different periods in the life of a single poet – and the grammar cited in (9) is a grammar of a single (long) poem. If the source-filter model could accurately predict frequencies of line types for individual poets, periods, or poems, that would be a remarkable result. However, it is not clear exactly how narrow the focus of the model's predictions ought to be.

This problem, however, is not specific to the source-filter model; it applies to any model of language variation, and especially to models that make predictions about patterns of frequencies rather than about more categorical phenomena. Should linguists attempt to write grammars for languages, for dialects, or for idiolects? There are potentially significant generalizations to be found at all these levels. This paper has taken a wide view of Russian iambic tetrameter and presented a grammar for a metrical tradition; it remains to be seen whether the variation within that tradition results from different metrical preferences, different poetic lexicons, random variability, or some other factor.

Finally, there is the question of how poets acquire their metrical grammars. In the case of the source-filter model (and other constraint-based theories of metrics), does the acquisition process involve only the ordering of a set of universal constraints (as in standard OT), or does the learner have to discover the constraints themselves as well as their ranking? And, in either case, what data does the learner rely on?

Some version of this question applies to any theory of generative metrics. It is made difficult to answer by the fact that standard linguistic arguments about learnability cannot necessarily be applied to poetry. All more or less normal children automatically learn to speak a language; not all children grow up to be poets. While generative metrics strives to capture 'natural' intuitions about what is metrical or unmetrical, the production of verse is generally considered to be an art. The procedures for the acquisition of poetic grammars are therefore much harder to limn than those that apply to ordinary language.

Despite these unanswered questions, though, the source-filter model has much to recommend it. In particular:

1. The model is able to predict that SSWS will be the most frequent line type, even though the metrical grammar prefers perfect adherence to the template (SSSS). This insight depends upon the ability to represent rhythm as the result of a negotiation between the language and the meter. In this respect, the source-filter model makes the principle of F$_{IT}$ explicit.

2. The model does not require an unreasonable number of constraints. The full ranking of the six line types can be achieved with four constraints, each of which can be formulated in terms of standard metrical constituents.

3. The model makes predictions about non-categorical phenomena without resorting to non-categorical constraint rankings. In this respect, the source-filter model addresses an issue raised by Guy (1997). Guy notes that standard OT, unlike the Variable Rule framework of Labov (1969) and Cedergren and Sankoff (1974), has difficulty dealing with the fact that variable phenomena do sometimes surface even in strongly unfavourable environments. "OT makes every constraint a knock-out, rendering invisible the effect of all lower-ranked constraints" (Guy 1997: 341); as a result, a candidate that violates a high-ranking constraint is predicted never to surface. The source-filter model, however, takes advantage of the fact that what eliminates a candidate from consideration is not such a violation *per se*, but rather the presence of another, more optimal candidate. Unlike standard OT, the source-filter model assumes that the set of candidates is finite and random rather than exhaustive. It thus predicts that a candidate that is dispreferred by a high-ranking constraint will occasionally be permitted, because sometimes the source will not supply a better alternative.

Other OT models of variation, such as those proposed by Anttila (1995), Boersma and Hayes (1999), and Hayes (2000), require constraints that are variably ranked. Anttila (1995) uses crucially unranked constraints to generate patterns of variation in Finnish genitives. This is a principled approach, but the number and granularity of the statistical patterns it can generate depend on the number of constraints involved. Hayes (2000) applies the overlapping constraints of Boersma and Hayes (1999) to account for patterns in English folk verse. This model can generate more complex patterns of numbers, but the rankings are considerably less constrained. The source-filter model, on the other hand, can produce fine-grained predictions without resorting to an infinitely divisible continuum of constraint rankings. It should be noted, however, that this approach is viable only when there is an identifiable source of variation that can serve as the input to a filter composed of categorically ranked constraints.

4. The source-filter model, like Friedberg's (1997) theory, makes good use of OT's inherent power to generate a harmonic ordering of an entire candidate set. Most phonological applications of OT simply use constraints to select a single candidate as the optimal output; in such cases, the theory vastly overgenerates judgments, since it generally does not matter which form is deemed second-, third-, or fifth-most harmonic. In the source-filter model, all the judgments matter.

In summary, then, the proposed source-filter model appears to be a promising and principled approach to the problems of generative metrics, and perhaps to those of linguistic variation more generally. Applied to verse, it provides a picture of the interaction between natural language and metrical structure, and in doing so it distinguishes the source of variability from the orderly grammar of poetry.

Notes

*   I would like to thank Elan Dresher and, especially, Nila Friedberg for inspiring and commenting on the work presented here. I am also grateful to the members of the phonology research group at the University of Toronto and to the audience at NELS 32 for their helpful comments on earlier versions of this paper. This research is supported in part by SSHRC grant #410-99-1309 to Keren Rice and Elan Dresher.

1. Lines like (4) are unmetrical for many poets, though licit for some. See Kiparsky (1977: 201-2) for a more detailed discussion.

2. Here and in the following discussion, four-letter abbreviations for line types indicate the realization of the four strong positions in the template. The letter S stands for a stressed syllable, W stands for an unstressed syllable, and X stands for any syllable.
3. This probability can be calculated for a line type L by multiplying (a) the probability that, out of three randomly chosen lines, none is more harmonic than L by (b) the probability that, in three randomly chosen lines no more harmonic than L, L itself occurs at least once. For the line types at the extremes of the hierarchy, this calculation is simple. In the case of the most harmonic line type (here, SSSS), probability (a) is necessarily 100%, and so the predicted frequency is equal to (b), which is the probability of selecting SSSS at least once. For the least harmonic line type (SWWS), probability (b) is necessarily 100%, and the predicted frequency is equal to (a), which is the probability of selecting SWWS all three times. The predicted frequencies of the other line types require somewhat more calculation, but are ultimately straightforward.

References

Anttila, Arno
    1995   Deriving variation from grammar: A study of Finnish genitives. Rutgers Optimality Archive ROA-63, http://roa.rutgers.edu/.

Bely, Andrei
    1910   *Simvolizm.* Moscow: Musaget'.

Boersma, Paul, and Bruce Hayes
    1999   Empirical tests of the Gradual Learning Algorithm. Rutgers Optimality Archive ROA-348, http://roa.rutgers.edu/.

Cedergren, Henrietta J., and David Sankoff
    1974   Variable rules: Performance as a statistical reflection of competence. *Language* 50: 333–55.

Coleridge, Samuel Taylor
    1991   Metrical feet: Lesson for a boy. In *The Norton Introduction to Literature,* ed. Carl E. Bain, Jerome Beaty, and J. Paul Hunter, 805. New York: Norton. Written [1806], originally published 1834 in *The Poetical Works of S.T. Coleridge*, H.N. Coleridge (ed.). London: William Pickering.

Dresher, Elan, and Harry van der Hulst
    1995   Head-dependent asymmetries in phonology. In *Leiden in Last: HIL Phonology Papers I*, Harry van der Hulst and Jan van de Weijer (eds.), 401–431. The Hague: Holland Academic Graphics.

Friedberg, Nila
 1997 Rules, tendencies, and the theory of meter, as exemplified by Russian verse. M.A. thesis, University of Toronto.
 2001 Metrical complexity in Russian iambic verse: A study of form and meaning. Doctoral dissertation proposal, University of Toronto.

Guy, Gregory
 1997 Violable is variable: Optimality Theory and linguistic variation. *Language Variation and Change* 9: 333–347.

Halle, Morris, and S.J. Keyser
 1971 *English Stress: Its form, Its Growth, and Its Role in Verse.* New York: Harper and Row.

Hanson, Kristin, and Paul Kiparsky
 1996 A parametric theory of poetic meter. *Language* 72: 287–335.

Hayes, Bruce
 2000 Faithfulness and componentiality in metrics. Ms., UCLA.

Hayes, Bruce, and Margaret MacEachern
 1996 Folk verse forms in English. Rutgers Optimality Archive ROA-119, http://roa.rutgers.edu/.

Hendriks, Petra, and Helen de Hoop
 2001 Optimality theoretic semantics. *Linguistics and Philosophy* 24: 1–32.

Jakobson, Roman
 1981 Linguistics and poetics. In *Selected Writings, Volume III: Poetry of Grammar and Grammar of Poetry*, ed. Stephen Ruby, 18–51. The Hague: Mouton. Originally published [1960] in *Style in Language*, T.A. Sebeok (ed.), Cambridge, Mass.: MIT Press.

King, Henry
 1973 The exequy. In *Poems, Elegies, Paradoxes, and Sonnets.* Facsimile, with an introduction by Eluned Brown. Menston: Scolar Press. Original edition [1657], London.

Kiparsky, Paul
 1975 Stress, syntax, and meter. *Language* 51: 576–617.
 1977 The rhythmic structure of English verse. *Linguistic Inquiry* 8: 189–247.

Labov, William
 1969 Contraction, deletion, and inherent variability of the English copula. *Language* 45: 715–762.

Pesetsky, David
 1997 Some optimality principles of sentence pronunciation. Proceedings of the "Good Enough" conference at MIT. Rutgers Optimality Archive ROA-184, http://roa.rutgers.edu/.

Prince, Alan, and Paul Smolensky
  1993 Optimality Theory: Constraint interaction in Generative Grammar. Ms., Rutgers University and University of Colorado at Boulder.
Taranovsky, K.F.
  1980 The rhythmical structure of Russian binary meters. In *Metre, Rhythm, Stanza, Rhyme,* edited and translated by G.S. Smith. Colchester: University of Essex. Original: [O ritmicheskoi strukture russkikh dvuslozhnykh razmerov'] published [1971] in *Poetika i stilistika russkoi literatury*, M.P. Alekseev et al. (eds.), Leningrad: Nauka.
Tomashevsky, Boris
  1929 *O stixe*. Munich: Fink.
Zhirmunsky, V.
  1966 *Introduction to Metrics: The Theory of Verse,* trans. C.F. Brown, ed. E. Stankiewicz and W.N. Vickery. The Hague: Mouton.

7. Russian meter

Generative metrics and the comparative approach: Russian iambic tetrameter in a comparative perspective*

Mihhail Lotman

1. Introductory notes

The model of generative metrics presented in this article differs in some aspects from that of Halle and Keyser (1972) and also Kiparsky (1973). It consists of three basic components: verse meter, a system of versification, and prosody. The metrical component is characterized by metrical rules (MR), the component of the system of versification by correspondence rules (CR), and the prosodic component by prosodic rules (PR). Metrical rules constitute the metrical structure of verse (the latter is understood here in a broad sense, including, for example, strophics),[1] correspondence rules constitute the number of rhythmical forms allowed in a given verse form, and prosodic rules constitute the prosodic structure of verse, including the transformations which evolve in language under the influence of verse meter.

2. Meter

Verse meter is an abstract structure which is organized according to the principles of translational symmetry; the elementary period of symmetry is called foot. Depending on how many types of elements are used to form a verse foot, the corresponding meters belong to metrical systems of 1st, 2nd, ..., n^{th} degree (henceforth MS^1, MS^2, ..., MS^n); in practical terms, MS^1 and MS^2 are most important.

MS^1 consists of chains composed from an alphabet which consists of one symbol, A. The delimiters of chains will be designated as &. Depending on how the composition of the chains is regulated, we can distinguish the meters shown in (1).

(1) (A) homometrical meters

    &&A&A&A&A&...   1-footed
    &&AA&AA&AA&...   2-footed
    ...
    &&A...A&A...A&A...A&...   n-footed
       n   n   n

(B) heterometrical positionally regulated meters

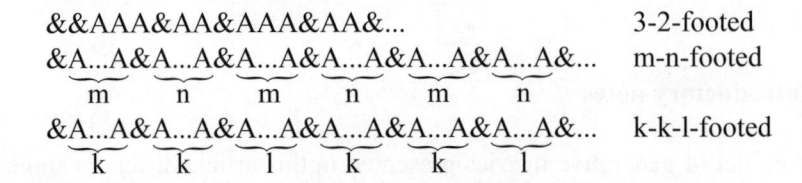

    &&AAA&AA&AAA&AA&...   3-2-footed
    &A...A&A...A&A...A&A...A&A...A&A...A&...   m-n-footed
      m   n   m   n   m   n
    &A...A&A...A&A...A&A...A&A...A&A...A&...   k-k-l-footed
      k   k   l   k   k   l

(C) heterometrical irregular meters

    &A...A&A...A&A...A&A...A&A...A&A...A&...   irregularly footed
      k   l   m   n   o   p

MS^2 consists of chains composed from an alphabet of two symbols, represented here as A and B. Note that I do not generally use symbols like W and S, which mark respectively weak and strong positions, since, in my view, weakness and strength do not belong to the sphere of metrics. All that is relevant about the symbols A and B is that they differ from each other. The content of that difference becomes evident only after correspondence rules are applied.

Examples of MS^2 are AB, ABB, ABA, ABBB, BBAB, ABBA, and so on. An important subgroup consists of feet where one of the symbols appears only once (it will be marked as A below), as shown for example in (2).

(2)   AB   ABB   ABBB   ABBBB
       BA   BAB   BABB   BABBB
                BBA   BBAB   BBABB
                         BBBA   BBBAB
                                       BBBBA

and so on.[2]

Like MS^1, verse feet in MS^2 are joined into metrical sequences of a higher level and can form isometrical and regulated or "free" nonisometrical meters.

MS^3 consists of chains composed from an alphabet of three symbols, MS^4 uses four symbols, and so on.

3. Systems of versification

In the following discussion we will proceed from the standpoint that verse is a realization of metrical structure in linguistic material. That is, verse is a double-coded system, coded linguistically and metrically. Using the structuralist oppositions *language vs. speech* and *meter vs. rhythm*, we could say that a verse message appears with respect to language in the function of speech and with respect to meter in the function of rhythm.

A system of versification (VS) is a set of correspondence rules which governs the relationship between the elements of metrical structure and certain elements of linguistic structure; in other words, the correspondence rules govern how meter is realized by means of natural language (NL). The generation of verse text could be represented with the following scheme:

(3) $\quad$ Meter $\xrightarrow{vs}$ NL $\longrightarrow$ Verse text

According to such a treatment, the system of versification is the central component of the verse mechanism, and therefore, the theory and typology of systems of versification should have a corresponding place in general verse theory. It is also clear that such a treatment eliminates the risk of confusing systems of versification with metrical or prosodic factors.

4. Preliminary example: Greek iambic dimeter

The metrical structure of verse does not depend on any concrete language; in other words, the chain ABABAB... can be realized as iambic in Greek, English, Finnish, or Chinese. But how this is realised depends on correspondence and prosodic rules. Such an approach offers great advantages not only in describing a particular verse, but in comparative analysis as well, both in synchronic and comparative-historical treatments. We will illustrate this approach with examples of iambic tetrameter, the metrical scheme of which is shown in (4).

(4)   &ABABABAB(A)&

We first come across verses that accord with this scheme in ancient Greece, where it was known as iambic dimeter. This meter appears rather infrequently, although we can see it in different genres, in lyric poetry as well as in drama. Its metrical scheme is slightly different from that of the iambic tetrameter shown above. Instead, it is a dipodic acatalectic verse, as shown in (5).[3]

(5)   **(MR$_{gr}$1)** &M& → &&D&D&&
       (MR$_{gr}$2) D → &F&F&
       (MR$_{gr}$3) F → &AB&

The expansion of the metrical scheme following MR1 is thus as in (6).

(6)   &&D&D&& ⇒ &&&F&F&&F&F&&& ⇒
        &&&AB&AB&&AB&AB&&&

A metrical analysis of iambic trimeter must refer not only to single positions, but also to verse feet and dipodies. Correspondence rules were quite simple. They were characterized by two separate but connected principles: one syllabic and one quantitative. The syllabic principle is regulated by CR1 (7).

(7)   **(CR$_{gr}$1)**   (i)   A → x, or
                                 A → xx

                   (ii)   B → x, or
                          B → xx

                   (iii) F → xx, or
                          F → xxx

That is, each A and B position can correspond to one or two syllables, but a foot can be only di- or trisyllabic.

The quantitative principle is regulated by CR2, shown in (8).

(8) **(CR$_{gr}$2)** (i)   A/&&___B → x
I.e., both long and short syllables can correspond to A in the initial position of a dipody.
(ii)   A/B&___B → ∪
I.e., only a short syllable can correspond to the A position inside a dipody.
(iii)   B → 2 moras
I.e., one long or two short syllables can occur in the B position.

An example is given in (9)[4].

(9)   A B   A B   A B A B
      | | ∧ | ∧ | | |
      τίς τὴν κεφαλὴν ἀπεδήδοκεν

In sum, the Greek iambic dimeter is a dipodic meter which belongs to the quantitative-syllabic versification system.[5]

5. The Russian iambic tetrameter

The Russian iambic tetrameter differs from the Greek dimeter both metrically and prosodically and belongs to the syllabic-accentual versification system. Its metrical scheme is as shown in (4). The following correspondence rules are valid here.

(10) **(CR$_{rus}$1)** One and only one syllable corresponds to each position A and B.

This rule is both simpler and stricter than the corresponding rule for Greek dimeter.

(11) **(CR$_{rus}$2)** (i)   A stressed syllable can correspond to an A position only if it is a monosyllabic word. For example,

& A   B A B A B A
Shvéd, rússkij, kólet, rúbit, rézhet (Pushkin)

(ii) An unstressed syllable of a polysyllabic word can correspond to a B position only if the stressed syllable of this word occurs in another B position. For example,

&A B A   B A B A B&
Kogdá ne v shútku zanemóg

$CR_{rus}2$ is the main rule for Russian syllabic-accentual verse. This rule is simpler and stricter than the Greek rule $CR_{gr}2$. All in all, the Russian tetrameter is simpler than the Greek dimeter with respect to both meter and correspondence rules.

$CR_{rus}2$ means that a monosyllabic word can occur in any position in the Russian iamb. It also means that in the Russian iamb a word boundary can occur after any position – there are no zeugmas in Russian verse. A more exact analysis will show that there are also certain rules in force that concern monosyllabic words. Georgij Shengeli (Shengeli 1921, 17) pointed out the significance of the syntactic factor for prosody.[6] Thus, a line of the kind in (12a) is quite permissible in Russian iambic trimeter, while the line in (12b) is not, even though both the distribution of stresses and the placement of word boundaries in (12b) seem to be isomorphic with (12a). (Note, however, that (12b) is quite appropriate in anapaestic dimeter.)

(12) (a)   Grozá. *Dózhd'* xlýnul. Lúch...
      (b)   Poshél *dózhd'*. Svétlyj lúch...

In both cases the metrical "transparency" of the iambic line is violated only by the monosyllabic word *dozhd'*. But, in fact, these lines are by no means isomorphic with each other: the rhythmical structure of the first line can be represented in the form (13a), and that of the second in the form (13b).

(13) (a) $[[[x\mathbf{X}]_\#]_\#]_\# \; [[[X]_\#]_\# \; [[\mathbf{Xx}]_\#]_\#]_\# \; [[[X]_\#]_\#]_\#$
      (b) $[[[x\mathbf{X}]_\#]_\# \; [[\mathbf{X}]_\#]_\#]_\# \; [[[Xx]_\#]_\# \; [[\mathbf{X}]_\#]_\#]_\#$

Hence, (12a) differs from (12b) both in syntagmatic boundaries and syntagmatic stress positions. Structures like (13b) are not permitted in the Russian iamb.

A third correspondence rule for Russian iambic tetrameter is given in (14).

(14) **(CR$_{rus}$3)** The syntagmatic stress can correspond only to a B position.

There is an additional rule in Russian syllabic-accentual verse which has no parallels in most verse traditions:

(15) **(CR$_{rus}$4)** Only a stressed syllable can correspond to the position directly before (A)&.

5.1. The prosodic rules of Russian iambic tetrameter

The prosodic rules of Russian iambic tetrameter are given below.

(16) **(PR$_{rus}$1)** Each vowel forms a syllable (there are no diphthongs nor elisions in standard Russian).

(17) **(PR$_{rus}$2)** A sequence of two vowels can form one syllable if it corresponds to one metrical position. For example,

&A B A B A B A B(A)&
Gráf v**ýi**gral dó klubníchki lákom (Brodsky)

(18) **(PR$_{rus}$3)** The sequence 'plosive + sonant' *(muta cum liquida)* at the end of a word can be considered a syllable if it occurs in an independent metrical position. For example,[7]

&A B AB AB A   B&
I rádiome**tr** treshchít (Brodsky)

(19) **(PR$_{rus}$4)** Any consonant or combination of consonants can form a syllable if (1) it is separated by word boundaries from the surrounding chains, and (2) it corresponds to any metrical position. For example,[8]

&A B   A B A B A B (A)&
Hm-hm, chitátel' blagoródnyj (Pushkin)

Whereas PR1–PR4 form the syllabic structure of iambic verse, the following rules govern its stress pattern.

(20) **(PR$_{rus}$5)** If the position of stress is determined by the standard rules of the language (as it is in most cases), then an iambic verse follows the usage of the language.

That is, in iambic verse transaccentuation is prohibited. (In Russian folk songs, by contrast, transaccentuation can be an important esthetic device.)

(21) **(PR$_{rus}$6)** If the standard rules of the language allow variation in the position of stress, then the position of stress is determined by the correspondence rules (i.e., stress occurs in the B position).

(22) **(PR$_{rus}$7)** The syntagmatic stress falls on the last full member of the syntagma.

5.2. Language prosody and verse prosody

PR$_{rus}$2–PR$_{rus}$4 do not contradict CR$_{rus}$1, since they do not allow the number of syllables in a verse to vary. At the same time, they violate the prosodic system of the Russian language. What is the linguistic mechanism of these violations? A brief answer follows.

It is necessary to differentiate prosodic elements at two levels: syllables and words. Syllables are segments distinguished by syllabic boundaries, culminating in their peak, which is usually a vowel; prosodic words are characterized by word boundaries and by word-level stress. PR$_{rus}$2 "erases" syllabic boundaries between the first and second syllable in [[vy]$_#$i]$_#$gral]$_#$]$_#$ ⇒ [[vyi]$_#$gral]$_#$]$_#$ and between the second and third in [[i[di[ot]$_#$]$_#$ ⇒ [[i[diot]$_#$]$_#$. In PR$_{rus}$3 and PR$_{rus}$4 the mechanism is the opposite: PR$_{rus}$3 produces syllabic boundaries before *muta cum liquida* if it is before a word boundary; thus, a disyllabic word [[ok[tjabr']$_#$]$_#$ becomes trisyllabic [[ok[tja]$_#$br']$_#$]$_#$ and tetrasyllabic [[ra[di[o]$_#$metr]$_#$]$_#$ becomes pentasyllabic [[ra[di[o]$_#$me]$_#$tr]$_#$]$_#$. PR4 reflects the fact that segments which do not contain any vowels are distinguished by word boundaries; this distinction creates syllabic peaks in these segments: [[hm]$_#$]$_#$ [[hm]$_#$]$_#$, or [[sh]$_#$]$_#$ [[slu]$_#$shaj]$_#$te]$_#$.

Verse prosody is the consequence of the transformation of language prosody resulting from its correspondence with meter.

6. Some typological remarks

Metrical rules are mostly the same in different verse traditions (although there is a certain variety here as well: for example, the dipodic structure of the ancient iamb or the position of the caesura in Sapphic hendecasyllabic verse in Greek and Latin). In contrast, prosodic rules mainly characterize each national tradition separately. Here, too, there are interesting questions connected with the transplantation of prosodic rules, for example, from ancient verse to new European verse. When Konrad Gessner in 1555 translated the prayer of *Pater Noster* in hexameters: *O Vatter vnser...*, he doubles the *t* in *Vater*, because according to Latin (but not to German) rules a long syllable would be formed in this way. Nevertheless, prosodical rules are in general limited to individual languages.

Hence, the central part of the model is the correspondence rules; these are extremely important for typological purposes. Let us compare the correspondence rules for the Russian iamb discussed above with the English and German iamb on the one hand, and, on the other hand, with the Estonian and Finnish iamb. The first thing we notice is that the typology of verse forms is not directly connected with kinship between languages: the English iamb is significantly different from the German iamb, as is the Estonian iamb from the Finnish iamb.

$CR_{rus}1$ (10). An analogous rule is valid in German, Finnish, Estonian, and many other national iambic traditions. In this respect, an important exception is the English iamb, where two syllables can correspond to an A positionn.[9]

$CR_{rus}2$ (11). This rule is valid in Estonian and some other iambic traditions. In English it is more liberal. The rule for the German iamb is stricter: (i) a stressed syllable, even if it is a stressed monosyllabic word, cannot correspond to an A position; (ii) an unstressed syllable of a polysyllabic word can occur in a B position only if it follows a stressed syllable. Thus, in the German iamb the word structure $[[xxX]_{\#}]_{\#}$ is not permitted at all, whereas the structure $[[Xxx]_{\#}]_{\#}$ is allowed.

It is difficult to explain such rigor in pure linguistic terms. The fact is that in most European verse traditions all iambic verse, including iambic tetrameter, is opposed to trochaic. In Estonian and Finnish verse the iamb represents *European* and *unusual* as opposed to *national* and *usual*. In Russian poetry – where the situation is especially interesting – the iamb is *European* and *usual* as opposed to the *national* and *unusual* trochee. In the English tradition, trochaic tetrameter is both *exotic* and *unusual*.

As for the German tradition, iambic tetrameter is primarily opposed not to trochaic tetrameter, but to *Knittelvers* – as *literary* and *regular* opposed to *popular* and *irregular*. So, German *Knittelvers* can be treated as a verse meter which has the same deep structure as iambic tetrameter, but different correspondence rules. *Knittelvers* resembles the English iamb in many ways, and it is not a coincidence that some German researchers tend to treat the English iamb as *Knittelvers*. In the English iamb the critical limit is not between mono- and polysyllabic words, but between mono- and disyllabic words on one hand, and polysyllabic words on the other; cf. Halle and Keyser's stress maxima rule (Halle and Keyser 1972, 223). However, Marina Tarlinskaja has demonstrated that there are important restrictions also for disyllabic words: words with the stress pattern $[[Xx]_\#]_\#$ are metrically much more frequent than those with $[[xX]_\#]_\#$ (Tarlinskaja 1976, 103–104).

The typological point of view allows us to discover some important regularities in Russian verse as well. The most frequent position in both English and Finnish verse is the initial position of a line.

Although more than 99% of Russian iambic lines satisfy the rule CR2 (ii), a small number of exceptions show a clear tendency to be concentrated at the beginning of the verse. This allows us to formulate two additional correspondence rules: CR5 and CR6.

(23) $(CR_{rus}5) \ \&AB \rightarrow [[Xx]_\#]_\#]_\#$

(24) $(CR_{rus}6) \ \&AB \rightarrow [[Xx]_\#]_\#$

$CR_{rus}6$ occurs more rarely and is a more emphatic violation of metrical tradition; in English verse both rules are quite usual.

Especially interesting in this respect are the Finnish and Estonian iambs, which are, in general, very strict. In these languages words stress is consistently placed on the first syllable. Therefore, there is no so-called "natural" basis for the iamb in these languages – words are either trochaic or dactylic. In order to avoid violating the main rule for syllabic-accentual verse, Estonian iambic verse has to begin with a monosyllabic word. Thus, the contracted scheme of the rhythm of iambic tetrameter is something like (25).

(25) x|XxXxXxX(x)

In other words, iambic tetrameter is a trochaic line which is preceded by a monosyllabic word. In Finnish verse, trisyllabic words are allowed at the beginning of a verse (26), but in all other positions the Finnish iamb is as strict as the Estonian one.

(26) $CR_{fin}5$ &ABA → $[[Xxx]_\#]_\#$,
or $[[[Xx]_\#x]_\#]_\#$

*syvä*sti aika uusi hengähtää (K. Kramsu 1883)

$CR_{rus}4$. This rule (the "stress constant" rule) is specific to Russian verse. An accentual constant also occurs in the second syllable of the Estonian iamb, for example. However, in contrast to the Estonian iamb, the Russian accentual constant is not determined by language – its nature is purely poetic. This rule governs more than 99.9% of Russian iambic verse. The lack of stress in a stress constant position is possible only in the case of acatalectic verse (male clause, cf. Lotman 1978):

(27)   ... BAB&&
$[[...Xxx]_\#]_\#$.

7. The rhythmic vocabulary of language and the strictness of verse

For syllabic-accentual verse the most important parameters of the word are the number of syllables it has and the position of stress. Consequently, the rhythmic vocabulary of language can be represented as follows:

(28) 1. $[x]_\#$
    1.1. $[[X]_\#]_\#$
    2.1. $[[Xx]_\#]_\#$
    2.2. $[[xX]_\#]_\#$
    3.1. $[[Xxx]_\#]_\#$
    3.2. $[[xXx]_\#]_\#$
    3.3. $[[xxX]_\#]_\#$
    and so on.

The order of appearance is important: usually, the higher the number, the more regulated its occurrence in verse.

Monosyllabic words are often ambivalent from the viewpoint of prosody: neither stressed nor unstressed, neither long nor short syllables can be syntagmatically opposed there. Therefore, such words play in a verse the role of *ancipitia*: they can occur in any position in at least the syllabic-accentual system of versification. Indeed, in Russian, English, Estonian, and Finnish verse there are no general limits in using monosyllabic words (however, cf. $CR_{rus}3$). The distribution of these is subordinated only to statistical regularities. For example, in Russian they very often occur at the beginning of a verse and in the positions of so-called weak ictuses; that is, in places where metrical ambivalence increases. But this is not the case in German verse, where monosyllabic words can occur only in a B position.

As for words with two or more syllables, the main rule for syllabic-accentual verse is that here stress can occur only in B positions ($CR_{rus}2$). In this sense the strictest is the Estonian iamb, which shows only few exceptions to this rule (in earlier occasions it is a poetical licence, later cases probably follow Finnish patterns).

In Russian verse, initially stressed disyllabic words can occur in the first position as well, but here we are clearly dealing with exceptions. Usually they result from following the sound of English verse and we find them more often in iambic pentameter than in iambic tetrameter.

As for English verse, the stress of disyllabic words can occur in A positions elsewhere than at the beginning of a verse. Here, trisyllabic complexes become critical; this is referred to as the stress-maxima rule by Halle and Keyser.

And finally, we can present the gradation of iambic tetrameter which proceeds from the strictness of the rules: German I4, Estonian I4, Russian I4, Finnish I4, English I4, and German *Knittelvers*.

Appendix: Symbols and abbreviations

A, B – metrical positions; & – delimitator; F – foot; D – dipody.
x – syllable; X – stressed syllable; **X** – syllable with syntagmatic stress.
$[...]_{\#}$ – syllabic boundaries; $[[...]_{\#}]_{\#}$ – word boundaries;
$[[[...]_{\#}]_{\#}]_{\#}$ – syntagmatic (phrase) boundaries.

Notes

* The writing of this paper was partly supported by ETF grant no 5243.
1. Strophical patterns and rhyme schemes can be treated as the realisation of the same metrical principles which form the meter of a verse line. For example, the scheme ABABAB... can characterize both the meter of a verse line and the rhyme pattern.
2. If we treat A and B as purely relative entities which acquire positive value only after the application of correspondence rules, then the question arises: why should we distinguish verse feet AB and BA? Indeed, both iambs and trochees, for example, can be derived from AB as well as from BA. The distinction is made based on both tradition (iambs and trochees not only have different surface structures, but different deep structures as well) and convenience: it would be impractical to define all the correspondence rules for each verse meter. In the present paper simplified versions of both metrical and correspondence rules are offered, for a more comprehensive treatment see Lotman 2000.
3. Metrical rules and schemes are presented in simplified form; for a more complete treatment see Lotman 2000.
4. Tis tên kephalên apedêdoken – who nibbled off the head of [sprat] (transl. by Benjamin Bickley Rogers).
5. In Greek iambic verse the quantitative principle is more important and stronger than the syllabic one. In this respect it differs from the Aeolian strophic verse, where the syllabic principle dominates over quantity. The Aeolian lyrical strophics belong to the syllabic-quantitative versification system (see also Lotman 1998).
6. Later, Paul Kiparsky (1973) drew attention to the same problem in English verse.
7. This example is especially effective also because here two phonologically identical sequences ...$tr]_\#]_\#$ $[[tr...$ are in succession; it constitutes a syllable at the end, but not at the beginning of a word.
8. Cf. Shengeli 1921, 11–12
9. Morris Halle and Samuel Jay Keyser claim that in iambic pentameter two syllables can also occur in a B position (Halle and Keyser 1972); according to this treatment, syllabic structure of the English iamb is similar to that of Greek (cf. $CR_{gr}1$). However, they do not provide any examples of actual verse practice to illustrate this statement.

References

Halle, M., and S.J. Keyser
    1972   The iambic pentameter. In: *Versification: Major Language Types. Sixteen Essays*, W.K. Wimsatt (ed.), 217–273. New York: Modern Language Association, New York University Press.

Kiparsky, P.
    1973   The role of linguistics in a theory of poetry. In: *Daedalus* 102: 231–244.

Lotman, M.
    1978   Stress and word boundary in qualitative verse. In: *Estonian Papers in Phonetics. Studies on Accent, Quantity, Stress, Tone. Papers of the Symposium (Tallinn, November 1978)*, Arvo Eek (ed.), 63–65. Tallinn: Academy of Sciences of the Estonian S.S.R. Institute of Language and Literature.
    1998   O sistemax stixoslozhenija (preimushchestvenno na materiale estonskogo i russkogo stixa). *Sign Systems Studies* 26, Tartu University Press, 201–255.
    2000   Russkij stix: Metrika, sistemy stixoslozhenija, prosodija (generativnyj podxod). *Sign Systems Studies* 28, Tartu University Press, 217–241.

Rogers, B.B. (transl.)
    1982   *Aristophanes, with the English Translation of Benjamin Bickley Rogers in Three Volumes*. Cambridge, Massachusetts: Harvard University Press; London: W. Heinemann.

Shengeli, G.
    1921   *Traktat o russkom stixe. Chast'I: Organicheskaja metrika*. Odessa [no publisher].

Tarlinskaja, M.
    1976   *English Verse: Theory and History*. The Hague-Paris: Mouton.

Structural dynamics in the Onegin stanza*

Barry P. Scherr

1. The Problem

The inner dynamics of the Onegin Stanza, created by Aleksandr Pushkin for his novel in verse, *Eugene Onegin*, have proved resistant to conventional analysis. On the one hand, the rhyme scheme implies that the form consists of three quatrains and a concluding couplet (4+4+4+2), much like the Shakespearean sonnet. On the other hand, the syntax does not necessarily adhere to this same division; in most stanzas at least one of the rhyme units does not conclude with a strong syntactic break. The goal here, then, is to analyze the tension between rhyme and syntax, and to formulate a hierarchical set of constraints which would account for the specific structural variety that this form exhibits.

Description of the Onegin Stanza:

(1)   Net: rano chuvstva v něm ostyli;   A
         Emu naskuchil sveta shum;   b
         Krasavicy ne dolgo byli   A
    4   Predmet ego privychnyx dum;   b
         Izmeny utomit' uspeli;   C
         Druz'ja i druzhba nadoeli,   C
         Zatem, chto ne vsegda zhe mog   d
    8   *Beef-steaks* i strasburgskij pirog   d
         Shampanskoj oblivat' butylkoj   E
         I sypat' ostrye slova,   f
         Kogda bolela golova;   f
    12   I xot' on byl povesa pylkij,   E
         No razljubil on nakonec   g
         I bran', i sablju, i svinets.   g

                            Pushkin, *Eugene Onegin*, I.37

(1a)   Yes – feeling early cooled within him;   A
              He came to loathe that worldly grind;   b
              Proud beauties could no longer win him   A
      4   and uncontested rule his mind;   b
              Constant inconstancy turns dreary;   C
              Of friends and friendship he grew weary: C
              One can't forever and again   d
      8   Chase with a bottle of champagne   d
              Beefsteak and Strasbourg liver pasty   E
              And scatter insults all around   f
              When senses swim and temples pound: f
      12   And so, although by temper hasty,   E
              Our lad at length was overfed   g
              With taunts and duels, sword and lead.   g

                                               trans. Walter Arndt[1]

The rhyme scheme differs from that of the Shakespearean sonnet (ababcdcdefefgg) only in lines 5–12: both have a concluding couplet, and the first quatrain is identical, except for the alternation of feminine and masculine rhymes – in Russian, unlike English, the length of the clausula (the syllables, if any, that follow the final ictus) is a key component in the description of rhyme schemes. Quatrains two and three vary from the English model in that the second contains two adjacent rhymes, while the third features enclosed rhyme. More crucially for our purposes, the rhyme scheme is far less useful for delineating inner divisions than it is in the Shakespearean sonnet, where strong syntactic breaks normally mark the borders between the internal quatrains. The first quatrain ends with a semi-colon, but so do lines 1, 2 and 5; lines 3 and 4 clearly form a unit (thanks to the enjambment between the lines), but it would be difficult to claim that the break after line 4 is any stronger than those after lines 2 and 5. If we look at the end of line eight, we will see that it is not followed by any punctuation at all; lines 7–11 form a single thought. The final couplet begins with the word "But" (*No* in the Russian), and taken by themselves these lines could well be said to play a similar role as the concluding couplet in a Shakespeare sonnet. However, the previous line, 12, with its initial word "And," in fact introduces this final segment of the stanza, which thus consists of three lines, rather than two.[2] For all its seeming variability (in comparison to the conventional sonnet), the Onegin Stanza does seem to be governed by certain structural parameters, or at least preferences. Yet scholars have struggled in their efforts to define those parameters in a manner that takes into full consideration the range of possibilities while offering a systematic explanation of the criteria that Pushkin employed.

2. Previous analyses

Leonid Grossman was among the first to point out that the structure of the stanza exhibited a range of possibilities. He essentially saw the main divisions as occurring after lines eight and twelve, thus resulting in a rising portion (the first two quatrains), a falling portion, and an independent coda (Grossman 1924, 121); he found the basic structure to be 4+4+4+2, but also, in about 1/3 of the cases (122 of 367) 4+4+3+3 (Grossman 1924, 127). The latter form resembles the Petrarchan sonnet, a point that Grossman emphasizes by quoting a pair of instances where Pushkin uses the same rhymes in the first and second quatrains, thereby creating a rhyme scheme reminiscent of that sonnet (AbAb AAbb Cdd Cee; cf. Baevskij 1990, who independently cites one of the same examples). Stankiewicz (1995), going more by a general impression than a precise count, finds a virtual balance between the two types (the 4+4+4+2 and 4+4+3+3); following Grossman, he states that the dominant larger structure is 8+6 (185–86).

These descriptions imply that the Onegin stanza is close to the sonnet, be it Shakespearean or Petrarchan, and that there is a clear division between the first eight and the final six lines. Vinokur (1941) is the first to examine carefully just what happens at the ends of quatrains, and he arrives at a quite different conclusion. He distinguishes three kinds of quatrain endings: those where there is a clear syntactic break (corresponding, as a rule, to the end of a sentence), those where there is a potential break (i.e., generally a clause boundary), and, third, those where the syntax requires that the sentence continue beyond the end of the quatrain. The ending of the first quatrain in the Onegin stanza exhibits the strongest breaks, coinciding either with the end of a sentence (71%) or clause (9%). For the second the corresponding figures are 51% and 12%; for the third both are 32% (186–7, 204). The final couplet, he notes, has the potential to exhibit independence, both syntactically and thematically (205), though in over one-third of the instances (cf. Grossman) the ending of the third quatrain is not separated from the final couplet. The most significant implication of his work is that the quatrain boundaries, other than that of the first, do not necessarily correspond to syntactic divisions. By showing that the break after the eighth line is weaker than that after the fourth, he largely invalidates the 8+6 schema and suggests that the structure is much more amorphous, and much less like that of a sonnet, than many have claimed.

Tomashevsky (1958) is close to Vinokur in his findings. Rather than look at just the borders of quatrains, he examines the punctuation at the end of all the lines, assigning relative strengths to each form of ending. He then expresses the strengths of the break at the end of each line in terms of a percentage, where 100% would mean that every line at that position in the poem's stanzas ends with a period or punctuation mark of similar strength, while 0% would indicate that none of the lines have any punctuation at all (cf. Table 1, first column). He notes that the first quatrain behaves much like an independent stanza, exhibiting a symmetrical structure in which the first two lines roughly mirror the last two. The second quatrain is much less autonomous, and its structure is not at all symmetrical. The third quatrain is hardly autonomous at all (118). Thus, it is difficult even to speak of lines 5–12 as forming quatrains in any conventional sense. Grinbaum (2000, 90) confirms the decreasing sense of closure after quatrains two and three.

Table 1. Line endings and average stressing.
First column: Calculations by Postoutenko (1998, 151) following methodology of Tomashevsky (1958, 118). Second column: from Gasparov (1989, 142, based on data in Shengeli [1923, 111]).
The second column is discussed below, in the section on rhythmical and syntactic data.

Line	Delineation of line endings	Average number of stresses per line
1.	31.9	3.39
2.	46.5	3.15
3.	24.2	3.17
4.	67.9	3.09
5.	38.5	3.24
6.	31.1	3.17
7.	36.0	3.10
8.	52.3	3.17
9.	36.0	3.22
10.	37.7	3.13
11.	34.4	3.13
12.	41.5	3.18
13.	28.4	3.22
14.	98.7	3.16

Tomashevsky (1958, 123–125) goes on to assert that the couplet following the third quatrain possesses an inner cohesion of its own, finding that even when the final two lines are not clearly divided from the preceding line or lines syntactically, they can be read independently. Consider the following example:

(2) Evgenij bez truda uznal
 Evgeny without difficulty learned
 Ego ljubvi mladuju povest',
 [of] his love [the] youthful tale,
 Obil'nyj chuvstvami rasskaz,
 Replete with feelings [a] story
 Davno ne novymi dlja nas.
 Long since not new for us   (II, 19, ll. 11–14)

The last four lines of the stanza all form a single sentence, but Tomashevsky's point is that the last two, if extracted from the stanza, could still be read on their own as a pithy saying or perhaps as the epigraph for a short story or novel: "A story replete with feelings long familiar to us." The same is true of the full Onegin stanza quoted earlier (1 and 1a); closure extends over the final three lines, but the last two, if printed separately, could form a self-contained unit. The special status that Tomashevsky assigns to the concluding couplet is more unqualified than Vinokur's and seems to have influenced Baevskij et al. (1997), who describe a computer analysis of the Onegin stanza that would search for similarities between what they call the body of the stanza (the first 12 lines) and the "tail" (the concluding couplet).

To summarize: one set of analyses claims a similarity between the Onegin stanza and the sonnet; a 4+4 structure at the beginning is followed by a 4+2 or 3+3 structure in the second half of the work. The other set implicitly sees the Onegin stanza as possessing a more distinctive structure, within which the initial quatrain provides one anchor and the concluding lines another, with a great amount of freedom in between.

3. Rhythmical and syntactic data

Table 2 shows the basic rhythmical data for *Eugene Onegin*. Russian words average over two syllables in length and contain just a single stress; as a result, while Russian poetry until very recent times obligatorily stressed the line-final ictus in syllabo-tonic verse, some of the other ictuses in binary (iambic and trochaic) poems are unstressed, because over an entire poem there will almost always be fewer stresses than ictuses. The percentages for this poem are typical for iambic tetrameter poetry in Pushkin's day: about a fifth of the ictuses are not stressed, the first ictus is stressed somewhat less often than the second, and the third or penultimate ictus is far less frequently fulfilled than the others. The first rhythmic form has fully stressed lines – just over ¼ of those in the poem. Three stresses appear in 63.8% of the lines (forms II–IV, where either the first, second or third ictus is not fulfilled). Both the first and third ictuses are not stressed in 9% of the lines (rhythmic form VI) and a very few lines omit stress on both the second and third ictuses (form V). The average number of stresses per line indicates an average of 44.5 stresses per 14-line unit; generally from 41 to 48 ictuses (out of 56) are stressed in each stanza.[3]

Table 2. Patterns of Stress in Eugene Onegin (based on Taranovsky (1953, Table 3))

A. Stressing by Ictus

I	II	III	IV	Avg.	Avg. # of stresses
84.4%	89.9%	43.1%	100.0%	79.4%	3.18

B. Rhythmic Forms

I	II	III	IV	V	VI	3-stress lines (II+III+IV)	2-stress lines (V+VI)
ssss	wsss	swss	ssws	swws	wsws		
26.8	6.6	9.7	47.5	0.4	9.0	63.8	9.4

While the overall data do not indicate anything out of the ordinary, the line-by-line figures for the average number of stressed ictuses yield some interesting data (Table 1, column 2). M. L. Gasparov (1989) was the first to focus on stress frequency throughout the stanza, paying particular attention to quatrains written in iambic or trochaic tetrameter. The frequencies vary by rhyme scheme and by meter, and, like the overall tendencies in stressing, evolve from one period to the next. One consistent feature is strong stressing on the stanza's first line. In AbAb quatrains of Pushkin's day, stressing also usually declined from the first line to the fourth. Both tendencies are evident in the first four lines of the Onegin stanza. The remaining quatrains also exhibit stronger stressing at the start (lines five and nine), as does the couplet (line 13), though the overall pattern of stressing is less clear after the first quatrain, perhaps in part because the rhyme schemes are also different.

This impression of a distinct first quatrain and weaker divisions over the rest of the stanza receives support from the figures in Table 1. A strong break occurs after the fourteenth line in nearly every stanza. Other than that, line boundaries are most prominent after the fourth line, in keeping with the concept of a clearly-defined first quatrain. The relative strength of line breaks after the second line (46.5, which is a higher figure than that at the quatrain boundary after the twelfth line) also implies that this first quatrain behaves much like an independent stanza, since this 2+2 internal structure is quite common in four-line stanzas. However, the demarcations of line endings are weaker after the eighth line than the fourth, and still weaker after the twelfth; what is more, the figures show roughly equal strengths for the breaks following lines 5–7 and 9–11, indicating a lack of internal structure for the quatrains occupying lines 5–8 and 9–12.[4]

4. A rule-based approach

The above analysis suggests that of the previous attempts to describe the Onegin stanza, Tomashevsky's comes closest to capturing the essence of the form: a relatively well-demarcated beginning, a clear sense of closure, and a highly varied set of possibilities among lines 5–12. And yet even his characterization neither explains the reasons for Pushkin's particular choices in creating his stanza nor fully elucidates the inner structure of this form. Of particular importance for my methodology are some of the techniques employed by Hayes and MacEachern (1998), who account for all the existing quatrain types in English folk verse by showing the interaction of various constraints on metrical well-formedness and saliency. However, there are two regards in which an examination of the Onegin stanza necessarily differs from their work on the folk verse quatrain. First, a 14-line stanza involves vastly more possibilities than a four-line unit. Hayes and MacEachern establish a set of five line cadences, leading to the theoretical possibility of 625 (5^4) quatrains, although admittedly only 21 quatrain types account for over 95% of the stanzas in their data base. Their cadences are not relevant for our study here, but if they were, we would be dealing with 5^{14} (or something over 6 billion) theoretically possible stanzas. The permutations are so much greater that it becomes necessary to look at units larger than the individual line in order to deal with the data in a practical fashion. Second, the question of well-formedness in literary verse necessarily involves issues of tradition and the consciousness of the author. Hayes and MacEachern assume, correctly I believe, that folk verse largely mirrors the well-formedness judgments of a language's native speakers. Such considerations certainly play a role in literary verse, but poets, in striving to be original or for other reasons, may resist rather than adhere to a language's inherent features and purposefully create ill-formed lines or stanzas.

Conversely, literary tradition can limit the range of poetic expression no less than inherent linguistic features. Let us note two instances in which Russian poets have obeyed rules stricter than those found in English. First, as we have already noted, until recent times the final ictus of a Russian syllabotonic line has been obligatorily stressed. Second, Russian does not allow what is often called "trochaic substitution" on a disyllabic word in an iambic line. Thus line 11 of Shakespeare's Sonnet 60 would be admissible in Russian ("Féeds ȯn thĕ rárĭtĭes...") since the trochaic beginning involves the monosyllabic words "feeds" and "on", but line 14 (Práisĭng thў wórth) would not be, since "praising" has two syllables.[5]

This latter limitation may in fact be influenced by linguistic qualities of Russian (Jakobson 1973). Indeed, many differences between English and Russian verse clearly stem from the specific prosodic features of each language. English, with its abundance of short words and relatively high frequency of stressed syllables, tends to fulfill the overwhelming majority of ictuses, while Russian, with longer words and less frequent stressing, leaves some pre-final ictuses unstressed in virtually every stanza. Thus, the set of principles adhered to by poets arises from a mixture of prosodic features and literary tradition; these affect everything from the nature of the individual verse line to the structure of the entire work.

Pushkin's Onegin stanza exhibits several qualities that have come to be associated with it on the few occasions when it has been used by later poets: *Eugene Onegin* is particularly long, but in other instances as well it is most often found in poetic works of substantial length; the meter is usually, though not always, iambic tetrameter; and a whimsical, self-aware manner allows the poet to break away from the basic form on occasion. An instance of Pushkin's whimsy is his assigning numbers to "missing" stanzas; the 389 numbered stanzas refer to only 366 actual stanzas, and of those three are left incomplete (Baevskij 1990, 53). In "The Tambov Treasurer's Wife," the longest of several works where Pushkin's immediate successor, Lermontov, employed the Onegin stanza, at least one line from 10 of its 54 stanzas is omitted (Pejsaxovich, 1969).

While such matters as genre and tone have little to do with the structural qualities of the Onegin stanza itself, several rules do determine the well-formedness of the stanza for Pushkin. Two rules are inviolable:

(3) The Onegin Stanza contains 14 lines.

(4) The rhyme scheme of the Onegin stanza is AbAbCCddEffEgg.

As we have just seen, incomplete Onegin stanzas occur, but they are just that: fragments, which are not structurally identical to the canonical form. The rhyme scheme, inviolable for Pushkin, does occasionally vary in works by other poets, but since the rhyme scheme is basic to the structure of this form, it seems best to consider such stanzas as falling outside the permissible bounds of the stanza.[6]

I will argue that the interaction of five violable rules largely accounts for the observed varieties of the Onegin stanza. The hierarchical ordering of their violability yields explanations for the frequency of observed structural types within the Onegin stanza and also helps account for the seemingly incompatible models of Grossman and Vinokur.

(5) Closure (C): Stanzaic endings are salient.

Broadly speaking, the longer the stanza, the greater the tendency for each stanza to be marked by a syntactic break. When, as in *Onegin*, the stanzaic structure is particularly long and complex, enjambment between stanzas must be sufficiently unusual so as to be highly marked; otherwise, the sense of the stanza as a separate unit will be lost. Actual enjambment between stanzas occurs only ten times within *Onegin* (Tomashevsky 1958, 114–15). Stanzas are very occasionally run together semantically despite strong syntactic breaks (i.e., a description or a specific action in one stanza continues without any shift in focus or emphasis into the next). This phenomenon, too, is rare; in the first chapter there are clear semantic as well as syntactic breaks after 53 of the 54 stanzas. Thus the "sense of closure" at the end of each stanza arises through semantic as well as syntactic means.

Tomashevsky's comment about the demarcation of the concluding couplet (1958, 123–125) is relevant here as well. Even when the final semantic grouping appears to extend over more than two lines, the final two lines are usually singled out by the paired masculine rhyme of that couplet, the aphoristic quality of those lines, and the frequent appearance in line-initial position of words that imply a final thrust ("And...", "Thus...") or a contrast to what has come before ("But...", "Although..."). Therefore this rhymed couplet, with its syntactic wholeness, helps to conclude the stanza and to demarcate it from that which follows.

(6) Opening (O): The beginnings of stanzas are salient.

While the effect of closure is generally clear (and its absence therefore stands as highly marked), the saliency of the opening tends to be weaker. The general principle is that the opening of a stanza is marked; however, this marking may be realized in a variety of ways, not all of which are necessarily present in a given stanza and most of which tend to be more subtle than the syntactic and semantic breaks that result in closure. One manifestation of saliency in the opening has already been discussed: stressing is generally heaviest on the first line of the stanza (cf. Gasparov 1989). In the Onegin stanza the saliency of the opening is further marked by the relatively well-formed opening quatrain, as noted by Vinokur (1941) and Tomashevsky (1958). In (1) all of the ictuses in the first line are stressed, and the hypermetrical stress on the stanza's initial word further emphasizes the beginning. Lines three and four are set off against one and two, imparting a sense of coherence to the quatrain. Missing is a semantic break coinciding with the end of the quatrain; line 5 is another in the series of parallel statements, and thus leaves the quatrain "semi-open." However, as indicated in the last column of Table 3, 40 of the 54 stanzas in Chapter I do have clear semantic and syntactic breaks after the fourth line. Further, the relatively high frequency of enjambment after the first and (especially) the third line, along with the number of breaks after line 2, are indicative of a strong 2+2 tendency, so that this opening quatrain often has the distinct appearance of a carefully crafted, symmetrical unit. In other words, the "sense of opening" is identical with the notion of a well-formed first quatrain. Note in this regard that the rhyme scheme for the first four lines, AbAb, consists of the most common pattern found in Russian quatrains; enclosed rhymes (as in the third quatrain) are significantly rarer in stand-alone quatrains, and two adjacent rhymes (the second quatrain) are rarer still. Hence it is only to be expected that this opening four-line unit would display a particularly strong cohesiveness, thereby imparting an initial sense of structure to the stanza.

The opening constraint tends to be less strictly observed than closure (e.g., over ¼ of the stanzas in Chapter I do not have a distinct boundary at the end of the first quatrain, while all observe syntactic closure at the end). This behavior suggests a parallel at the level of the stanza to the principle of "beginnings free, endings strict" which appears in various descriptions of the verse line (Kiparsky 1975; cf. Hayes 1989, 222 and 257).

Table 3. Punctuation, Enjambment, and Structural Divisions in Chapter I (N=54)

Line	(none)	,	;	... or –	:	? or !	.	# of enj.	# of breaks
1.	19	21	4	1	4	4	1	14	2
2.	7	23	12	0	3	4	5	5	11
3.	27	22	0	1	0	3	1	20	1
4.	3	9	12	0	2	6	22	3	40
5.	12	23	8	0	2	5	4	10	3
6.	20	20	6	0	3	4	1	16	8
7.	14	19	7	1	3	2	8	11	13
8.	14	14	8	1	2	2	13	14	25
9.	18	26	5	0	1	1	3	16	7
10.	13	31	5	0	2	1	2	11	8
11.	15	27	6	0	0	2	4	11	16
12.	9	27	9	2	1	4	2	7	23
13.	28	21	2	0	3	0	0	21	4
14.	0	0	0	0	0	9	45	0	53

(7) Grouping (G): Avoid syntactical-semantic units longer than five or shorter than 2 lines.

The quatrain is by far the most popular stanza length for Russian poetry. Long non-stanzaic poems, as well as long stanzas, tend to divide into shorter units, usually of two or four lines. Longer groupings do occur within individual stanzas; for instance, in *Onegin*, I.11 the verb *umel* ("knew how to") in the first line is followed by a dozen infinitives over the first twelve lines, each of which mentions another of Onegin's talents, with a thirteenth infinitive appearing in the final couplet. In a way all 14 lines go together, but an ellipsis at the end of line 12 suggests that the two groupings should be 1–12 and 13–14. However, this structure is unusual; by my count, the 54 stanzas in the first chapter contain 161 clear breaks before the last line (cf. Table 3), or about 3 per stanza, resulting in an average of four units per stanza. This finding is not out of keeping with the frequent appearance of such structures as 4+4+4+2 and 4+4+3+3.

(8) Matching (M): Syntactic and semantic boundaries match those of rhyme subsets within a larger structure.

This tendency appears in much Russian (and not only Russian) poetry. The frequency of stressing from line-to-line in many 8-line stanzas rhymed ababcdcd follows the same pattern that would be seen in two independent quatrains (Gasparov 1989, but only for iambic, not trochaic poems), and these 8-line stanzas also display a high percentage of syntactic breaks at the juncture between the two quatrains. Both the 4+4+4+2 and the 4+4+3+3 structures for the Onegin stanza could be described as symmetrical in this regard, because they do correspond with rhyme units: AbAb / CdCd / EffE / gg and AbAb / CdCd / Eff / Egg.

(9) Blurring (B): In an integral stanzaic structure the syntactic and semantic boundaries of the whole take precedence over those of rhyme subsets.

Roughly speaking, (9) is the obverse of (8). Pospelov (1990) has made the point that asymmetrical structures are quite common in *Onegin*, and that very often shifts in verb tense help intensify demarcations that do not coincide with those implied by the poem's rhyme scheme. Column 2 of Table 1 (cf. Gasparov 1989) indicates that while the first four lines of the Onegin stanza exhibit the same decline in stressing from beginning to end that occurs in independent quatrains, lines 8 and 12 exhibit a rise rather than a decline in stressing at the end of the subunit, thereby blurring any "boundary" between quatrains. Furthermore, preliminary work by Mihhail Lotman (personal communication) has indicated that frequently a break occurs at the mid-point of the stanza (after line 7); note, in fact, that Table 1, column 2 shows particularly low stressing on line 7, which would be consistent with its marking the end of a structural unit.

All of this implies that two opposing principles contend with each other in the Onegin stanza. On the one hand, much poetry exhibits a tendency toward structures in which rhyme units match syntactic and semantic groupings (i.e., matching) – a phenomenon that certainly occurs frequently in *Onegin* and one which many scholars have been pre-inclined to see as overwhelmingly dominant. Pushkin, however, at the same time strove for maximal freedom within his stanza, often allowing his syntactic boundaries to occur outside the boundaries of rhyme sets. He did not always privilege the subunits suggested by the rhyme scheme, but instead saw the stanza in its entirety as a basic building block for his long poem. At the same time, rather than obliterate the boundaries suggested by the internal stanzaic subgroups, he tends to "blur" them, so that major syntactic breaks often occur at the end of line 7 as well as line 8, at the end of line 11 almost as often as at the end of line 12.

The punctuation that Pushkin employed in the first chapter of *Onegin* (Table 3) illustrates how the two opposing tendencies play themselves out.[7] A comma or the lack of any punctuation would generally signal that no sharp break occurs; the other forms of punctuation indicate at least the potential for a break. However, as indicated in (1), lines 4–5, the appearance of the same form of punctuation at closely-spaced intervals – be it as strong as a semicolon, as in (1), or even a period – may indicate a listing rather than semantic breaks. Table 3 shows that demarcations after lines 3 or 13 are rare (in 49 of 54 instances there is either a comma or no punctuation at all); hence these lines tend to be closely tied to the following lines (4 and 14 respectively), which in turn are likely to conclude with a break. More significantly, this table reveals certain hidden dynamics of the Onegin stanza. It is not so much that Pushkin deflates the expectation of a break after lines 8 and 12, but that he makes these two breaks "movable," thereby blurring the structure. Note that there are breaks 40 times after line 4, a number virtually matched by the totals for lines 7 *and* 8 (=38) and for lines 11 *and* 12 (=39). Note, too, that the breaks after lines 7 and 8 are more likely to coincide with the end of a sentence, whereas those after 11 and 12 do so less often – that is, in keeping with Lotman's observation, the break near the mid-point of the poem is generally stronger than the penultimate break.

As Table 3 implies, and as a stanza-by-stanza analysis of Chapter I confirms, the various constraints work in conjunction to create specific stanza types. Closure (C) is the most stringent of the constraints under which the Onegin stanza is created. Even in the one instance in Chapter I where the subject matter from one stanza clearly continues into the next, the first of these (numbered 57, because this chapter has several "missing" stanzas that figure in the count) would still appear to have a distinct conclusion, if considered on its own, and thus it, too, observes (C). The next two constraints are roughly equal in rank: Opening (O) is considered violated when the first four lines do not form a closed quatrain and Grouping (G) when more than five consecutive lines are not divided by a strong semantic or syntactic break. Of Chapter One's 54 stanzas, 14 do not observe (O) and 11 do not observe (G). Note that for Matching (M) to occur, both (O) and (G) must be observed; all three occur in 21 of the stanzas. However, fourteen of those that exhibit both (O) and (G) still exhibit a blurring of the underlying structure created by the rhyme units (B). While the (B) stanzas may or may not observe (O) and (G), the (M) stanzas are all alike:

(10)   COGM: 21   COGB: 14   CGB: 8   CB: 6   COB: 5

As an example of the most common stanzaic type, see (11):

(11)   Nashel on polon dvor uslugi;
            K pokojniku so vsex storon
            S"ezzhalis' nedrugi i drugi,
     4   Oxotniki do poxoron.
            Pokojnika poxoronili.
            Popy i gosti eli, pili,
            I posle vazhno razoshlis',
     8   Kak budto delom zanjalis'.
            Vot nash Onegin sel'skij zhitel',
            Zavodov, vod, lesov, zemel'
            Xozjain polnyj, a dosel'
     12   Porjadka vrag i rastochitel',
            I ochen' rad, chto prezhnij put'
            Peremenil na chto-nibud'.   Pushkin, *Eugene Onegin*, I.53

(11a)   He found the manor full of mourners,
            Connections dear and not so dear,
            Who had converged there from all corners;
     4   All funeral fans, it would appear.
            They laid to rest the late lamented,
            Then, dined and wined and well-contented,
            The priests and guests left one by one,
     8   Gently, as from a job well done.
            There was Eugene, a landed squire,
            Of forests, waters, mills galore
            The sovereign lord – he who before
     12   Had been a scamp and outlaw dire –
            And pleased to see his life's stale plot
            Exchanged for – well, no matter what.   Trans. Walter Arndt

The opening is clearly delineated, with a fully-stressed first line and a clear break after line 4. The next four lines also form a definite unit, following the rhyme scheme, while the next four lines develop yet another theme, which receives a whimsical conclusion in the final couplet. Yet what is most interesting about the Onegin stanza is not these instances, which many scholars have considered to be the predominant if not the only kind (and where the Onegin stanza seems structurally similar to the Shakespearean sonnet), but the amount of asymmetry that results in other stanzas (see, for example, [1]), sometimes due to the violation of (O) or (G) (or both) and sometimes because Pushkin simply chooses to avoid co-incidence of the rhyme and syntactic units in lines 5–12. Pushkin, faced with the competing rules, created stanzas with matching rhyme and semantic units more often than any other single type. However, the frequency with which he violated at least one of (O), (G) and (M) makes the majority of the stanzas "blurred," accounting for the variety and richness displayed by the Onegin stanza, as well as for the sense that it is indeed an independent stanzaic form, distinctly different from the sonnet, where violations of (M) are much rarer.[8]

Subsequent appearances of the Onegin stanza do not always follow this usage precisely. For instance, Lermontov, in "The Tambov Treasurer's Wife," delineated the quatrains far more strongly than did Pushkin; if Tomashevsky's methodology yielded a relative strength of 67.9 at the end of line 4 and 52.3 at the end of line 8 (cf. Table 1), then for Lermontov the corresponding figures are 85.6 and 78.8 (Postoutenko 1998). Pushkin himself chose to go in the other direction; the unfinished poem "Ezerskij," begun after he completed *Onegin*, consists of fifteen Onegin stanzas, only three of which exhibit (M), and only six a clearly defined opening quatrain. Thus Pushkin seems to have been moving further away from the internal structure that has caused some to see in the Onegin stanza a resemblance to the sonnet. Indeed, by weakening the regularity of the opening quatrain and by allowing for entire runs of lines with strongly marked enjambment, as he does in the very opening stanza of this later poem, Pushkin made it still harder to speak of subunits or quatrains within the Onegin stana.. Thus he was coming to treat this long stanza as a minimal structural unit, giving it the fully independent status enjoyed by the quatrain and other shorter stanzaic forms.[9]

Notes

* For comments on an earlier version of this paper, I am grateful to Elan Dresher, Nigel Fabb, Colleen Fitzgerald, Nila Friedberg, Paul Kiparsky, Emily Klenin, and Mihhail Lotman.

1. The Arndt translation follows not only the precise rhyme scheme of the Russian, but also, insofar as possible, the syntactic structure and the punctuation found in the original.
2. Wachtel 1998 (124–5) analyzes the second stanza of the poem, pointing out that there, too, the syntactic breaks do not match those of the quatrains. He also notes (122) that Pushkin in general showed little interest in the sonnet, which emerged as a significant form in Russian only after he had started to write *Onegin*.
3. Grinbaum 2000 (especially in the first two sections of chapter three) offers more detailed analysis of average stressing in the Onegin stanza.
4. Other kinds of internal structure also occur. Lilly 1995 (36) has pointed to a high degree of parallelism that appears with some frequency in lines 5–6 (rhyming CC); the role that parallelism plays at various points in the stanza requires further investigation.
5. For a detailed discussion of this rule, see Jakobson 1973.
6. Thus the sixteenth of eighteen stanzas in Maksimilian Volosin's "Pis'mo" rhymes AbAbCCddEEfGGf, with the third quatrain following rather than preceding the "final" couplet, and the masculine and feminine clausulae reversed on all six final lines (on Volosin's use of the Onegin stanza, see Scherr 1991).
7. As the commentary below in the text implies, the final two columns of Table 3 cannot be derived directly from the information in the previous columns, since (a) the absence of punctuation does not necessarily result in enjambment, and (b) the presence of "strong" punctuation, such as a period or question mark, does not always indicate a semantic break.
8. As Paul Kiparsky has observed, it is possible to consider the structure as essentially binary, with anchors at the beginning and the end, since (C) and (O) are the strongest rules.
9. For these reasons Mihhail Lotman (personal communication) has said that "Pushkin comes at the end of the Onegin stanza's tradition." In the variability that he achieved with the inner structure as well as in the ease with which he manipulated the form, he attained a level of perfection greater than that achieved by any of the subsequent poets who adopted this stanza.

References

Baevskij, V. S.
    1990   Strofa i rifma v "Evgenii Onegine". In: *Pushkinskie chtenija: Sbornik statej,* S. G. Isakov (ed.), 44–57. Tallinn: Eesti raamat.
Baevskij, V. S., et al.
    1997.   Struktura Oneginskoj strofy: K teorii teksta i giperteksta (Komp'juternyj analiz). Russkaja filologija 1997 (Uchenye zapiski Smolenskogo gos. ped. universiteta), 115–120.

Gasparov, M. L.
1989   Stroficheskij ritm v russkom 4-stopnom jambe i xoree. In: *Russian Verse Theory: Proceedings of the 1987 Conference at UCLA,* Barry P. Scherr and Dean S. Worth (eds.), 133–147. Columbus, Ohio: Slavica.

Grinbaum, O. N.
2000   *Garmonija stroficheskogo ritma v èstetiko-formal'nom izmerenii (na materiale 'Oneginskoj strofy' i russkogo soneta).* St. Petersburg: Izdatel'stvo Sankt-Peterburgskogo universiteta.

Grossman, Leonid
1924   Oneginskaja strofa. In: *Pushkin: Sbornik pervyj,* N. K. Piksanov (ed.), 117–161. Moscow: Gosudarstvennaja izdatel'stvo.

Hayes, Bruce
1989   The prosodic hierarchy in meter. In: *Phonetics and Phonology, vol. 1: Rhythm and Meter,* Paul Kiparsky and Gilbert Youmans (eds.), 201–260. San Diego: Academic Press.

Hayes, Bruce, and Margaret MacEachern
1998   Quatrain form in English folk verse. *Language* 74: 473–507.

Jakobson, Roman
1973   Ob odnoslozhnykh slovakh v russkom stikhe. In *Slavic Poetics: Essays in Honor of Kiril Taranovsky,* Roman Jakobson, C. H. van Schooneveld, and Dean S. Worth (eds.), 239–252. The Hague: Mouton.

Kiparsky, Paul
1975   Stress, syntax and meter. *Language* 51: 576–616.

Lilly, Ian K.
1995   *The Dynamics of Russian Verse.* Nottingham: Astra Press.

Pejsaxovich, M. A.
1969   Oneginskaja strofa v poèmax Lermontova. *Filologicheskie nauki* 12/1: 25–38.

Pospelov, N. S.
1990   Sintaksicheskij stroj Oneginskoj strofy v sootnoshenii s ee metricheskim chleneniem i v sootvetstvii s osobennostjami v postroenii ee vremennnogo plana. In his *Mysli o russkoj grammatike: Izbrannye trudy,* 165–173. Moscow: Nauka.

Postoutenko, K. Ju.
1998   Oneginskij tekst v russkoj literature. Pisa: Dipartimento di linguistica, Università degli Studi di Pisa.

Pushkin, Aleksandr
1964   *Polnoe sobranie sochinenija v desjati tomax. 3rd ed. vol. 5: Evgenij Onegin, Dramaticheskie proizvedenija.* Moscow: Nauka.
1981   *Eugene Onegin.* Translated by Walter Arndt. 2nd ed. New York: E. P. Dutton.

Scherr, Barry P.
1991 Maksimilian Voloshin and the search for form(s). *Slavic and East European Journal* 35: 518–536.

Shengeli, G. A.
1923 *Traktat o russkom stixe. Chast' pervaja: Organicheskaja metrika.* 2nd ed. rev. Moscow and Petrograd: GIZ.

Stankiewicz, Edward
1995 The Onegin stanza revisited. *O Rus! Studia litteraria slavica in honorem Hugh McLean,* Simon Karlinsky et al. (eds.), 176–192. Oakland: Berkeley Slavic Specialties.

Taranovsky, Kiril
1953 *Ruski dvodelni ritmovi, I-II.* Monograph Series, Serbian Academy of Sciences, no. 217: Language and Literature Section, vol. 5. Belgrade: Nauchna knjiga.

Tomashevsky, B. V.
1958 Strofika Pushkina. *Pushkin: Issledovanija i materialy, II* 49–184.

Vinokur, G. O.
1941 Slovo i stix v Evgenii Onegine. In *Pushkin: Sbornik statej,* A. M. Egolin (ed.), 155–213. Moscow: Goslitizdat.

Wachtel, Michael
1998 *The Development of Russian Verse: Meter and Its Meanings.* Cambridge: Cambridge University Press.

8. Classical and Roman metrics

The ancient iambic trimeter: a disbalanced harmony*

Maria-Kristiina Lotman

1. The origin and the metrical structure of iambic meters

There is a general understanding that there were no iambic structures in Indo-European metrics: in those meters the configuration of accents had no role at all; quantity was regulated only at the end of a verse (the so-called quantitative verse-end), and, accordingly, the smallest symmetrical unit was not a verse foot, but a verse line.

Iambic meters did not evolve until the gradual regulation of long and short syllables in Ionian quantitative metrics (see White 1912: IX), whereby iambic trimeter became the most important meter. Its creator (or at least the first classic author to use it) is traditionally thought to be the 7th century lyrical poet Archilochos, but already in the archaic period it was associated with quite different themes: from the serious politics to the satirical and even scurrilous poetry, which, supposedly, has also given the meter its name. Trimeter appears occasionally as the meter of epitaphs and dedicatory inscriptions (West 1982: 39–40).

The metrical structure of iambic trimeter is based on the alternation of short and long syllables, whereby long (and later also short) syllables can be resolved into two short ones. The result of this license is an unusual verse with complicated structure, where not only the number of syllables, but also the number of moras is unstable: the duration of the unresolved iambic foot is three moras, the dactylic foot which is the result of a resolution of a strong position is also tri-moraic, and the "anapaestic" foot resulting from the resolution of a weak position has a duration of four moras. By the classical period the variations of the iambic trimeter are already so free that, for example, in the case of comic trimeter it is often difficult to find any iambic basis at all. Thus, the schematic representation of the meter involves several complications.

Let us look, for instance, at how the iambic trimeter was featured in the 19th century. In that period, a quite typical understanding of this structure is the following (Rossbach, Westphal 1856: 181):

(1)   ˘ ´́́ ˘ – | ˘ ´́ ˘ – | ˘ ´ ˘ –
      ⎵⎵⎵⎵⎵⎵⎵⎵ ⎵⎵⎵⎵⎵
         Arsis   Thesis

This scheme is, on the one hand, rather detailed, attributing to the iambic trimeter even features that are not in fact in correspondence with its actual prosody (e.g., describing the metrical structure with ictus). On the other hand, it is at the same time too general – it does not show all the possible transformations of meter, illustrating only the instability of its moraic structure, thus implying that the syllabic structure of the verse does not vary at all.

The metrists of the 20th century generally avoid the schematic representations of comic trimeter and have usually given the schemes of only the lyric and tragic trimeter; see, for example, the scheme of tragic trimeter by Dietmar Korzeniewski which, in contrast to that of August Rossbach and Rudolf Westphal, also reflects the possible resolutions and bridges (Korzeniewski 1989: 54), as shown below:

(2)   x ⌢˘ | ⌢x | ⌢˘ | ⌢x : ⌢˘ – |||

Another example is the scheme of archaic trimeter by Martin L. West (West 1982: 40), as shown in (3):

(3)   X̆ ⌣ ˘ ⌣ x : ⌣ x : ⌣ x — ˘ —

Mikhail Gasparov's scheme (Gasparov 1989: 74) draws together the essential features of the Greek and Roman lyric, tragic, and comic trimeter as follows:

(4)   Lyrics and tragedy   x — ˘ — x | — ˘ | — x — ˘ x
      Greek comedy   X̆ ⌣ ˘̆ ⌣ X̆ | ⌣ ˘̆ | ⌣ X̆ ⌣ ˘ x
      Roman comedy   X̆ ⌣ X̆ ⌣ X̆ | ⌣ X̆ | ⌣ X̆ ⌣ ˘ x

In comparison with the 19th century schemes, the ones by Korzeniewski, West, and Gasparov are significantly more comprehensive. Korzeniewski's scheme not only represents the positions of bridges and caesuras, but also differentiates them by the frequency of recurrences. Gasparov's scheme, although it does not show bridges, includes all the possible forms of the iambic trimeter; in contrast to other such schemes, in his scheme the final syllable is correctly represented as anceps. However, all the above-mentioned schemes have two important deficiencies: 1) an abstract scheme and its typical realization are not distinguished; 2) verse is not treated integrally, but rather every position (at best, every verse foot) is considered separately. Proceeding from this treatment, in the Roman trimeter, for example, the number of syllables could vary within the range of 12–22 syllables. But in reality there appear to be no 22 syllabic verses in poetic practice. In the material of the present study the maximum number of syllables was 17 and even this occurred extremely rarely and only in Roman comedy. Therefore, there must be a principle which regulates syllabism and which has not been considered in the treatments given above.

Specifically, the possible number of syllables must be limited by a correspondence rule, according to which resolution can take place only in the weak or in the strong position, but never in both at the same time. According to this rule, in the case of the resolved weak position the strong position could be filled only with a di-moraic syllable and, consequently, a verse foot can have a maximum of three syllables.

The existing approaches discussed earlier treat the Roman trimeter only as a quantitative-syllabic structure. The configuration of accents is not given. In contrast to these approaches, Friedrich Crusius (1961) gives a scheme which also exhibits the accentual positions of the verse, but which is still based on the same principles as the schemes discussed above. It is shown in (5).

(5) ⏑⏑ ⏑⏑́ ⏑⏑ ⏑⏑́ ⏑⏑ ⏑⏑́ ⏑⏑ ⏑⏑́ ⏑⏑ ⏑⏑ ⏑⏑́

In addition to traditional treatments there is also an attempt to present generative models of iambic trimeter (Prince 1989: 61–64), as shown below in (6). In comparison with the traditional treatment the benefit of Prince's scheme is, above all, that the hierarchical relations of meter have been clearly pointed out. But a problem emerges in displaying the possible transformations; this scheme does not illustrate the internal relations of a foot. This is because Prince's approach does not proceed from the actual generative analysis, but rather is based on the traditional treatment. Furthermore, Prince does not specify whether he considers the verse feet to be real entities, or whether he adopts the idea of Halle and Keyser's (1971), who do not. In reality, Prince's model is only the reformulation of the problem in other terms: it does not proceed from the generative approach and therefore offers no solutions.

(6) Tragedy

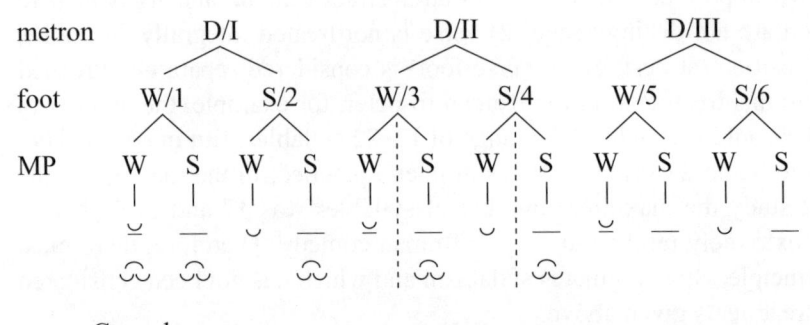

```
metron         D/I            D/II           D/III
              /   \          /    \         /    \
foot        W/1   S/2      W/3    S/4     W/5    S/6
            / \   / \      / \    / \     / \    / \
MP         W  S  W  S    W : S  W : S    W  S   W  S
           |  |  |  |    | : |  | : |    |  |   |  |
           ⌣  —  ⌣  —    ⌣ : —  ⌣ : —    ⌣  —   ⌣  —
           ~  ~     ~      ~      ~
```

Comedy

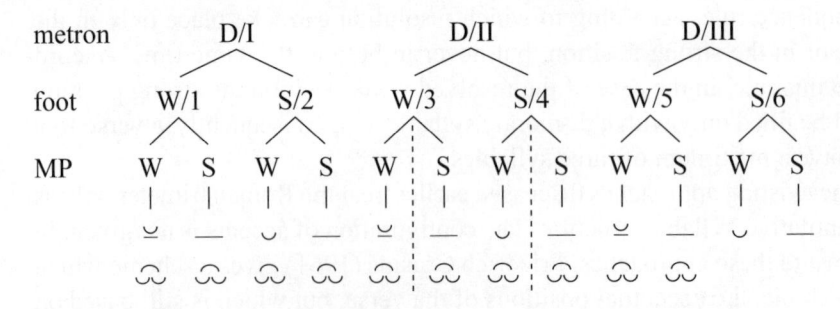

```
metron         D/I            D/II           D/III
              /   \          /    \         /    \
foot        W/1   S/2      W/3    S/4     W/5    S/6
            / \   / \      / \    / \     / \    / \
MP         W  S  W  S    W : S  W : S    W  S   W  S
           |  |  |  |    | : |  | : |    |  |   |  |
           ⌣  —  ⌣  —    ⌣ : —  ⌣ : —    ⌣  —   ⌣  —
           ~  ~  ~  ~    ~ : ~  ~ : ~    ~  ~
```

The basis for the present study is a generative model consisting of three levels: metrical rules (MR) which determine the metrical structure of verse, correspondence rules (CR) which fix the possible transformations of meter, and prosodic rules (PR) which govern the prosodic structure of verse (Lotman 1996).

2. The Greek iambic trimeter

2.1. The archaic trimeter

The freedom which characterized the classical trimeter had not yet evolved in archaic period. The resolutions took place only in the first anceps and in long positions of the first two dipodies; the verse end was invariably x—⌣—.

The deep structure of the archaic trimeter could be represented in the following way:

(7) &&&AB&AB&&AB&AB&&AB&AB&&& →
&&&F&F&&F&F&&F&F&&& → &&D&D&D&& → &L&.[1]

Here we can see the clear hierarchy of the meter: the minimal element of the verse structure is position (A, B). Positions join up to verse feet (F); verse feet, in turn, are united into dipodies (D), which make up the line (L).

The metrical rules are quite simple: the basic alphabet of this meter consists of two symbols; thus, we are dealing with the metrical system of the second degree (MS^2; see also Lotman 1998: 1860–1861).

The following correspondence rules are applied:[2]

2.1.1. The syllabic rules

$CR_{Gr.A}1$: Position A corresponds to one syllable
A → x

$CR_{Gr.A}1a$: As a result of resolution, the first **anceps** can be filled with two syllables:

&&A_1 → x x

$CR_{Gr.A}2$: Position B corresponds to one syllable.
B → x

$CR_{Gr.A}2a$: As a result of resolution, B positions of the first, second and third feet can be filled with two syllables:

B_1–B_3 → x x
For example, Archilochus 21A, 2^3:

(8) οὐδ' ἐρατός, οἷος ἀμφὶ Σίριος ῥοάς.

$CR_{Gr.A}3$: A verse foot corresponds to two or three syllables:

F_1–F_3 → x x, x x x

$F_4-F_6 \to x\ x$

$CR_{Gr.A}4$: Resolutions occur only once or, in some cases, twice per verse, whereby two short syllables are not separated with a word boundary, as if they were carrying a memory of their former unity (Gasparov 1989: 74). This rule restricts the number of syllables in a line:

$L \to$ 12–14 syllables

2.1.2. Quantitative rules

$CR_{Gr.A}5$: One short (monomoraic) or one long (dimoraic) syllable corresponds to position &&A.

$\&\&A \to \underline{\cup}$

$CR_{Gr.A}5a$: The first anceps can be filled with two short syllables.

$\&\&A_1 \to \cup\cup$

$CR_{Gr.A}5b$: Position &A corresponds to one short syllable.

$\&A \to \cup$

$CR_{Gr.A}6$: B positions correspond to one long (dimoraic) or two short (monomoraic) syllables.

$B \to —$

$CR_{Gr.A}6a$: B positions of the first two dipodies can be filled with two short syllables.

$B_1-B_3 \to \cup\cup$

$CR_{Gr.A}7$: A verse foot can be tri- or tetra-moraic:

$\&\&F \to$ 3–4 moras
$\&F \to$ 3 moras

CR_{Gr.A}8: Accordingly, the possible number of moras per line is restricted in the following way:

L → 18–21 moras

2.1.3. The prosody of archaic trimeter

PR_{Gr.A}1: Elision is considered an ordinary feature of natural language, a sign of a continuous utterance, leaving no pause between the words (Allen 1973: 226–227; West 1982: 11). Elision is quite common in archaic iambus, as, for example, in Semonides 6.1[4]:

(9)   γυναικὸς οὐδὲν χρῆμ̲' ἀνὴρ λῄξεται

or Archilochos 27.2[5]:

(10) σήμαινε καί σφεας ὄλλυ̲' ὥσπερ ὀλλύεις.

PR_{Gr.A}1a: The so-called **prodelision** is only an occasional phenomenon in the early iambus, as, for example, in Archilochus 24[6]:

(11) καὶ δὴ ̲'πίκουρος ὥστε Κὰρ κεκλήσομαι.

PR_{Gr.A}2: Correption, i.e., the shortening of a long vowel or a sequence of vowels before another vowel, is mostly characteristic to epic and elegy, but can also be found in lyrical poetry, for example, in Semonides 8[7]:

(12) ὥσπερ ἔγχελυς κατὰ γλ̲ο̲ι̲ο̲ῦ.

PR_{Gr.A}3: In the case of synizesis or synecphonesis, two or more vowels which initially belong to separate syllables are amalgamated into one heavy syllable, as in Archilochus 25[8]:

(13) Οὔ μοι τὰ Γύγ̲ε̲ω̲ τοῦ πολυχρύσου μέλει,
      οὐδ' εἷλέ πώ με ζῆλος οὐδ' ἀγαίομαι
      θ̲ε̲ῶν ἔργα, μεγάλης δ' οὐκ ἐρ̲έ̲ω̲ τυραννίδος·
      ἀπόπροθεν γάρ ἐστιν ὀφθαλμῶν ἐμῶν.

PR$_{Gr.A}$4: **Hiatus**, which is generally avoided in Greek language, occurs in the Ionic iambus only with pronouns ἐ, οἱ, ἑό, and following ἤ (West 1982: 15, Allen 1973: 225).

PR$_{Gr.A}$5: The consonantalization of ι and υ between a consonant and another vowel in the same word is only an exceptional phenomenon in early Greek poetry, generally used to accommodate a name (West 1982: 14).

PR$_{Gr.A}$6: The **syllable-releasing** function of *muta cum liquida* is not characteristic of early iambic poetry, that means, stop plus liquid clusters close the syllable, as, for example, Semonides 7.21[9]:

(14) τὴν δὲ πλάσαντες γηΐνην Ὀλύμπιοι.

2.2. The tragic trimeter

2.2.1. The early tragedy (Aeschylus and Sophocles)

In comparison with the archaic trimeter, both the syllabic regulation and quantitative structure became more liberal: consequently, resolutions started to occur in the second half of the verse as well, and "anapaestic" feet were permitted more frequently. Thus, the correspondence rules need to be readjusted.

First of all, CR$_{Gr.A}$1a and CR$_{Gr.A}$5a are applied more extensively:

CR$_{Gr.T}$1a: &&A → x x
&A$_4$ → x x

CR$_{Gr.T}$5a: &&A → UU
&A$_4$ → UU

For example, see Sophocles *Oedipus at Colonus* 1[10]:

(15) Τέκνον τυφλοῦ γέροντος Ἀντιγόνη, τίνας.

Even more liberal are the **resolutions of principitia**, as in CR2a and CR6a of the archaic trimeter in tragedy:

CR$_{Gr.T}$2a: B$_1$–B$_5$ → x x
CR$_{Gr.T}$6a: B$_1$–B$_5$ → UU

See, for example, Aeschylus *The Seven against Thebes* 703[11]:

(16) χάρις δ' ἀφ' ἡμῶν ὀλ<u>ομέ</u>νον θαυμάζεται.

As a result, the syllabic structure of a foot is as follows:

$CR_{Gr.T}3$: A verse foot corresponds to two or three syllables:

$F_1-F_5 \rightarrow x\,x, x\,x\,x$
$F_6 \rightarrow x\,x$

Due to the occasional admission of "anapaests" in the fourth foot, the quantitative regulation of a line changes as well:

$CR_{Gr.T}8$: L → 18–22 moras

The prosody of tragic trimeter differs to a certain extent from that of archaic iambus.

$PR_{Gr.T}1$: Elision is a very common prosodic feature not only in archaic iambus but also in tragic trimeter, as in Aeschylus' *Eumenides* 186–188[12]:

(17) ἀλλ'_οὗ καρανιστῆρες ὀφθαλμωρύχοι
δίκαι σφαγαί τε σπέρματος τ'_ἀποφθορᾷ
παίδων κακοῦται χλοῦνις, ἠδ'_ἀκρωνία.

$PR_{Gr.T}2$: The rule of correption is applied to a certain extent in tragedy as well, especially in Sophocles (West 1982: 11), for example, in Sophocles *Antigone* 535[13]:

(18) φήσεις μετασχεῖν ἢ 'ξομεῖ τὸ μὴ_εἰδέναι;

or Aeschylus *Eumenides* 85[14]:

(19) ἄναξ Ἄπολλον, οἶσθα μὲν τὸ μὴ_ἀδικεῖν.

$PR_{Gr.T}3$: In tragic trimeter also synizesis occurs.

PR$_{Gr.T}$4: Hiatus in tragedy occurs before and after exclamations and urgent imperatives, after τι and in phrases εὖ ἴσθι, εὖ οἶδα but also next to ἤ, e.g., Aeschylus The Seven against Thebes 202[15]:

(20) ἤκουσας ἢ οὐκ ἤκουσας, ἢ κωφῇ λέγω;

PR$_{Gr.T}$5: The consonantalization of ι and υ appears as an exception in tragedy.

PR$_{Gr.T}$6: *Muta cum liquida* with the syllable-releasing function is quite common in tragic trimeter, as for example, in Aeschylus' *Eumenides* 124–125[16]:

(21) ᾤζεις, ὑπνώσσεις· οὐκ ἀναστήσῃ τάχος;
       τί σοι πέπρωται πρᾶγμα πλὴν τεύχειν κακά;

2.2.2. The metrical innovations by Euripides

Euripides further loosens the metrical restrictions. First, in his trimeter A positions can be resolved at any place of the verse (however, the resolved A2 are rather exceptional).

CR$_{Gr.T}$1a: A → x x
CR$_{Gr.T}$5a: A → ᴗᴗ

See, for example, Euripides' *The Bacchantes* 230[17]:

(22) Ἀκταίονός τε μητέρ', Αὐτονόην λέγω.

Second, resolutions start to occur more frequently, and the restriction that a foot can be resolved only once or twice per verse becomes looser.

Thus, CR4 is not strictly valid in Euripides' trimeter (although, there are still more verses without any resolutions at all than with resolutions, the highest rate being 34,7% in *Orestes*, according to West 1982: 85).

In comparison with the early tragedy, there are no principal differences between the prosody of trimeter by Euripides and that found in early tragedy.

2.3. The trimeter of comedy

The evolution towards more liberal syllabic structure reaches its peak: the looseness of verse is most apparent at the rhythmic level. For example, the percentage of verses with resolution becomes extremely high (47% by Aristophanes, 53% by Menander[18]), and the restrictions on the number of possible resolutions per line cease to be valid. Therefore, the version of $CR_{Gr.A}4$ for comic trimeter is as follows:

L → 12–16 syllables[19]

The admission of "anapaests" in the second foot increases the possible quantity of a line:

$CR_{Gr.C}8$: L → 18–23 moras.

Anapaestic structures can occur in any of the first five feet of the comic trimeter, which, in contrast to the **melic** iambic verse, is considered a special feature of the spoken comic iambus (White 1912: 44). See also the rules $CR_{Gr.T}1a$ and $CR_{Gr.T}5a$. Aristophanes' *The Frogs* 47[20] provides an example:

(23) τίς ὁ νοῦς; τι κόθορνος καὶ ῥόπαλον ξυνηλθέτην

The main prosodic licences of the comic trimeter are PR1, PR4 and PR6:

$PR_{Gr.C}1$ and $PR_{Gr.C}1a$:

Elision and **prodelision** are regular also in comedy, e.g., Aristophanes *The Clouds* 60–62[21]:

(24) μετὰ ταῦθ᾽, ὅπως νῷν ἐγένεθ᾽ υἱὸς οὑτοσί,
      ἐμοί τε δὴ καὶ τῇ γυναικὶ τἀγαθῇ,
      περὶ τοὐνόματος δὴ ᾽ντεῦθεν ἐλοιδορούμεθα.

($PR_{Gr.C}4$) In certain cases hiatus is admitted, e.g., Aristophanes *The Clouds* 746[22]:

(25) ὦ Σωκρατίδιον φίλτατον. τί, ὦ γέρον;

See also $PR_{Gr.T}6$ (§ 2.2.1).

2.4. The trimeter of the Hellenistic tragedy

The tragic trimeter of the Hellenistic period is stricter than the trimeter of classical tragedy. First of all, the "anapaestic" feet are rare and occur only in the fifth foot (West 1982: 159), i.e., as a rule, A positions are not resolved:

$CR_{Gr.H}1: A \to x$
$CR_{Gr.H}1a: A_5 \to x\,x$
$CR_{Gr.H}5: A \to \cup$
$CR_{Gr.H}5a: A \to \cup$

B positions can be resolved only in the second, third, and fourth foot (ibid.):

$CR_{Gr.H}2: B \to x$
$CR_{Gr.H}2a: B_2-B_4 \to x\,x$
$CR_{Gr.H}6: B \to \cup$
$CR_{Gr.H}6a: B_2-B_4 \to \cup\cup$

As a result, the syllabic structure of a foot is as follows:

$CR_{Gr.H}3$: Two or three syllables correspond to a verse foot:

$F_2-F_5 \to x\,x, x\,x\,x$
$F_1, F_6 \to x\,x$

Resolutions are rare (1 per 78 verses; ibid.), accordingly, the number of syllables in a line is quite stable:

$CR_{Gr.H}4:$
$L \to 12–13$ syllables

The quantitative structure of a verse is subject to the following rule:

$CR_{Gr.H}8:$
$L \to 18–21$ moras

The prosody is strict, and elision and hiatus are only occasional.

3. The Roman trimeter

3.1. The trimeter of early comedy

The main differences between the Roman and Greek trimeter are the following: a) the weakening of quantitative oppositions (the replacement of a short syllable with a long one is allowed everywhere except the sixth feet; therefore, every A position is quantitatively an anceps and, thus, the Roman trimeter is usually called a *senarius)*; b) the change from the accentual principle to the quantitative and syllabic principle that partly compensates the weakness of quantitative oppositions (see also Beare 1968: 323). The deep structure of early Roman comic senarius is as follows:

(26) &&AB&AB&AB&AB&AB&AB& →
&&F&F&F&F&F&F&& → &L&

3.1.1. The syllabic rules

$CR_{Lat.C}1$: Position A corresponds to one syllable or a sequence of two syllables, but the latter one can occur only if a B position of this foot is filled with one syllable.

A → x
A → x x / __ x

$CR_{Lat.C}2$: Position B corresponds to one syllable or a sequence of two syllables, but the latter possibility can occur only if a A position of this foot is filled with one syllable.

B → x
B → x x / x __

$CR_{Lat.C}3$: As a consequence, a verse foot corresponds to two or three syllables:
F → x x, x x x

$CR_{Lat.C}3a$: Occasionally, both A and B positions of the same feet can be resolved and, especially in the first feet, **proceleusmatics** are allowed (Raven 1965: 51–53):

F → x x x x

There are no restrictions of the place or number of resolutions in a line, except for the last foot, which remains unresolved. We can even come across a few lines, where all the possibilities for resolutions are realized, for example, in Plautus' *Three Bob Day* 177[23]:

(27)   an ego alium dominum paterer fieri hisce aedibus? ($CR_{Lat.C}4$)

L → 12–17 syllables

3.1.2. The quantitative rules

$CR_{Lat.C}5$: An A position corresponds to one long syllable, one short syllable or a sequence of two short syllables, but the latter one can occur only if a strong position is filled with one syllable.

A → ⏑
A → ⏑⏑/__ x

$CR_{Lat.C}6$: B positions correspond to one long syllable or a sequence of two short syllables, but the latter possibility can occur only if A position is filled with one syllable.

B → __
B → ⏑⏑/ x __

CR7 and CR8 have no importance in Latin verse since Latin is not a mora-counting language (see also Lotman 2001: 551).

3.1.3. The accentual rules

As it has already been noted, the role of accent in the early Latin trimeter is to balance the weakness of quantitative structure. This function of accent becomes particularly obvious in the central part of the verse, that is, in the second, third, and fourth foot, where, in weak positions, word-accents are generally avoided, while there is a strong tendency to fill the strong positions with stressed syllables:

$CR_{Lat.C}9$: $A_2–A_4 \rightarrow x$
$CR_{Lat.C}10$: $B \rightarrow \acute{x}$

See, for example, Plautus' *The Captives* 172–173[24]:

(28)   Ita di deaeque faxint. Set numquo foras
       Vocatus [es] ad cenam? Nusquam, quod sciam.

In this example we can clearly see how the accent contributes to the structure of the verse until the last two feet, where, instead, it conflicts the iambic pattern and, thus, strengthens the effect of the quantitative structure.

$CR_{Lat.C}10a$: In resolved feet, word accents usually occur in the first syllable of the resolved strong position:

$B \rightarrow \acute{x} x / x \underline{}$

Consequently, the most common form of a resolved foot in iambic verse is x x́ x, as, for example, in Terence's *The Brothers* 493[25]:

(29)   Sin aliter animus voster est, ego Demea.

$CR_{Lat.C}10b$: On certain occasions, when a stressed syllable occurs in a strong position, the quantity of the rest of the syllables in a given foot may become irrelevant and the foot may become subject to accentual rules. This rule causes, for example, the phenomenon which is traditionally treated as iambic shortening, that is, a long syllable adjacent to a stressed syllable can be treated as short.

3.1.4. Prosodic rules

As for the prosodic rules, here PR1, PR3, PR4 and PR6 apply:

$PR_{Lat.C}1$: Elision of both long and nasalized vowels as well as of diphthongs is a common feature of the early Latin verse (Allen 1973: 145), as in Plautus' *The Braggart Warrior* 491–493[26]:

(30)   Perii hercle: hic ad me recta habet rectam viam.

Metu̱o̱ illaec mihi res ne malo magno fuat,
Quant_um_ hunc audivi facere verborum senem.

PR$_{Lat.C}$1a: In the case of the copula *es* or *est* the so-called **prodelision** or **aphaeresis** took place, in which the beginning of the second word was elided, as in Plautus *The Captives* 125[27]:

(31)   Set satis verbor_umst_: cura quae iussi atque abi.

PR$_{Lat.C}$3: Synizesis is often used with words in *ea* (e.g., eadem), *eo* (e.g, deorum), *ei* (e.g., deinde), *eu* (e.g., meum), *ie* (e.g., diebus), *ua* (e.g., tua), *ue* (e.g., fuere), *ui* (e.g., fuisti), *uo* (e.g., suo), for example, in Terence's *The Brothers* 114[28]:

(32)   T_uo_m filium dedisti adoptandum mihi.

PR$_{Lat.C}$4: Hiatus is only an exceptional phenomenon in early trimeter, appearing occasionally at a caesura or **diaeresis** (Raven 1965: 28), as in Plautus' *Amphitryo* 874[29]:

(33)   Esse adsimulab_o_ atque in horum familiam.

PR$_{Lat.C}$6: In the early Latin trimeter, **muta cum liquida** generally releases a syllable (Allen 1973: 137), as in Terence's *The Brothers* 391[30]:

(34)   Pat_ris_, et facilitas prava. Fratris me quidem.

3.2. The Roman lyrical trimeter

As in the trimeter of Greek tragedy, here the first position of every dipody is **anceps**, that is, a long, a short, or two short syllables can occur in this position, while the second weak position of a dipody is always short. Therefore, the rules CR$_{Lat.L}$1–CR$_{Lat.L}$6 are analogical to CR$_{Gr.T}$1–CR$_{Gr.T}$6.

Yet there is a constraint on resolution in A positions:

CR$_{Lat.L}$1a: $A_1, A_5 \rightarrow x\ x$
CR$_{Lat.L}$5a: $A_1, A_5 \rightarrow \cup\cup$

As a result, lyric poets like Horace and Martialis have anapaestic patterns only in the first and the fifth feet.

In addition to these rules, CR9 and CR10 are valid here as well. In other words, the accent continues to play a role in verse structure, for example, in Horace's *Epodes* 17, 53–59[31]:

(35)   quid obseratis auribus fundis preces?
       non saxa nudis surdiora navitis
       Neptunus alto tundit hibernus salo.
       inultus ut tu riseris Cotytia
       volgata, sacrum liberi Cupidinis,
       et Esquilini pontifex venefici
       impune ut Urbem nomine impleris meo?

Prosody is much stricter than in comedy; however, elision (PR1) is allowed.

In addition, *muta cum liquida* can sometimes have a syllable-lengthening function ($PR_{Lat.L}6$): see **sacrum** in the preceding example (Horace's *Epodes* 17, 57).

3.3. The trimeter of the late Roman tragedy

The main source here is, of course, Seneca's creation. For the most part, Seneca follows the same rules as Roman lyric poets do. However, there are some additional restrictions.

The first position of the fifth foot is very rarely filled with a short syllable. A long syllable generally corresponds to this position (Crusius 1961: 77):

($CR_{Lat.C}5$) A_5 → —

See, for example, Seneca's *Medea* 253–257[32]:

(36)   non esse me qui sceptra violentus geram
       nec qui superbo miserias calcem pede,
       testatus equidem videor haud clare parum
       generum exulem legendo et adflictum et gravi
       terrore pavidum, quippe quem poenae expetit...

The resolution of the fifth **princeps** is exceptional, as, for example, in Seneca's *Medea* 266[33]:

(37) tu, tu, malorum machinatrix <u>facino</u>rum.

There are some instances of **proceleusmatic** feet (see $CR_{Lat.C}3a$), as in Seneca's *Medea* 488[34]:

(38) <u>tibi patria</u> cessit, tibi pater, frater, pudor

or Seneca Phaedra 1275[35]:

(39) <u>patefacite</u> acerbam caede funesta domum.

In contrast to Horace and Martialis, "anapaests" can also occur in the third foot:

$(CR_{Lat.T}1a)$ &&A → x x
$(CR_{Lat.T}5a)$ &&A → ⌣⌣

The prosodic rules are principally the same as in lyrical trimeter.

4. Conclusion

The deep structure of the ancient iambic trimeter demonstrates a perfect translational symmetry in all its hierarchical levels. Its surface structures, on the other hand, are striving to break this symmetry. Thus, the beginning of a verse is never the same as its central part, while the end is regulated by completely different correspondence rules. This pattern characterizes the syllabic rules (e.g., in Roman senarius the first foot can have 2–4 syllables, while the sixth is always disyllabic), as well as the quantitative rules (e.g., allowing anapaestic structures only in a few determined positions), and accentual rules (cf., the accented central part of the Roman senarius as opposed to its quantitative ending).

Notes

* The author of this paper is grateful to the Estonian Science Foundation (grant no 5243).
1. A and B mark here different metrical positions, F verse feet, D dipodies, L verse line, and metrical boundaries.
2. The rules are based primarily on the statistics by Joseph Marie Descroix (1931: 112–113). For the analysis of archaic choliamb see Lotman 2004.
3. oud' eratos, hoios amphi Sirios rhoas – [there's no country...] so lovely as the banks of the Siris (transl. by John Maxwell Edmonds).
4. gunaikos ouden chrêm'_anêr lêixetai – A man wins himself nothing whatsover [that is better than a good] wife (transl. by John Maxwell Edmonds).
5. sêmaine kai spheas ollu'_hôsper ollueis – reveal [the guilty] and destroy them as Thou ever dost (transl. by John Maxwell Edmonds).
6. kai dê_'pikouros hôste Kar keklêsomai – and I shall be called a soldier of fortune like a Carian (transl. by John Maxwell Edmonds).
7. hôsper egxelus kata gloiou (transl. by John Maxwell Edmonds).
8. Ou moi ta Gugeô tou poluchrusou melei, / oud' eile pô me zêlos, oud' agaiomai / theôn erga, megalês d' ouk ereô turannidos: / apoprothen gar estin ophthalmôn emôn – I care not for the wealth of golden Gyges, / nor ever have envied him; I am not jealous / of the works of Gods, and I have no desire for lofty despotism; / for such things are far beyond my ken (transl. by John Maxwell Edmonds).
9. tên de plasantes gêinên Olumpioi – Another the Olympians fashioned of Earth (transl. by John Maxwell Edmonds).
10. Teknon tuphlou gerontos Antigonê, tinas – Child of an old blind sire, Antigone, what [region...have we reached?] (transl. by Francis Storr).
11. charis d' aph' hêmôn olomenôn thaumazetai – The service they value at our hands is that we perish (transl. by Herbert Weir Smyth).
12. all'_hou karanistêres ophthalmôruchoi /dikai sphagai te spermatos t'_apophthorai / paidôn kakoutai chlounis, êd'_akrônia – No, your place is where there are sentences to beheading, gouging out of eyes, / and cutting of throats; where, by destruction of the seed, / the manhood of youth is ruined, where men are mutilated (transl. by Herbert Weir Smyth).
13. phêseis metaschein ê 'xomei to mê_eidenai –Didst thou too abet [this crime] or dost abjure all privity? (transl. by Hugh Lloyd-Jones).
14. anax Apollon, oistha men to mê_adikein – Lord Apollo, thou knowest not to be unrighteous (transl. by Herbert Weir Smyth).
15. êkousas ê_ouk êkousas, ê kôphêi legô? – Dost hear or not? Or am I speaking to the death? (transl. by Herbert Weir Smyth).
16. ôizeis, hupnôsseis: ouk anastêsêi tachos? / ti soi peprôtai pragma_plên teuchein kaka? – Thou moanest, slumberest. Wilt thou not arise at once? / What task hath been allotted thee save to work ill? (transl. by Herbert Weir Smyth).

17. Aktaionos te mêter', Aut<u>ono</u>ên legô – Autonoe withal, Actaeon's mother (transl. Arthur S. Way).
18. In this chapter the statistics by John Williams White (1912) have been used.
19. Although theoretically the lines with 17 and even 18 syllables would also be possible (cf., the two exceptional cases of anapaests in the sixth feet in Aristophanes; White 1912: 38), such verses are not found in actual poetic practice.
20. <u>tis ho nous</u>? ti kothor<u>n</u>os kai <u>rhopalon</u> xunêlthetên – A club and buskin! What's it all about? (transl. by Benjamin Bickley Rogers).
21. meta tau<u>th'</u>, hopôs nôin egene<u>th'</u> huios houtosi, / emoi te dê kai têi gunaiki tagathêi, / peri tounomatos dê '<u>n</u>teuthen eloidoroumetha – (transl. by Benjamin Bickley Rogers).
22. ô Sôkratidion filtaton. <u>ti, ô</u> geron? – Oh, here, dear Socrates! Well, my old friend (transl. by Benjamin Bickley Rogers).
23. Or was I to let this house fall into other hands (transl. by Paul Nixon).
24. The gods and goddesses be with you! I say, though, – you haven't been invited out / to dinner anywhere? Nowhere, to my knowledge (transl. by Paul Nixon).
25. If your intentions are different, I, Demea [will strain every nerve] (transl. by John Sargeaunt).
26. O Lord, I'm done for! He's making straight for me, straight! / I'm afraid I've got into a frightful fix by this affair, / from what I heard the old fellow say (transl. by Paul Nixon).
27. But enough of this. Mind my orders and be off with you (transl. by Paul Nixon).
28. You gave me your son to adopt (transl. by John Saurgeaunt).
29. I will pretend to be [Amphitryon] and [confound] this family (transl. by Paul Nixon).
30. Father's [mildness] so easy-going, quite wicked. [I am... ashamed] of my brother (transl. by John Sargeaunt).
31. Why dost thou pour forth prayers to ears whose gates are barred? / Not deafer to shipwrecked sailors are the cliffs / that wintry Neptune beats with swelling surge! / Thou to laugh with impunity at divulging the Cotytian / rites and the orgies of Cupid unrestrained! / Thou, the minister of Esquiline incantation, / to fill the town with talk of me and reap no punishment (transl. by Charles Edwin Bennett).
32. That I am not one to wield the sceptre with violence / nor to trample upon misery with haughty foot, / methinks I have not unclearly shown / by choosing for son-in-law an exile, crushed and stricken with heavy / fear, on whom [Acastus...] demands for punishment (transl. by Frank Justus Miller).
33. Thou, thou contriver of wickedness (transl. by Frank Justus Miller).
34. For thee my country has given place, for thee father, brother, maidenhood (transl. by Frank Justus Miller).
35. Open the bitter house with deadly murder.

References

Allen, William Sidney
    1973   *Accent and Rhythm. Prosodic Features of Latin and Greek: A Study in Theory and Reconstruction*. Cambridge: Cambridge University Press.
Beare, William
    1968   *The Roman Stage*. London: Methuen.
Bennett, Charles Edwin
    1968   *The Odes and Epodes / Horace; with an English Translation by C. E. Bennett*. Cambridge, Massachusetts: Harvard University Press; London: William Heinemann.
Crusius, Friedrich
    1961   *Römische Metrik: eine Einführung*. München: Max Hueber.
Descroix, Joseph Marie
    1931   *Le trimètre iambique (des iambographes à la comédie nouvelle)*. Macon: Protat frères.
Edmonds, John Maxwell (ed.)
    1982   *Elegy and Iambus: Being the Remains of All the Greek Elegiac and Iambic Poets from Callinus to Crates, Excepting the Choliambic Writers, with the Anacreontea. In Two Volumes, Newly Edited and Translated by J. M. Edmonds*. Cambridge, Massachusetts: Harvard University Press; London: William Heinemann.
Gasparov, Mikhail
    1989   *Ocherk istorii evropejskogo stixa*. Moskva: Nauka.
Korzeniewski, Dietmar
    1989   *Griechische Metrik*. Darmstadt: Wissenschaftliche Buchgesellschaft.
Halle, Morris, and Samuel Jay Keyser
    1971   *English Stress: Its Form, Its Growth, and Its Role in Verse*. New York: Harper & Row.
Lloyd-Jones, Hugh, and Nigel Guy Wilson (eds.)
    1990   *Sophoclis fabulae*. Oxford: Clarendon Press.
Lotman, Mihhail
    1996   Russkij stix: osnovnye razmery, vxodjashchie v evropeiskij metricheskij fond. In: *Słowiańska metryka porownawcza. VI Europejskie wcorce metryczne w literaturach słowiańskich*, L. Pszczolowska, D. Urbanska (eds.), 259–340. Warszawa: Instytut Badań Literackich.
    1998   Värsisüsteemidest (peamiselt eesti ja vene värsi näitel). *Akadeemia* 10: 1846–1874; 11: 2058–2078.
Lotman, Maria-Kristiina
    2001   Prosody and versification systems of ancient verse. *Sign System Studies* 29.2: 535–561.

2004   Choliamb: its metre, rhythm and semantics. *Acta Collegii Humaniorum Estoniensis* 4: 142–163

Miller, Frank Justus (transl.)
1979   *Seneca in Ten Volumes. Tragedies I–II with an English Translation by Frank Iustus Miller.* Cambridge, Massachusetts: Harvard University Press; London: W. Heinemann.

Nixon, Paul (transl.)
1984   *Plautus, with an English Translation by Paul Nixon I–V.* Cambridge, Massachusetts: Harvard University Press; London: W. Heinemann.

Prince, Alan
1989   Metrical Forms. *Phonetics and Phonology. Vol. 1. Rhythm and Meter,* Paul Kiparsky and Gilbert Youmans (eds.), 45–80. San Diego: Academic Press.

Raven, David S.
1965   *Latin Meter.* London: Faber and Faber.

Rogers, Benjamin Bickley (transl.)
1982   *Aristophanes, with the English Translation of Benjamin Bickley Rogers in Three Volumes.* Cambridge, Massachusetts: Harvard University Press; London: W. Heinemann.

Rossbach, August, and Rudolph Westphal
1856   *Griechische Metrik.* Leipzig: B. G. Teubner.

Sargeaunt, John (transl.)
1983   *Terence, with an English Translation by John Sargeaunt I–II.* Cambridge, Massachusetts: Harvard University Press; London: W. Heinemann.

Smyth, Herbert Weir (transl.)
1988.   *Aeschylus, with an English Translation by Herbert Weir Smyth I.* Cambridge, Massachusetts: Harvard University Press; London: W. Heinemann.

Storr, Francis (transl.)
1981.   *Sophocles, with an English Translation by F. Storr I.* Cambridge, Massachusetts: Harvard University Press; London: W. Heinemann.

Way, Arthur S. (transl.)
1966   *Euripides with an English Translation by Arthur S. Way II.* London: W. Heinemann; Cambridge, Mass.: Harvard University Press.

West, Martin Litchfield
1982   *Greek Meter.* Oxford: Clarendon Press.

White, John Williams
1912   *The Verse of Greek Comedy.* London: MacMillan and Co.

Author index

Aeschylus, 294–296
Allen, William Sydney, 293–294, 301–302
Andrzejewski, Bogumil and I. M. Lewis, 204–205
Anttila, Arto, 8, 33–36, 39, 215, 246
Archilochos, 287, 291, 293
Aristophanes, 297, 306
Árnason, Kristján, 157, 159–161, 164, 167
Arnold, Matthew, 60, 68, 69, 82, 89
Attridge, Derek, 152, 156, 166

Baevskij, Vadim S., 163, 165, 168
Bailey, James, 3, 59, 157, 212
Bely, Andrei, 3, 211–213, 225, 235
Biggs, Henry, 60
Browning, Robert, 57, 63, 68, 85
Byron, George Gordon, 55, 57, 61, 67–70

Chaucer, Geoffrey, 56
Cole, Deborah, 108
Coleridge, Samuel Taylor, 54, 70, 234

Donne, John, 55–58, 64, 71–72, 122, 126, 212
Dresher, Elan, 217, 221, 228, 236

Fabb, Nigel, 77, 78, 80, 81, 85–86, 88, 89, 195, 197, 199, 203–204
Fitzgerald, Coleen, 108, 190, 193, 200, 204, 215
Friedberg, Nila, 27, 46, 212, 213, 224, 228, 233, 236–241, 244, 246
Frost, Robert, 53–63, 67, 69, 71–72

Gasparov, Mikhail, 3, 56, 61, 71, 212, 270, 272, 276, 2278, 288–289, 292

Getty, Michael, 154, 215, 228
Golston, Chris, 27, 111, 118, 120, 130, 193, 204, 215, 217
Grinbaum, O.N., 270, 282
Grossman, Leonid, 269, 275

Halle, Morris, 54, 56, 57, 77, 80, 89, 93, 113, 124, 174, 190, 211–212, 236, 253, 262, 264, 265, 289
Hammond, Michael, 108, 176, 190
Hanson, Kristin, 2, 7, 58, 63, 108, 112–113, 115, 117, 122, 124, 129, 130, 152, 158, 164, 166, 174, 187, 193, 217–218, 228, 236, 238
Hayes, Bruce, 2, 7, 8–19, 21–22, 24–35, 37, 41, 43–47, 59, 88, 107, 112, 128, 136, 138, 152, 156, 164, 165–166, 174, 189, 190, 198–195, 204, 205, 211, 212, 215–217, 228, 236, 246, 273–274, 277
Holmes, Oliver Wendell, 135, 146
Horace, 303–304

Idsardi, William, 82

Jackendoff, Ray, 7
Jakobson, Roman, 1, 61, 64, 87, 152, 166, 233, 274, 282
Jaamac Cumar Ciise, Sheekh, 196

Karpeles, Maud, 8–11, 24, 46–47
Keats, John, 63, 67–68, 70
Keyser, Samuel Jay, 54, 56–57, 89, 93, 113, 124, 174, 190, 211–212, 236, 253, 262, 264, 265, 289
Kiparsky, Paul, 2, 7, 45, 47, 56–57, 58, 63, 108, 111–115, 117, 118–124, 126–128, 130, 144, 152, 158, 166, 174, 187, 193, 211–212, 215, 217,

Kiparsky, Paul *(continued)*, 218, 228, 236, 238, 246, 253, 265, 277, 282
Korzeniewski, Dietmar, 288

Lehiste, Ilse, 173, 176–177, 184–190
Lehrdahl, Fred, 7
Lermontov, Mikhail, 71, 225–226, 274, 281
Lilly, Ian, 282
Longfellow, Henry Wadsworth, 15, 135–146
Lomonosov, Mikhail, 218–219, 223–226, 228, 238
Lotman, Mihhail, 263, 265, 290, 291
Lotman, Maria–Kristiina, 300, 305

MacEachern, Margaret, 2, 7–19, 21–22, 25–35, 37, 41, 44–47, 136, 189, 190, 204, 212, 215–217, 228, 236, 273–274
Martialis, 303–304
McCarthy, John and Alan Prince, 93, 108, 228
Menander, 297
Milton, John, 1, 68, 70, 115
Miyashita, Mizuki, 175, 186, 193

Orwin, Martin, 194, 199, 204, 205

Petrarch, 56, 64, 269
Plautus, 300–302
Pope, Alexander, 1, 54–55, 61–62, 64, 70, 72
Prince, Alan, 2, 7, 93, 108, 113, 135, 136, 138, 144, 215, 228, 233, 289–290
Pushkin, Aleksandr, 212–214, 221–222, 224–226, 237, 257, 259, 267, 269, 272–275, 278–282

Raven, David, 299, 302
Ritchie, Jean, 8
Russom, Geoffrey, 89, 154–155

Scherr, Barry P., 213, 282
Semonides, 293–294
Seneca, 303–304
Service, Robert, 93–94, 97, 103, 107–108
Shakespeare, William, 53–55, 58–59, 64, 67–71, 111–131, 136, 267–269, 274, 281
Sharp, Cecil, 8–11, 24, 46–47
Shelley, Percy Bysshe, 57–59, 63, 65–70
Shengeli, Georgij, 258, 265, 270
Sievers, Eduard, 151, 153–155, 159, 162
Smolensky, Paul, 2, 93, 106, 136, 215, 217, 228, 233
Sophocles, 294–295
Sperber, Dan and Deirdre Wilson, 77–78, 86

Taranovsky, Kiril, 3, 212–214, 226, 228, 233, 235, 240, 242, 272
Tarlinskaja, Marina, 3, 54, 55, 56, 59, 65, 66, 71, 84, 111–112, 114, 128–129, 136, 212, 213, 227, 262
Tennyson, Alfred Lord, 67–68, 70
Terence, 301–302
Tomashevsky, Boris, 3, 57, 212–213, 239, 270–271, 273, 275–276, 281

van der Hulst, Harry, 217, 228, 236

Wachtel, Michael, 282
West, Martin, 89, 287–288, 293–296, 298
White, John Williams, 287, 297, 306
Wordsworth, William, 67–68, 70
Wyatt, Thomas, 56, 64, 71, 122, 126

Yeats, William Butler, 68
Youmans, Gilbert, 2, 111–112, 119–122, 124–125, 130–131, 138, 174

Subject and language index

accentual meter, 60, 80, 136
accentual-syllabic (or syllabo-tonic) meter, 56, 61, 80, 136, 238, 257–264, 272
alliterative poetry, 151–167, 195
anapest, 14, 15, 93–111, 136, 144
anapestic-iambic meter, 93, 107
Arabic, 80, 89, 91

beat 2, 8–12, 15, 21–22, 29–39, 46, 84–98, 100, 103–104, 106–108, 151, 154, 157, 160–165, 173–192
empty beat, 9, 10, 22, 188
Beowulf, 80, 89, 151, 152–155, 167, 169, 229

cadence, 9, 16, 29, 32, 56, 140, 143, 273
cadentiality, 29, 30, 165–166
caesura, 46, 94, 107, 137, 144, 195, 205, 261, 289, 302
catalexis, 127, 128, 162, 165, 166
closure, 15, 16, 23, 24, 46, 165, 270–279
colon, *see also* half-line, 83, 113, 129, 151–153, 159–165, 176, 186, 191, 237
complexity, 26, 27, 37, 48, 62, 90, 211–232, 235, 248
couplet, 15–26, 29–30, 34–46, 190, 267–271, 282, 275–277, 281, 282

dactyl, 135–146, 262, 287
dactylic hexameter, 135–146
disyllables, 156, 164, 260, 262, 264, 274, 304
dolnik, 46, 54, 136, 147
duration, phonetic, 173–192
Dyirbal, 81, 89

Eddic meter, 151–170
English
  anapestic-iambic meter, 93, 107
  folk verse, 2, 3, 7–48, 136, 137, 246, 273, 274, 283
  iambic pentameter, 53–74, 77, 80, 113, 114, 118, 159, 195
enjambment, 268, 275–277, 281, 282
Estonian, 2, 176, 261–264

Finnish, 2, 193, 246, 255, 261–264

generative metrics, 84, 93, 130, 203, 204, 211, 236, 245, 246, 253
German, 136, 138, 151, 152, 153, 154, 261, 262, 264
Germanic, 151–170
grid, 7–12, 15, 21, 29, 33, 84, 85
  bracketed grid theory, 77, 80, 81, 84

Greek, Ancient, 2, 80, 138, 195, 255, 257, 258, 261, 265, 288–298
  Greek iambic trimeter, 257, 287–288, 290–298

Half-line, 21, 23, 25, 137, 152, 155, 193–205, 216
Hemistich, *see also* half-line, 21, 23, 26, 36, 46, 57, 58, 61, 216–219, 228, 236, 237, 241
hexameter, 135–146, 261
hiatus, 294–298, 302

Japanese, 2, 173–192, 193, 194
  haiku, 173, 174, 175, 176, 177, 184, 186, 187, 190
  tanka 173–190

Kuhn's law, 160, 167

Latin (or Roman) meter, 2, 138, 195, 261, 298–304
　Roman iambic trimeter, 287–288, 298–304
lexical stress, 84, 93–98, 103–105, 107, 125
long meter, 15, 42

markedness, 27, 28, 35, 36, 39, 40, 43, 46
metricality, 53–74
monosyllables, 11, 56–58, 62–71, 77, 85–87, 89, 95–101, 105, 106, 164
mora, 2, 80, 115, 158, 173–208, 257, 287–288, 292–298, 300
moraic trochee, 115, 164, 193–195, 199–204
music, 2, 7, 8, 12, 14, 16, 29, 42, 47, 151, 152, 165, 166, 187
musical performance, 8, 12, 15

Old English, 152, 156, 189
Old Norse 151–170
Optimality Theory, 2, 7, 8, 93, 136, 215, 233
　constraints, 1, 2, 7–50, 93, 102, 105, 106, 107, 211, 212, 215–225, 233, 236–240, 245, 246, 267, 273, 279
　faithfulness, 21, 28, 29, 37–43, 46, 168, 238
　local conjunction, 93, 106, 217, 228
　null parse, 101, 102, 216, 219, 228
　partial ranking, 33–35, 39, 44, 215, 246
　stochastic OT, 7, 8, 27, 33, 34, 35, 215, 246

parallelism, 12, 15, 18, 22, 23, 25, 29–32, 36–44, 46, 88, 282

prose 39, 55, 56, 61, 65, 81, 112, 124, 135, 152, 166, 240–244
quatrain, 7–50, 151–170, 188, 267–273, 276–279, 281, 282

Relevance Theory, 77, 78, 79, 86
resolution, 80, 114, 115, 164, 195, 287–304
　anti-resolution, 93–110
rhyme, 1, 13, 14, 15, 16, 19, 20, 24–28, 45–47, 78–81, 88, 97, 265, 267–282
Russian, 136, 156, 211–284
　folk verse, 156, 260
　formalism, 57
　iambic tetrameter, 267–284, 211–232, 233–250, 253–266
　Onegin stanza, 267–284
　school of metrics, 3, 57, 212, 213, 233, 270, 272, 276

Sanskrit, 80, 89
short meter, 30, 42
Somali, 193–208
　Masafo verse 193–208
sonnet, 56, 64, 78, 79, 86, 88, 111–115, 119–130, 136, 267–271, 281, 282
source-filter model, 233, 239–246
stanza, 7–50, 78, 151–157, 162–166, 224, 267–284
stress maximum, 57, 58, 62, 65, 84, 89, 262, 264
syllabic meter, 115
symmetry, 217, 220, 222, 223, 228, 237, 241, 253, 304

ternary meter, 60, 61, 136, 141–144
trochaic substitution, 135, 141, 146, 274
truncation, 162, 165, 166

List of contributors

Kristján Árnason
University of Iceland
Iceland
kristarn@rhi.hi.is

Deborah Cole
University of Texas-Pan American
USA
dcole@rgv.rr.com, dcole@panam.edu

B. Elan Dresher
University of Toronto
Canada
dresher@chass.utoronto.ca

Nigel Fabb
University of Strathclyde
United Kingdom
N.Fabb@strath.ac.uk

Colleen M. Fitzgerald
Texas Tech University
USA
colleen.fitzgerald@ttu.edu

Nila Friedberg
Portland State University
USA
nfriedbe@pdx.edu

Daniel Currie Hall
University of Toronto
Canada
daniel.hall@utoronto.ca

Michael Hammond
University of Arizona
USA
hammond@u.arizona.edu

Kristin Hanson
University of California, Berkeley
USA
khanson@socrates.berkeley.edu

Paul Kiparsky
Stanford University
USA
kiparsky@csli.stanford.edu

Maria-Kristiina Lotman
University of Tartu
Estonia
Maria.Lotman@mail.ee

Mihhail Lotman
University of Tartu
Estonia
mihhail@ehi.ee

Mizuki Miyashita
University of Montana
USA
Mizuki.Miyashita@mso.umt.edu

Barry Scherr
Dartmouth College
USA
Barry.P.Scherr@Dartmouth.EDU

Marina Tarlinskaja
University of Washington
USA
marinat@u.washington.edu

Gilbert Youmans
University of Missouri-Columbia
USA
youmansg@missouri.edu